TEXTILE PRACTICES
FORTY FEMALE ARTISTS AND DESIGNERS
FROM EUROPE

TEXTILE PRAKTIKEN
VIERZIG KÜNSTLERINNEN UND GESTALTERINNEN
AUS EUROPA

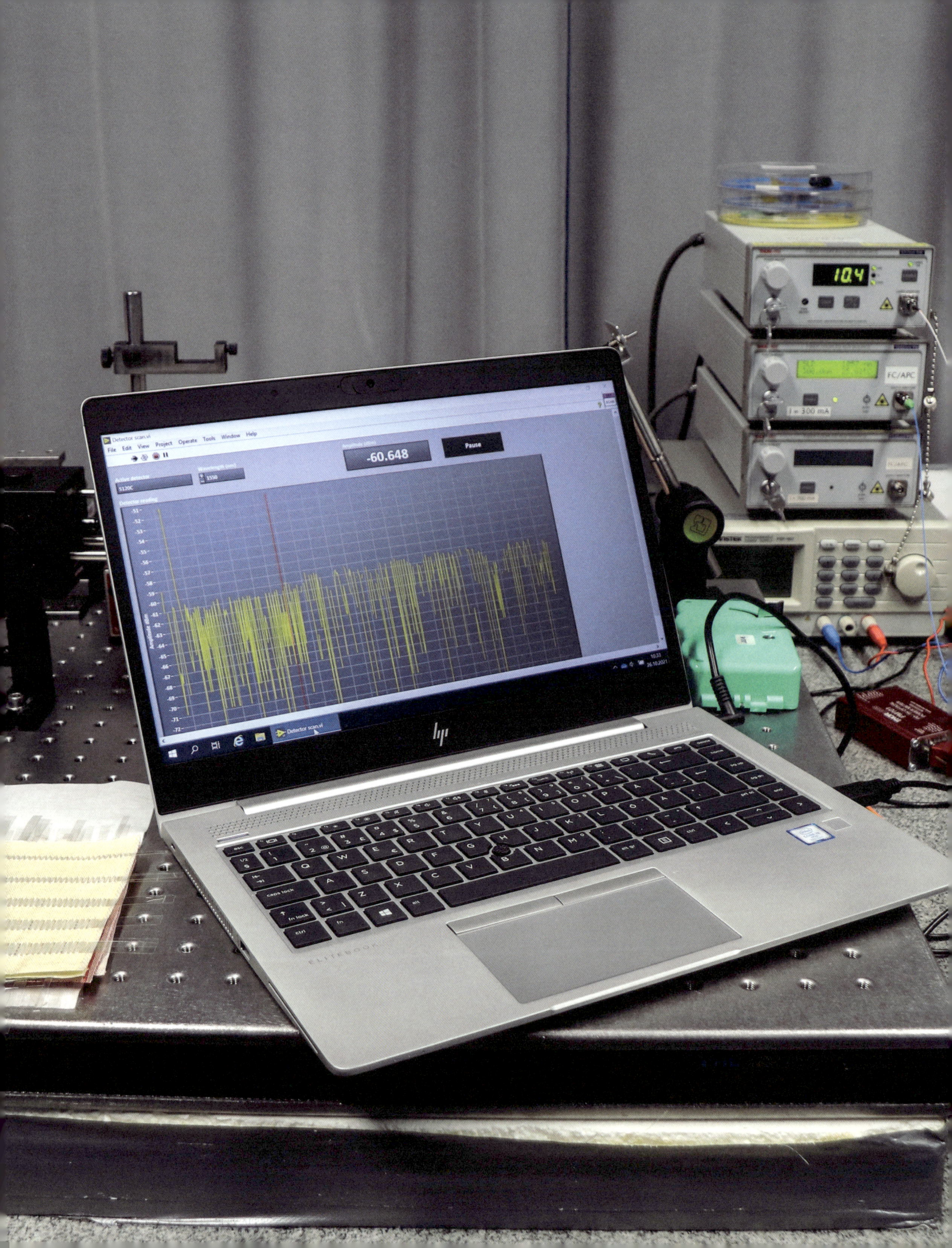

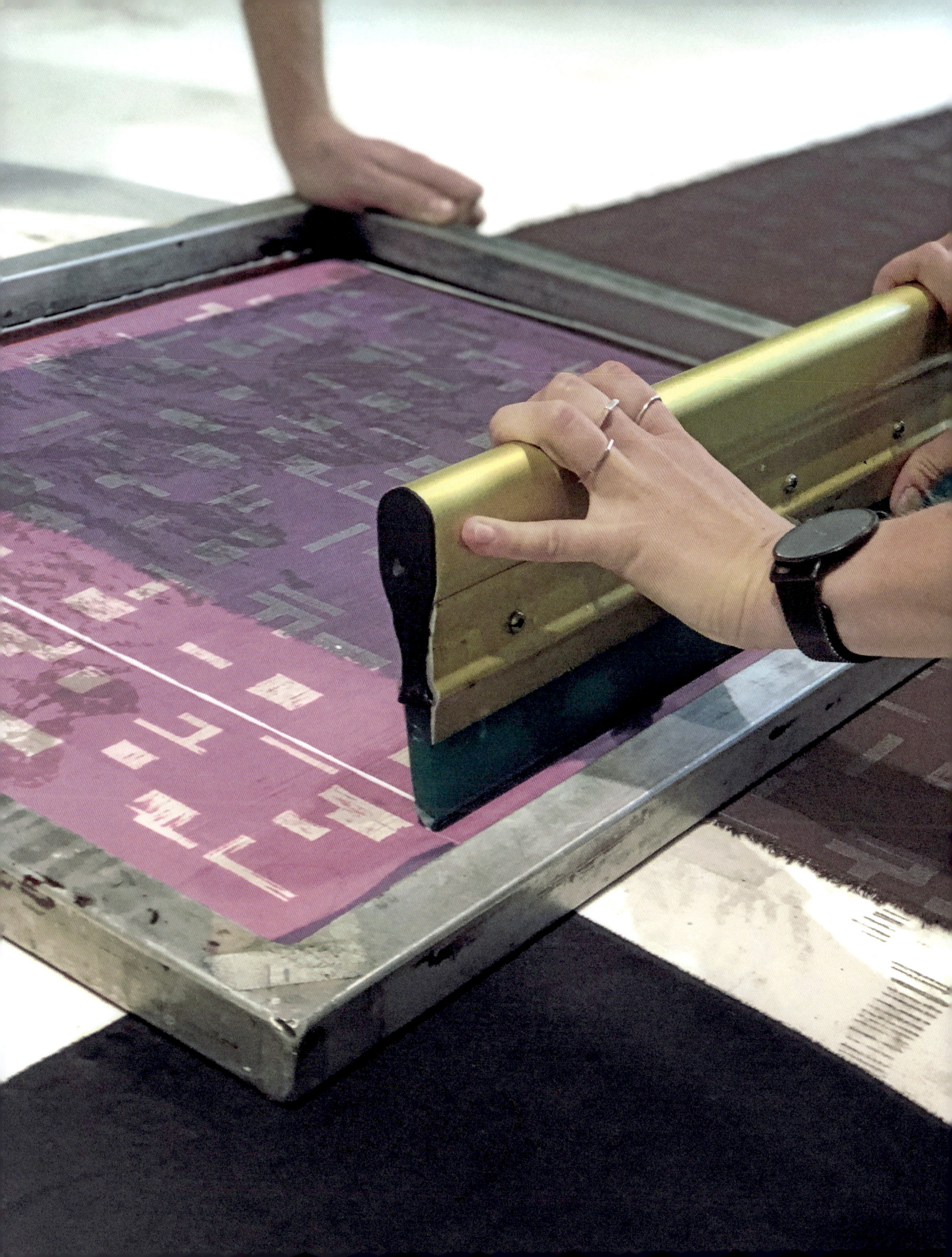

PREFACE
STEPHANIE KAHNAU

VORWORT

Women and textiles are often thought of as belonging together, and they do indeed seem to be closely associated with one another. Still, why should that be so? Viewed from the historical standpoint, women have surely not always voluntarily opted for working with textiles but have been pressured into taking on particular roles that have been societally allocated to them and with which they have been expected to comply. Nevertheless, they have so often become deeply passionate about handling this material, developing an artistic idiom and, concomitantly, promoting self-determined practices that articulate powerful dissent to assumptions that the only function textiles have is providing women with an artisanal pastime. In that sense, textiles have become not only a tool but also a means for expression: sensitive, political, defiant.

This context shapes the question the present book sets out with: what happens when women not only feel assigned to textiles but also consciously take on the debate about this field?

It is not about identifying a singular woman in textiles – but making many visible: it is about individual stances, differing life realities, manifold approaches to work. This volume views itself as a stage for polyphony: it collates positions that deal with analogue techniques or use digital tools that are intersectionally positioned between art, design and research.

In their full spectrum textiles belong to humanity's earliest forms of cultural expression and of artisanal arts – women have always been key vehicles for and designers of that culture. Whether weaving, knitting, tufting, dyeing or printing, textile skills have been handed down for generations, often privately, even secretly, or in everyday settings, and have remained invisible in many art historical narratives or have not attracted the attention they deserve.

After all, textiles are not just material – they are a medium. For centuries women have used textiles to show they are caring, to tell stories, to mark allegiances or to create art or artisanal spaces that stand on the symbolic plane for feminist self-determination, visibility and resistance and thus enable a form of empowerment. The works assembled in this illustrated book show how multifaceted these forms of expression have grown – between tradition and innovation, between body and space, between function and speculation.

The force field of textile and body runs through many of the works collected here. For textiles are often body-hugging – they literally touch us. And it is in this very closeness that the functional, critical, fragile and poetic potential of many textile works unfolds.

Drawing on a virtually infinite pool of impressive works encountered in the course of research, this book concentrates on forty twentieth- and twenty-first-century female positions from the European region. Not to perpetuate a Western perspective, but rather to mark a point of departure and, we hope, to inspire more publications that can enlarge the angle of vision with an approach based on sound research. The women who are the protagonists presented here are engaging with the interfaces between creation, art, design, materials development and crafts.

All designers presented in this book can draw on professional experience with textiles as a medium or with specific textile-related techniques. The history of the formal career paths embarked on by each individual plays a minor role in the presentation, even if many of the women introduced here have a background of training in textiles. The illustrations reproducing their works play a pivotal role in the presentation of the stances represented by the designers. This documentary approach is accompanied by introductory texts as well as four guest essays that expand the perspectives on textile practices by idiosyncratic theoretical positions.

Finally, but not least importantly, the presentation is forward-looking. At a time when resources are running short, identities are fluid and production methods are being called into question, the social and political significance of textile praxis is mounting. The women designers featured here demonstrate that textiles are not a fringe phenomenon in the history of art and design but rather represent a call for rethinking them from other angles. Textiles stand for an autonomous, wide-ranging history of traditions and today still represent a powerful medium for contemporary creativity.

In order to experience the contents of this book from a spatial and tactile perspective, an exhibition is planned for 2027 in collaboration with the Staatliches Textil- und Industriemuseum Augsburg (State Textile and Industry Museum in Augsburg), tim for short. Showing textile-related design in a museum context has, fortunately, become an increasingly frequent occurrence and for some time has been an established practice. Although progress has obviously been made, a great deal of hidden potential remains to be tapped into. With the planned exhibition we would like to steer these developments into clear channels and share in actively shaping the course they take.

DE Frauen und Textilien werden oft zusammengedacht und scheinen eng miteinander verbunden zu sein. Doch warum ist das so? Historisch gesehen haben sich Frauen sicherlich nicht immer freiwillig für die Arbeit mit Textilien entschieden, sondern wurden durch gesellschaftliche Zuschreibungen und Erwartungen in bestimmte Rollen gedrängt. Trotzdem entwickelten sie immer wieder eine tiefe Leidenschaft im Umgang mit dem Material, eine künstlerische Sprache und damit selbstbestimmte Praktiken, die einen kraftvollen Widerspruch zu Annahmen formulieren, Textil hätte seine einzige Funktion darin, Frauen einen handwerklichen Zeitvertreib zu bieten. Textilien wurden in diesem Sinne nicht nur Werkzeug, sondern auch Ausdrucksmittel - sensibel, politisch, widerständig.

Dieser Zusammenhang bildet die Ausgangsfrage des vorliegenden Buches: Was passiert, wenn Frauen sich dem Textilen nicht nur zugewiesen fühlen, sondern sich die Auseinandersetzung mit diesem Bereich bewusst aneignen?

Dabei geht es nicht um eine Identifizierung der Frau im Textilbereich - sondern um die Sichtbarmachung von vielen: Um individuelle Haltungen, unterschiedliche Lebensrealitäten, vielfältige Arbeitsweisen. Dieser Band versteht sich als Bühne für eine Vielstimmigkeit: Er versammelt Positionen, die sich mit analogen Techniken beschäftigen oder digitale Tools nutzen, die sich an der Schnittstelle zwischen Kunst, Design und Forschung bewegen.

Textilien in ihrer vollen Bandbreite gehören zu den ältesten kulturellen Ausdrucksformen und Dokumenten der Handwerkskünste der Menschheit – Frauen waren und sind zentrale Trägerinnen sowie Gestalterinnen dieser Kultur. Ob gewebt, gestrickt, getuftet, gefärbt oder bedruckt: Textiles Wissen wurde über Generationen hinweg oft im Privaten, im Verborgenen oder auch im Alltäglichen weitergegeben – und blieb dabei in vielen kunsthistorischen Erzählungen unsichtbar oder erlangte nicht die Aufmerksamkeit, die es verdient hat.

Denn Textil ist nicht nur Material – es ist Medium. Frauen haben es über Jahrhunderte hinweg genutzt, um Fürsorge zu zeigen, Geschichten zu erzählen, Zugehörigkeit zu markieren oder künstlerisch oder gestalterisch Räume zu schaffen, die symbolisch für feministische Selbstbestimmung, Sichtbarkeit und Widerstand stehen – und damit eine Form von Ermächtigung ermöglichen. Die in diesem Bildband versammelten Arbeiten zeigen, wie facettenreich sich diese Ausdrucksformen bis heute entwickelt haben – zwischen Tradition und Innovation, zwischen Körper und Raum, zwischen Funktion und Spekulation.

Das Spannungsfeld von Textil und Körper zieht sich dabei durch viele der hier versammelten Arbeiten. Denn Textilien sind häufig körpernah – sie berühren uns buchstäblich. Und gerade in dieser Nähe entfaltet sich das funktionale, kritische, fragile und poetische Potenzial vieler textiler Werke. Aus einer kaum zu überblickenden Fülle eindrucksvoller Arbeiten, die im Zuge der Recherche zusammengetragen wurden, konzentriert sich dieses Buch auf 40 ausgewählte weibliche Positionen des 20. und 21. Jahrhunderts aus dem europäischen Raum. Nicht, um die westliche Perspektive zu perpetuieren, sondern um einen Ausgangspunkt zu setzen und hoffentlich weitere Publikationen anzuregen, die diesen Blickwinkel fundiert erweitern können. Die vorgestellten Akteurinnen bewegen sich an den Schnittstellen zwischen Gestaltung, Kunst, Design, Materialentwicklung und Handwerk.

Alle in diesem Band vorgestellten Gestalterinnen können auf eine professionelle Beschäftigung mit dem Medium Textil oder mit spezifischen textilen Techniken zurückgreifen. Dabei spielt der jeweilige formale Werdegang eine untergeordnete Rolle – auch wenn viele der vorgestellten Frauen einen textilen Ausbildungshintergrund mitbringen. Die Abbildungen der Arbeiten spielen eine zentrale Rolle bei der Präsentation der vorgestellten Positionen: die Vielfalt und Ausdruckskraft textiler Arbeiten soll sichtbar werden. Begleitet wird dieser dokumentarische Ansatz von einleitenden Texten sowie vier Gastbeiträgen, die Perspektiven auf textile Praktiken um eigensinnige theoretische Positionen erweitern.

Nicht zuletzt soll der Blick in die Zukunft gerichtet werden. In einer Zeit, in der Ressourcen knapp, Identitäten im Wandel sind und Produktionsmethoden hinterfragt werden, erhält textile Praxis zunehmend gesellschaftliche und politische Bedeutung. Die hier vorgestellten Gestalterinnen zeigen: Textil ist kein Randphänomen der Kunst- oder Designgeschichte, sondern fordert dazu auf, das historische Gewebe hinter dem Textil, die kulturellen Praktiken und Einschreibungen infrage zu stellen – oder aus anderen Perspektiven zu denken. Textil steht für eine eigenständige, weite Historie von Überlieferungen und stellt bis heute ein kraftvolles Medium zeitgenössischer Gestaltung dar.

Um den Inhalt dieses Buches auch räumlich und haptisch erfahrbar zu machen, ist in Zusammenarbeit mit dem Staatlichen Textil- und Industriemuseum Augsburg – kurz: tim – eine Ausstellung für das Jahr 2027 geplant. Textile Gestaltung im musealen Kontext zu zeigen, ist erfreulicherweise seit einiger Zeit zunehmend etabliert. Dennoch bleibt noch viel Potenzial ungenutzt. Mit der geplanten Ausstellung möchten wir diesen Entwicklungen eine klare Richtung geben und sie aktiv mitgestalten.

TEXTILE PRACTICES
ART, CREATIVITY, DESIGN AND CRAFTS
STEPHANIE KAHNAU

TEXTILE PRAKTIKEN: KUNST, GESTALTUNG,
DESIGN UND HANDWERK

Textile praxis moves along a sliding scale between art, creativity, design and crafts, a scale that enables practitioners to transgress boundaries, to develop interstitially between categories and to explore new spaces. It is in this complexity that its potential lies. Before we address the multilayered contexts of textiles, however, the various terms that surface in relation to this medium must be subjected to a brief semantic search.

Textile work is often viewed as a crafts activity and, thus, traditionally assigned to the decorative or applied arts field. This classification often has a pejorative connotation, as if crafts were less relevant or less 'art-related', although both complex technological and creative processes play a role here. Yet the very fact that many techniques have to be executed 'by hand' and are not, therefore, reproducible by machine makes what is known as the applied arts a demanding field, one that is relevant and well worth knowing about, which deserves to be given a closer look.

In parallel there is the term 'design', which is used nowadays for manifold conceptual processes. Historically, the term derives from the Latin *designare*–which, apart from 'to design', also stands for 'designate', 'earmark' or 'plan'. Based on the Latin, the noun *disegno* became commonplace usage in the Italian Renaissance as a term that denoted both the idea entertained by an artist as well as their ability to give form to it in drawing. Thus the drawing represented a necessary transitional stage, as it were, for the intended work and its given form – alongside architecture, sculpture and painting, this was ultimately also true of tapestry weaving. In the Bauhaus era that contradictory locus was transferred to industrial contexts under the heading of 'Functionalism' and was, therefore, viewed as the shaping foundation for what would later be subsumed under the term 'textile design'. In the 1950s and 1960s the term began to resurface more frequently in specialist academic circles, training programmes and university courses and gradually became standard usage. Contemporary usage defines textile design as the conception and designing of textile surfaces, patterns or structures with a view to application, reproducibility and functionality. The focus is often on collaboration with industry or commercially viable fashion brands. Digital designing processes, serial production and the aim of positioning textiles in contexts of concrete application are typical of this trend. In German-speaking countries the term Gestaltung also exists, but it has no direct match in English. It is often used in contradistinction to the contemporary term 'design' to indicate a stance taken up against the superficial decoration of consumer objects. Hence Gestaltung means, on the one hand, to give form to something from within its intrinsic functional context while transcending that context. On the other hand, the term concedes awareness of aesthetic-artistic expression. In the latter sense, the term 'textile design' also belongs in this semantic grouping; accordingly, it designates a form being developed from within through the deliberate choice of material but also includes the dimension of a degree of experimental artistic openness that can reveal new perceptions.

In comparison, there is the broadly defined and continuously changing term 'art'. If you take a look at its derivation as well – Latin *ars* – it is concerned, at least in line with its etymological interpretation, with skilfulness, a skill as learnt, but also craft. This term can be traced back, to greatly simplify matters, semantically to the ancient Greek *tékhne* and *poiesis*; even though the two terms are to be differently interpreted, the former connotes technical skill applied with a specific aim whereas the latter means 'making', that is, the process of producing. In the modern age, finally, an individualistic definition of art has been added that sees human activity as creative, which has quite often led to exaltation or overhyping of the term 'art'. Textile art, too, has suffered from this development by being dismissed as a manual activity and viewed purely as 'women's work'. And all this, despite textile art being closely linked with tékhne, for it entails proceeding technically in a way based on learnt skill yet nonetheless has the potential for developing artistic experiential spaces.

This is precisely the point at which an inclusive approach to looking at textile work sets in: how textile practices, as can be investigated on the basis of the following stances, are often positioned on a sliding scale between the terms explained above. When does a textile object belong to everyday life and when is it a museum piece? Think of tapestry: where does the mundane utilitarian object that is a 'carpet' end and where does the depth of field that makes it art begin? And what about fashion: from what point on does it merge with its functional character in everyday wear and when does it stand out to such an extent that it changes physical perceptions and behaviours?

EXAMPLE FOR A QUIPU, OR PERUVIAN KNOT-RECORD, TAKEN FROM LESLIE LELAND LOCKE, "THE ANCIENT QUIPU, A PERUVIAN KNOT RECORD", AMERICAN ANTHROPOLOGIST, 14, 1912, PLATE XXII; ORIGINAL CAPTION: "THE NUMBER OF PENDENT CORDS (95) IS INDICATED BY KNOTS ON THE ENDS OF THE MAIN CORD. B8705 AMERICAN MUSEUM OF NATURE"

DE Textile Praxis bewegt sich zwischen Kunst, Gestaltung, Design und Handwerk. Sie erlaubt es, Grenzen zu überschreiten, sich zwischen den Kategorien zu entwickeln und neue Räume zu erkunden. Gerade in dieser Vielschichtigkeit liegt ihr Potenzial. Bevor wir uns aber den vielschichtigen Kontexten des Textils widmen, bedarf es einer kurzen Verortung der verschiedenen Begriffe, die im Bezug zu diesem Medium auftauchen.

Textile Arbeit wird häufig als handwerkliche Tätigkeit verstanden und damit traditionell dem Bereich des Kunsthandwerks zugeordnet. In dieser Einordnung schwingt nicht selten eine Abwertung mit, als wäre das Handwerk weniger relevant oder weniger »künstlerisch«, obwohl hier sowohl komplexe, technologische wie auch kreative Prozesse eine Rolle spielen. Doch grade die Tatsache, dass viele Techniken »durch die Hand« hergestellt werden müssen und eben nicht maschinell reproduzierbar sind, macht das sogenannte Kunsthandwerk zu einem anspruchsvollen und wissensrelevanten Bereich, der es verdient, näher betrachtet zu werden.

Parallel dazu steht der aus dem Englischen übernommene Begriff »Design«, wie er heute verwendet wird, für diverse Entwurfsprozesse. Historisch ist dieser auf das lateinische *designare* zurückzuführen – was neben »entwerfen«, auch für »bezeichnen«, »vorsehen« oder »planen« steht. Darauf basierend wurde in der italienischen Renaissance der Begriff *disegno* geläufig, der sowohl die Idee des Kunstschaffenden als auch dessen gestaltgebendes, zeichnerisches Vermögen bezeichnete. Die Zeichnung bildete damit eine Art notwendiges Übergangsstadium für das angestrebte, formgewordene Werk – neben Architektur, Bildhauerei und Malerei galt dies letztlich auch für Gobelins.

In der Zeit des Bauhauses wurde jenes Spannungsfeld unter dem Stichwort des Funktionalismus in industrielle Zusammenhänge überführt und damit prägende Grundlage für das, was später unter dem Begriff »Textildesign« verstanden wurde. Ab den 1950er- und 1960er-Jahren tauchte der Begriff vermehrt in akademischen Fachkreisen, Ausbildungen und Studiengängen auf und setzte sich allmählich im Sprachgebrauch durch. Im zeitgenössischen Verständnis bezeichnet Textildesign die Konzeption und den Entwurf von textilen Flächen, Mustern oder Strukturen mit Blick auf Anwendung, Reproduzierbarkeit und Funktionalität. Häufig steht dabei die Zusammenarbeit mit Industrie oder Modeunternehmen im Vordergrund. Typisch sind digitale Entwurfsprozesse, serielle Produktion und der Anspruch, das Textil in konkrete Gebrauchszusammenhänge zu überführen.

Im deutschsprachigen Raum existiert zusätzlich der Begriff »Gestaltung«, der im Englischen keine direkte Entsprechung hat. Er wird häufig in der Abgrenzung zum zeitgenössischen Begriff »Design« genutzt, um sich gegen die oberflächliche Dekoration von Konsumgegenständen zu positionieren. Unter Gestaltung versteht man daher einerseits, einer Sache aus ihrem intrinsischen Funktionszusammenhang heraus eine Form zu geben. Der Begriff räumt andererseits ein Bewusstsein für einen ästhetisch-künstlerischen Ausdruck ein. In diesem Sinne reiht sich auch der Begriff der Textilgestaltung ein; entsprechend bezeichnet er, dass eine Form von innen heraus durch eine gezielte Materialwahl entwickelt wird, und schließt zudem mit ein, dass in einem derartigen Prozess eine gewisse experimentelle, künstlerische Offenheit steckt, die neue Wahrnehmungen eröffnen kann.

Demgegenüber steht der weit gefasste und sich stetig im Wandel befindende Begriff der »Kunst«. Betrachtet man auch hier die Wortherkunft - etwa das lateinische *ars* - geht es hier, zumindest der etymologischen Deutung nach, um Geschicklichkeit, Fertigkeit, aber auch um Handwerk. Dieser Begriff lässt sich, sehr vereinfacht gesprochen, im Altgriechischen auf *téchne* und *poiesis* zurückzuführen - auch wenn diese Begriffe verschieden ausgelegt werden, konnotiert ersterer das technische, auf ein Ziel gerichtetes Herstellungswissen, während letzterer das Machen, sprich, die Hervorbringung meint. Daran knüpft in der Neuzeit schließlich ein individualistisches Kunstverständnis an, die menschliche Tätigkeit als eine schöpferische aufzufassen, was nicht selten zur Überhöhung des Kunstbegriffs führte. Darunter litt nicht zuletzt auch die Textilkunst, die als handwerkliche Tätigkeit abgetan und rein als »weibliche Arbeit« angesehen wurde. Dabei steht Textilkunst in enger Verbindung zur *téchne*, denn es ist ein auf Wissen basierendes, technisches Vorgehen und birgt gleichwohl das Potenzial, künstlerische Erfahrungsräume zu entwickeln.

Ein inklusiver Ansatz in der Betrachtung textiler Arbeit setzt genau hier an: Wie anhand der folgenden Positionen erkundet werden kann, bewegen sich textile Praktiken nicht selten zwischen den oben aufgeführten Begriffen. Wann gehört ein textiles Objekt in den Alltag und wann ins Museum?

Women and textiles: unheeded but making an impact

The cultural relevance of creativity in textiles is often misjudged – and likewise the leading role of the woman as an acteur in artistic processes. The contrasting field between specialist expert skills and social inequality is still clinging to textile praxis and was the point of departure for this book.

Textile practices imply far more than merely designing surfaces. They are about precise, exploratory investigation of structures on a small scale; they are about developing materials that possess functional, aesthetic and cultural implications and command the interplay of perfecting and improvisation with a variety of production techniques.

These facets are revealed in very different ways by the acteurs. Each position presented in the following illustrates this in its own, characteristic way. The present book focuses on the diversity of textiles, which are constantly being enriched by a complex interplay of material and form, body and space; aesthetic and functional qualities, tactile stimuli and cultural significance are interwoven in them: from textile art – for instance, in Caroline Achaintre and Joana Schneider (p. 63 and p. 187) – through 'intelligent' textiles that react to touch or reveal physical condition, as in Iga Węglińska (p. 211), on up to innovative acoustic materials developments as exemplified by Annette Douglas (p. 91) or approaches to sustainable production such as the Cradle to Cradle principle championed by Sabrina Stadlober (p. 191). In fact, the question of responsible handling of resources, material origins and processing informs virtually all works presented.

Nevertheless, textile work often remains in the background although, or perhaps also because, its outcomes are often part of a larger creative process. The impact it makes often develops only in an interdisciplinary context – such as fashion, interior design or product design – one reason why this diverse (professional) field is still underrepresented in the public perception. The present book would like to contribute to giving this activity, which although in part unnoticed nonetheless makes an impact, higher visibility for a broader public.

Textiles as a (world) language

The cultural depths of the field of textiles can also be plumbed via the medium of language. As far as terminology is concerned, 'textile(s)', as Christina Leitner, head of the Textiles Zentrum Haslach (Austria)

describes it in her guest essay (p. 40), refers not only to the material and crafts aspects. It links practical with poetic, communication with art, and thus opens up multilayered semantic contexts. Leiter elucidates this polysemy by addressing holistic perception, social nexus and knowledge retention.

Viewed from the historical angle, 'textiles' does not surface as a generic concept for materials and techniques until the close of the nineteenth century. Yet thinking in terms of textiles is much older: it belongs to humanity's earliest cultural technologies. Textiles functioned as barter goods, as means of payment, or were the expression of social and cultural affiliation. There are textile-based metaphors, sayings and idiomatic expressions in almost all languages: we 'spin yarns', 'get tied up in knots', 'untangle knotty problems' or 'link up with someone' and in this way are constantly and unwittingly referring to the worldwide cultural technology of weaving. These expressions occur not just in sayings but also in Greek myths and tales, such as Penelope weaving in The Odyssey or in the Arachne myth, as Silke Geppert points out in her essay (p. 44). One impressive example of the link between textiles and language comes from South America and specifically derives from the Inca. For a long time this was assumed to be a culture that managed without a writing system. Yet the Inca, as Sabine Hyland, a cultural anthropologist and ethnohistorian, has worked out, had a complex medium for storing information: what are called quipus (khipus).[1] These are known to have been cords in a variety of colours and deliberately knotted at certain points. According to Hyland, they functioned as information storage and communication devices. Numerical data could be transmitted by the position, number and type of knot – quipus might be defined as early textile-based coding or information systems.

Language interwoven with thinking in terms of textile also developed idiosyncratically in the industrialised West: invented in the early nineteenth century, the Jacquard loom is viewed as a precursor of programming, hence of the computer, because it was controlled by chains of punched cards. The British mathematician Ada Lovelace (1815–1852) contributed substantially to the development of both the loom and the computer.[2] She is viewed as a pioneering computer scientist. Along with Charles Babbage (1791–1871) she is credited with developing the conception of the Analytical Engine, one of the earliest calculating machines. Ada Lovelace bequeathed an appo-

ADA LOVELACE, DAGUERREOTYPE BY ANTOINE CLAUDET, C. 1843 (CROPPED)

Man denke an den Gobelin: Wo hört der alltägliche Gebrauchsgegenstand »Teppich« auf und wo beginnt seine künstlerische Bildtiefe? Und wie verhält es sich in der Mode: Ab wann geht sie mit ihrem funktionalen Charakter in der Alltagsbekleidung auf und wann tritt sie derart in den Vordergrund, dass sie körperliche Wahrnehmungen und Verhaltensweisen verändert?

Frauen und Textilien: Unbeachtet, aber wirkungsvoll

Die kulturelle Relevanz von textiler Gestaltung wird häufig verkannt – ebenso wie die tragende Rolle der Frau als Akteurin in künstlerischen Prozessen. Dieses Spannungsfeld zwischen fachlichen Expertisen und gesellschaftlicher Ungleichheit begleitet die textile Praxis bis heute und war Ausgangspunkt für dieses Buch.

Textile Praktiken implizieren weit mehr als das bloße Entwerfen von Oberflächen. Es geht um eine präzise, erforschende Auseinandersetzung mit Strukturen im Kleinen – um Materialentwicklung, die über funktionale, ästhetische und kulturelle Tragweite und das Zusammenspiel von Perfektionierung und Improvisation mit verschiedenen Herstellungstechniken verfügt.

Diese Facetten werden durch die Akteure:innen sehr unterschiedlich erschlossen. Jede der im Folgenden vorgestellten Positionen veranschaulicht dies auf charakteristische Weise. Im Zentrum des vorliegenden Bandes steht die Vielfalt des Textils, das sich immer wieder durch ein komplexes Zusammenspiel von Material und Form, Körper und Raum anreichert; ästhetische und funktionale Qualitäten, taktile Reize und kulturelle Bedeutungen verweben sich darin: von textiler Kunst – etwa bei Caroline Achaintre oder Joana Schneider (S. 63 und 187) – über »intelligente« Textilien, die auf Berührung reagieren oder körperliche Zustände sichtbar machen, so bei Iga Węglińska (S. 211), bis hin zu innovativen akustischen Materialentwicklungen wie bei Annette Douglas (S. 91) oder nachhaltigen Produktionsansätzen wie dem Cradle-to-Cradle-Prinzip von Sabrina Stadlober (S. 191). Dabei zieht sich die Frage nach einem verantwortungsvollen Umgang mit Ressourcen, Materialherkunft und Weiterverarbeitung durch nahezu alle vorgestellten Arbeiten.

Jedoch bleibt die textile Arbeit häufig im Hintergrund, obwohl oder vielleicht auch weil deren Resultate häufig Teil eines größeren gestalterischen Prozesses sind. Ihre Wirkung entfaltet sich oft im Zusammenspiel mit anderen Disziplinen – etwa Mode, Innenarchitektur oder Produktdesign – ein Grund, weshalb dieses vielseitige (Berufs-)Feld in der öffentlichen Wahrnehmung noch immer unterrepräsentiert ist. Das vorliegende Buch möchte dazu beitragen, die in Teilen unbemerkte, aber wirkungsvolle Tätigkeit für ein breites Publikum sichtbarer zu machen.

Textil als (Welt-)Sprache

Die kulturelle Tiefe des Bereichs Textil erschließt sich auch über das Medium der Sprache. Terminologisch verweist ›Textil‹, wie die Leiterin des Textilzentrums Haslach (Österreich), Christina Leitner in ihrem Gastbeitrag beschreibt (S. 40), nicht nur auf das Materielle und Handwerkliche. Es verbindet das Praktische mit dem Poetischen, die Kommunikation mit der Kunst – und eröffnet so vielschichtige Bedeutungszusammenhänge. Leitner zeigt diese Mehrdeutigkeit auf, indem sie ganzheitliche Wahrnehmung, gesellschaftliche Verbindung und Wissensspeicherung adressiert.

Historisch gesehen tauchte »Textil« als Oberbegriff für Materialien und Techniken erst Ende des 19. Jahrhunderts auf. Doch das textile Denken ist viel älter: es gehört zu den ersten Kulturtechniken der Menschheit. Textilien fungierten als Tauschgut, Zahlungsmittel oder sie waren Ausdruck sozialer und kultureller Zugehörigkeit. In fast allen Sprachen finden sich textile Metaphern, Sprichwörter oder Redewendungen: Wir »spinnen Geschichten«, »verstricken uns«, »entwirren Zusammenhänge« oder »knüpfen Verbindungen« und nehmen so immer wieder unbewusst Bezug auf die global verbreitete Kulturtechnik des Webens. Diese findet sich nicht nur in den Sprichwörtern, sondern in griechischen Mythen und Erzählungen, wie der webenden Penelope in der Odyssee oder in der Sage über Arachne wieder, worauf Silke Geppert in ihrem Beitrag verweist (S. 44).

Ein eindrucksvolles Beispiel der Verbindung von Textil und Sprache stammt aus dem südamerikanischen Raum und geht zurück auf die Inka. Lange Zeit wurde davon ausgegangen, dass diese Kultur ohne eigenes Schriftsystem auskam. Doch verfügten die Inka, wie es die Kulturanthropologin Sabine Hyland herausgearbeitet hat, über ein komplexes Medium der Informationsspeicherung: die sogenannten Quipus.[1] Als solche gelten Schnüre in unterschiedlichen Farben und mit bewusst gesetzten Knoten. Laut Hyland dienten sie der Speicherung und Übermittlung von Informationen. Durch Position, Anzahl und Art der Knoten konnten numerische Daten weitergegeben

site description of the relationship between language and textiles: 'We may say most aptly that the Analytical Engine weaves Algebraic patterns, just as the Jacquard loom weaves flowers and leaves.'[3] She described computing as weaving thoughts, as a logical linkage of data and commands, similar to the linkage between warp and weft threads. Lovelace envisaged the computer as a loom for ideas – a poetic as well as technological metaphor.

Catrin Lorch (also see her essay on p. 52), theorist and weaver, has developed another interesting way of accessing textiles by honing her approaches through art historical observations and aesthetic theories. In so doing she shifts the focus from the 'finished product' to the initiation of processes. This take on the field of textiles lends it a performative character. Subsuming her art under the heading 'Action Weavings' (after Travis Meinolf), Lorch stages textile actions to bring people together, open discussions and create networks.

From craft to art form

Studying designers such as Otti Berger and Gunta Stölzl (see p. 71 and p. 199) vividly evokes the formative yet ambivalent role of the textile workshop at the Bauhaus. Although women at the Bauhaus were often banished from other divisions of the school and 'assigned' to weaving, that was where they developed creative independence and technical innovation and also attained enormous economic importance. Traditional weaving techniques were associated with an abstract language of forms, and, alongside functional objects, aesthetic paradigms emerged to shape what is known as the avant-garde of Modernism and its visual strategies. Although the allocation of gender roles was still relatively conservative, the status of the Bauhaus ensured that textiles were acknowledged for the first time as a profession in their own right,[4] which went beyond the 'decorative' arts and the presumed 'women's work' associated with them. Nonetheless, decades would pass before the women artists at the Bauhaus were sufficiently honoured for their work: it was not until 2018 that a grand retrospective at Tate Modern in London was devoted to Anni Albers, to take one example. After the Second World War, textile design underwent palpable change. Technological advances and new materials opened up additional application possibilities. Synthetic fibres began to be used more in the 1950s and 1960s and influenced the textile creative repertoire. Textiles became increasing-ly technologised and consequently more synthetic – not just for furnishings or interiors but also for innovative applications in architecture or space travel. New processes including digital printing, heat setting (thermofixation) and lamination are just a few facets of this trend.

In parallel, textile design played a key role in rebuilding post-war daily life, particularly in the interior decoration and furnishing sectors. Demand for functional modern materials surged, and designers such as Lucienne Day (p. 83) and Marli Ehrman created textiles in keeping with the times for a broader section of the population. Thus design became a means of expression that was no longer exclusively elite but actually a part of everyday life.

In the 1960s and 1970s the textile arts came to be more highly appreciated, which is shown by the founding of the Biennales internationales de la Tapisserie Lausanne),[5] which took place from 1962 until 1995; thanks to those events modern textile art was first able to assert itself as an autonomous art form. At the same time women artists began to reinterpret textiles as a form of expression for the feminist movement, physicality and space and to make them visible within social contexts. With three-dimensional, sculptural works they blew narrow notions of what textile art should be wide open. Biennials and triennials followed in the Netherlands, the Scandinavian countries and also in Germany.

Textiles became sculpture, installation, social gesture, an institution of feminist empowerment. Synthetic materials such as nylon or fibreglass were added to the vibrant mix. Artists including Magdalena Abakanowicz (p. 59), Hannah Ryggen and Lenore Tawney abandoned the classic picture format to work with soft handmade materials, often in large formats and in three dimensions. What is known as Soft Sculpture emerged as a deliberate countermovement opposed to the prevailing sculpture of post-war Modernism, so often interpreted as 'masculine'. Textile materials united the intimate, physical and fragile with political, feminist and socially critical content.

Even after the demise of the Lausanne Biennial the field remained lively: in Germany initiatives were founded such as the Deutsche Gruppe Textilkunst (German Textile Art Group), which participated in further developing and interconnecting this profession.

It was not until the early 2000s that the picture began to change noticeably, a development that was driven forwards not least

werden – die Quipus können somit als frühtextile Codierungs- oder Informationssysteme verstanden werden.

Auch in der westlichen Industrialisierung entwickelt sich das sprachlich-textile Denken auf eigenwillige Weise: Der Jacquard-Webstuhl, entwickelt im frühen 19. Jahrhundert, gilt aufgrund seiner Lochkartensteuerung als Vorläufer der Programmierung und damit des Computers. Dazu hat die britische Mathematikerin Ada Lovelace (1815–1852) maßgeblich beigetragen.[2] Sie gilt als Pionierin der Informatik. Gemeinsam mit Charles Babbage (1791–1871) war sie an der Konzeption der Analytical Engine beteiligt – einer der ersten Rechenmaschinen. Ada Lovelace benannte die Beziehung zwischen Sprache und Textil treffend: »We may say most aptly that the Analytical Engine weaves Algebraical patterns, just as the Jacquard loom weaves flowers and leaves.«[3] Sie beschrieb das Rechnen als Weben von Gedanken, als ein logisches Verknüpfen von Daten und Befehlen, ähnlich der Verbindung von Kett- und Schussfäden. In ihrer Vision wurde der Computer zum Webstuhl für Ideen – eine poetische und zugleich technische Metapher.

Einen weiteren interessanten Zugang zum Textil entwickelt die Theoretikerin und Weberin Catrin Lorch (vgl. auch ihr Beitrag auf S. 52), indem sie ihre Ansätze durch kunsthistorische Beobachtungen und ästhetische Theorien schärft. Dabei verlagert sie den Schwerpunkt vom »fertigen Produkt« zur Eröffnung von Prozessen. So erhält der Bereich Textil einen performativen Charakter. Unter dem Begriff des sogenannten »Action Weavings« (nach Travis Meinolf) inszeniert Lorch textile Aktionen, um Menschen zu verbinden, Diskurse zu eröffnen und Netzwerke zu schaffen.

Vom Handwerk zur Kunstform

Durch die Auseinandersetzung mit Gestalterinnen wie beispielsweise Otti Berger oder Gunta Stölzl (s. S. 71 und 199) lässt sich die zugleich prägende und ambivalente Rolle der Textilwerkstatt am Bauhaus eindrücklich nachvollziehen. Obwohl Frauen dort oftmals aus anderen Bereichen der Schule verdrängt und der Weberei »zugewiesen« wurden, entwickelten sie gerade dort gestalterische Eigenständigkeit, technische Innovation und erzielten zudem eine große wirtschaftliche Bedeutung. Traditionelle Webtechniken wurden mit abstrakter Formensprache verbunden und es entstanden neben neuen funktionalen Objekten auch ästhetische Paradigmen, die die sogenannte Avantgarde der Moderne und ihre Bildstrategien prägten. Trotz der noch immer relativ konservativen Rollenverteilung ermöglichte der Status des Bauhauses die Anerkennung des Bereichs Textil erstmals als eigenständiges Metier, das über die »angewandte« Kunst und die damit verbundene, vermeintliche »Frauenarbeit« hinausgeht. Gleichwohl wurden die Künstlerinnen des Bauhauses erst nach vielen Jahrzehnten umfassend für ihr Werk gewürdigt – so wurde zum Beispiel Anni Albers erst im Jahr 2018 eine große Retrospektive in der Tate Modern in London gewidmet.

Nach dem Zweiten Weltkrieg erlebte die textile Gestaltung einen spürbaren Wandel. Technologischer Fortschritt und neue Materialien eröffneten dem Textildesign zusätzliche Wirkungsmöglichkeiten. Kunstfasern kamen in den 1950er- und 1960er-Jahren verstärkt zum Einsatz und beeinflussten das gestalterische Repertoire. Textilien wurden zunehmend technisiert und damit synthetischer – nicht nur für Möbel oder Innenräume, sondern auch für innovative Anwendungen in Architektur oder Raumfahrt. Neue Verfahren wie Digitaldruck, Thermofixierung oder Laminierung sind einige Aspekte davon.

Parallel dazu spielte Textildesign eine zentrale Rolle beim Wiederaufbau des Nachkriegsalltags – insbesondere im Wohn- und Möbelbereich. Die Nachfrage nach funktionalen, modernen Stoffen stieg an, und Designerinnen wie Lucienne Day (S. 83) oder Marli Ehrman entwarfen zeitgemäße Textilien für eine breite Bevölkerungsschicht. So wurde Gestaltung nicht mehr ausschließlich elitäres Ausdrucksmittel, sondern Teil des alltäglichen Lebens.

In den 1960er- bis 1970er-Jahren stieg die Anerkennung textiler Künste, etwa durch die Gründung der Internationalen Biennale der Tapisserie in Lausanne,[5] die von 1962 bis 1995 stattfand, und dank der sich die moderne Textilkunst als eigenständige Kunstgattung erstmalig durchsetzte. Gleichzeitig begannen Künstlerinnen, das Textil als Ausdrucksform feministischer Bewegung, Körperlichkeit und Raum neu zu interpretieren und innerhalb gesellschaftlicher Zusammenhänge sichtbar zu machen. Sie sprengten mit dreidimensionalen, skulpturalen Arbeiten die engen Vorstellungen von Textilkunst. Es folgten Biennalen und Triennalen in den Niederlanden, Skandinavien und auch in Deutschland.

Textil wurde Skulptur, Installation, soziale Geste, zur Institution feministischer Ermächtigung. Synthetische Materialien wie Nylon oder Glasfaser flossen mit ein und Künstlerinnen wie Magdalena Abakanowicz (S. 59), Hannah Ryggen oder Lenore Tawney

by a new generation of curators - among them women in decision-making positions. They made a point of focusing on textiles. By 2014 there were more exhibitions devoted solely to textiles in Europe and the US, among them *Fiber: Sculpture 1960-Present* in Boston and *Kunst & Textil* (Art & Textile) in Wolfsburg. The French art historian and curator Christine Macel, who curated the 57th Venice Biennale in 2017, is ultimately credited with presenting a wide range of choice textile works at that event and thus communicating the mass appeal of textiles as equals in the field of contemporary and fine arts.

As the above-outlined dynamics vividly exemplify, textiles were subject to a variety of influences in the past century and, concomitantly, to constant changes in the way they were perceived and evaluated. In any case, the ever widening rediscovery of textiles is all the more gratifying to see. More and more contemporary exponents of the fine arts, including Hanne Friis (p. 107), are finding out about textiles as a rewarding medium. This trend can also definitely be traced to the art market, which is in a position to exploit the textile sector to the fullest. For all its inherent ambivalence, this economic dynamo is also contributing to textiles - and with them the stances taken by women artists - being currently more highly visible than ever. In both galleries and the museum context the question arises of what the presentation possibilities are for textile works, which are quite often treated like pictures: flat, framed, hung on the wall in compliance with conservation dictates. Yet, unlike a conventional painting, textile works always have an intended reverse side, a second level that is often more informative than the front: it reveals technical details, traces of process and the material properties specific to a work.

Sabine Flaschberger, curator at the Museum für Gestaltung Zürich, has pointedly addressed this multidimensionality under the auspices of *Textile Manifeste - von Bauhaus bis Soft Sculpture* (Textile Manifestos - From Bauhaus to Soft Sculpture). In a deliberately chosen exhibition concept she thematised the multidimensionality of textile praxis. Her curatorial approach appears particularly impressive in the way a work by the textile artist Lissy Funk is presented, which she reconstructs in a guest essay for this book (p. 48).

Between traditional and contemporary technologies

Textile practices have only succeeded in evolving into the phenomena they represent today because they continue from where protracted, historically evolving processes have left off. The making of a fibre, a yarn, a fabric, and suchlike cannot really be imagined without specialist skills being handed down. And that means these traditional techniques are in a close relationship with time - not just because they have evolved historically but also because they can only be translated into individual creative praxis through practitioners' personal involvement with them. Textile practices are premised on slowness and contemplation - even though they are being continually developed. An inertia seems to cling to textiles that runs counter to the high-paced living of our era.

An opposing dynamic has shown up since the introduction of digital media: they contribute substantially to accelerating our production processes, consumer behaviour and everyday living and to 'optimising' these, and their salient features include virtual character, seamless interfaces and automation. The digital acceleration of the present has evidently awakened in us a new yearning for the analogue and for experiential tactility. Alfhild Külper (p. 151) is one artist who deliberately creates counter-spaces to digital dynamism with her works - they are soft and physically experienceable. In her hands, textiles can be experienced not only as a technical aid but also as a stance: physically demanding, deaccelerated, unfathomable, gruelling, sensuous. Many of the artists represented in this book emphasise physical work and view textiles as a form of resistance against virtual striving for efficiency.

Other textile practices, by contrast, consciously affirm the digital age. Stances such as those taken by Pauline van Dongen and Sofía Guridi (p. 87 and p. 115) represent a move towards technoid practices. They research integrating electronic technologies into textiles and using them to make textiles manipulable for contemporary needs - for instance, generating electricity through the solar cell fabrics that exemplify smart textiles.

This book is intended to reveal how wide-ranging textile creativity is - in all its cultural depth, its aesthetic impact and its social relevance - with reference to the forty examples chosen. To avoid squeezing diversity into a rigid schematic framework, we have eschewed chronological ordering and opted for an alphabetical arrangement by category - like a glossary that invites users to browse, linger and discover.

[1] See on this Sabine Hyland, 'Writing with Twisted Cords: The Inscriptive Capacity of Andean Khipus', *Current Anthropology* 58, no. 3 (June 2017), pp. 412–419, https://doi.org/10.1086/691682, last retrieved 3 March 2025.

[2] See, for instance, Sadie Plant, 'The Future Looms: Weaving Women and Cybernetics', *Body & Society* 1, no. 3–4 (November 1995), https://monoskop.org/images/1/13/Plant_Sadie_1995_The_Future_Looms_Weaving_Women_and_Cybernetics.pdf, last retrieved 14 September 2024, and Matteo Pasquinelli, *Das Auge des Meisters: Eine Sozialgeschichte künstlicher Intelligenz* (Münster: Unrast, 2024), pp. 80-85.

[3] Philip Morrison and Emily Morrison, *Charles Babbage and His Calculating Engines: Selected Writings by Charles Babbage and Others* (New York: Dover, 1961), p. 252, quoted in Plant, 'The Future Looms', p. 50.

[4] See Ulrike Müller, *Bauhaus-Frauen: Meisterinnen in Kunst, Handwerk und Design* (Berlin: Insel, 2021), p. 11, p. 43.

[5] See on this the foreword written by the former president of the Bayerische Akademie der Schönen Künste München, Professor Gerd Albers, in *Erste Biennale der Deutschen Tapisserie*, compiled by the Bayerische Akademie der Schönen Künste München, exh. cat. 1978, p. 9.

verließen das klassische Bildformat und arbeiteten mit weichen, handgefertigten Materialien – häufig in großen und dreidimensionalen Formaten. Die sogenannte Soft Sculpture entstand als bewusste Gegenbewegung zur dominanten, oft als »maskulin« verstandenen Bildhauerei der Nachkriegsmoderne. Textile Materialien verbanden das Intime, Körperliche, Fragile mit politischen, feministischen und gesellschaftskritischen Inhalten.

Auch nach dem Ende der Lausanner Biennale blieb das Feld in Bewegung: In Deutschland gründeten sich Initiativen wie die »Deutsche Gruppe Textilkunst«, die an der Weiterentwicklung und Vernetzung dieses Metiers beteiligt waren.

Erst zu Beginn der 2000er-Jahre veränderte sich das Bild deutlich. Was nicht zuletzt durch eine neue Generation von Kurator:innen – darunter vermehrt Frauen in Entscheidungspositionen – vorangetrieben wurde. Sie richteten den Fokus gezielt auf das Textile. Ab 2014 kam es vermehrt zu reinen Textilausstellungen in Europa und den USA, wie etwa *Fiber: Sculpture 1960-Present* in Boston oder *Kunst & Textil* in Wolfsburg. Schließlich war es die französische Kunsthistorikerin und Kuratorin Christine Macel, die 2017 auf der von ihr kuratierten 57. Biennale von Venedig eine reiche Auswahl textiler Arbeiten präsentierte und damit die die Gleichberechtigung des Textilen im Bereich der zeitgenössischen bzw. bildenden Kunst massenwirksam kommunizierte.

Wie man exemplarisch an den hier dargestellten Dynamiken sehen kann, unterlag das Textile im letzten Jahrhundert verschiedenen Einflüssen und, damit verbunden, einer sich stetig verändernden Aufmerksamkeit und Wertschätzung. Umso erfreulicher ist die sich weiter ausdehnende Wiederentdeckung des Textilen. Immer mehr zeitgenössische bildende Künstler:innen, wie etwa Hanne Friis (S. 107), entdecken das textile Medium für sich. Diese Bewegung lässt sich sicherlich auch auf den Kunstmarkt zurückführen, der den textilen Bereich ausschöpfen kann. Trotz der ihr innewohnenden Ambivalenz, trägt auch diese wirtschaftliche Dynamik dazu bei, dass die Sichtbarkeit des Textils – und damit auch von verstärkt weiblichen Positionen – derzeit so groß ist wie nie. Wie in den Galerien, so stellt sich auch im musealen Kontext die Frage nach den Präsentationsmöglichkeiten von textilen Werken, die nicht selten wie Bilder behandelt werden: flach, gerahmt, nach konservatorischen Vorgaben an die Wand gehängt. Doch im Unterschied zur gängigen Malerei besitzen textile Ar-

beiten immer auch eine intendierte Rückseite – eine zweite Ebene, die oft aufschlussreicher ist als die Vorderseite. Sie offenbart technische Details, Spuren des Prozesses und die Materialität des Werks.

Sabine Flaschberger, Kuratorin am Museum für Gestaltung Zürich, hat sich im Rahmen der Ausstellung *Textile Manifeste - von Bauhaus bis Soft Sculpture* gezielt mit dieser Mehrdimensionalität auseinandergesetzt. In einem bewusst gewählten Ausstellungskonzept thematisierte sie die Mehrdimensionalität textiler Praxis. Besonders eindrücklich erscheint ihr kuratorischer Ansatz in der Präsentation einer Arbeit der Textilkünstlerin Lissy Funk, die sie in einem Gastbeitrag für dieses Buch rekonstruiert (S. 48).

Zwischen tradierten und zeitgenössischen Technologien

Textile Praktiken konnten sich bis zu ihren heutigen Erscheinungsformen nur ausbilden, weil sie an langwierige, historisch gewachsene Prozesse anknüpfen. Die Herstellung einer Faser, eines Garns, eines Gewebes usw. sind ohne die Überlieferung von fachlichem Wissen kaum denkbar. Und so stehen diese traditionellen Techniken in einem engen Verhältnis zur Zeit – nicht nur, weil sie historisch gewachsen sind, sondern auch, weil sie erst durch persönliche Auseinandersetzung in eine eigene, kreative Praxis überführt werden können. Textile Praktiken setzen – auch wenn sie immer wieder weiterentwickelt werden – Langsamkeit und Kontemplation voraus. Dem Textil scheint eine Trägheit anzuhaften, die der Schnelllebigkeit unserer Zeit entgegenwirkt.

Eine gegensätzliche Dynamik zeichnet sich seit der Einführung der digitalen Medien ab; sie tragen maßgeblich dazu bei, unsere Produktionsprozesse, das Konsumverhalten oder Alltagsleben zu beschleunigen und zu »optimieren«. Charakteristisch sind ihr virtueller Charakter, die glatten Interfaces und die Automation. Die digitale Beschleunigung unserer Gegenwart hat offenbar eine neue Sehnsucht nach dem Analogen, dem haptischen Erleben geweckt. Künstlerinnen wie Alfhild Külper (S. 151) schaffen mit ihren Arbeiten bewusst Gegenräume zu digitalen Dynamiken – weich und körperlich erfahrbar. Textil wird hier nicht nur als technisches Hilfsmittel, sondern auch als Haltung erfahrbar: körperlich fordernd, entschleunigt, abgründig, zermürbend, sinnlich. Viele der im Buch vertretenen Künstlerinnen betonen die physische Arbeit und betrachten das Textil als eine Form des Widerstands gegen virtuelles Effizienzstreben.

Andere textile Praktiken affirmieren hingegen bewusst das Digitale. Positionen wie Pauline van Dongen oder Sofía Guridi (S. 87 und 155) stehen für eine solche Hinwendung zu technoiden Praktiken. Sie erforschen, wie sich elektronische Technologien in das Textil integrieren lassen und wie diese für aktuelle Bedarfe das Textil manipulierbar machen können – wie zum Beispiel die Generierung von Energie durch textile Solarzellen, die exemplarisch für die sogenannten Smart Textiles stehen.

Mit den 40 ausgewählten Positionen soll dieses Buch das breite Spektrum textiler Gestaltung sichtbar machen – in seiner kulturellen Tiefe, seiner ästhetischen Kraft und seiner gesellschaftlichen Relevanz. Um die Vielfalt nicht in ein starres Schema zu pressen, haben wir bewusst auf eine chronologische Ordnung verzichtet und eine alphabetische Kategorisierung gewählt – ähnlich einem Lexikon, das zum Blättern, Verweilen und Neuentdecken einlädt.

[1] Vgl. dazu Sabine Hyland, »Writing with Twisted Cords: The Inscriptive Capacity of Andean Khipus«, in: *Current Anthropology*, 58/ 3 (Juni 2017), hg. v. Caroline Schuster und Catherine J. Frieman, S. 412-419, https://doi.org/10.1086/691682, zuletzt aufgerufen am 3.3.2025.
[2] Vgl. etwa Sadie Plant, »The Future Looms: Weaving Women and Cybernetics«, in: Body & Society, vol. 1, Nr. 3-4, November 1995, https://monoskop.org/images/1/13/Plant_Sadie_1995_The_Future_Looms_Weaving_Women_and_Cybernetics.pdf, zuletzt aufgerufen am 14.9.2024, sowie Matteo Pasquinelli, *Das Auge des Meisters. Eine Sozialgeschichte künstlicher Intelligenz*, Münster, Unrast, 2024, S. 80-85.
[3] Philip Morrison und Emily Morrison, *Charles Babbage and His Calculating Engines: Selected Writings by Charles Babbage and Others*, New York, Dover, 1961, S. 252; zitiert nach Plant, »The Future Looms: Weaving Women and Cybernetics«, S. 50.
[4] Vgl. Ulrike Müller, *Bauhaus-Frauen. Meisterinnen in Kunst, Handwerk und Design*, Berlin, Insel, 2021, S. 11 u. 43.
[5] Vgl. dazu das Vorwort des damaligen Präsidenten der Bayerischen Akademie der Schönen Künste, Prof. Gerd Albers, in: *Erste Biennale der Deutschen Tapisserie*, hg. v. d. Bayerischen Akademie der Schönen Künste München, Ausstellungskatalog 1978, S. 9.

I   FOUR PERSPECTIVES FROM THE   VIER PERSPEKTIVEN AUS DER
      THEORY OF TEXTILES   TEXTILEN THEORIE

THE UNIVERSAL LANGUAGE OF TEXTILES AND
THE ART OF CONNECTING
CHRISTINA LEITNER

DIE UNIVERSELLE SPRACHE DES TEXTILEN UND
DIE KUNST DER VERBINDUNG

EN 'Textiles' is a phenomenon familiar to all of us yet difficult to grasp in all its implications. Merely defining textiles as a group of materials and fibres would be overly simplistic. Subjecting the word 'textile' to closer scrutiny, one realises that the term derives from the Latin verb *texere*, one of the meanings of which is 'to join together'. The word 'text' also derives from that Latin verb. Just as a text is given meaning only through the skilful composition of individual words, so is this also true of textile surfaces: it is the skilful interweaving of individual loops and knots, the skilful cabling of threads or the compressing of fibres that produces a compact yet flexible fabric. Textiles are built up of many minute, usually nondescript individual elements: from fibre to thread to surface, all the way up to a three-dimensional object. The creative process can be influenced at more points than is possible in any other medium. It doesn't take much to start. That explains why textile structures stand at the beginning of human cultural expression. It is due simply to the perishability of the material and probably also to the usually female connotations associated with this craft that social anthropology and archaeology have been unable to pinpoint an 'age of textiles' as one of the earliest epochs of civilisation.

Anyone who studies textiles dares to look beneath the surface. Practitioners of textiles are interested in the inner blueprints of things; they want to understand the grammar of textile fabrics and to know the inner workings of what holds the world together. We live in an age in which we are largely preoccupied with using smooth surfaces and, although we can skilfully use all sorts of digital tools, often do not understand how they function. Their tactile and sensory qualities enable textiles to contribute substantially to promoting holistic perception and getting to the bottom of things again. For many people, making something from scratch entirely by hand is not only a satisfying experience; neurological research has indicated that autonomous design and 'the intelligence of the hands' also influence our thought structures. Anyone who is engaged in making textiles experiences the power of connections and cultivates the art of assembling – an experience that is also of great value for interpersonal relationships and can be read as symbolic of social cohesion.

Textiles lead us into all sorts of cultures and can function worldwide as a non-verbal means of communication. The stories concealed in textiles tell of humanity's creative powers, of locally available materials, of cultural and individual needs and collective codes. Textiles can be interpreted as the universal human language, for despite all the dazzling array of sophisticated variants and the abundance of distinctive textures that have been developed over the course of history, textile systems can be broken down worldwide into only a few elemental principles that are applied in all cultures: twisting, looping, intertwining and knotting.

It's often stories about women that are concealed in the fibres, threads and surfaces. The products and their makers tend, on the one hand, to be underappreciated and textiles viewed as the fortuitous spin-off from the whirl of female activities. On the other hand, many fairy tales and myths deal with women spinning and weaving, who quite frequently decide by their actions the fate of humanity. In those stories women are not necessarily portrayed as positive figures; nonetheless, they are empowered to act, and thus woman's potential role in social contexts is made clear. Textile crafts, cult and religion are here closely associated with each other: collectively they define status and social affiliation. The value assigned to textiles and the ability to make them can, therefore, vary widely, depending on the context.

Since textiles accompany human life from birth to death, they are vehicles for imparting diverse items of information and creating identities. Textiles are in both the literal and the figurative sense absorbent, and not only do they assimilate the individual stories of their makers; they also have the capacity to store the zeitgeist of their time. Those who decode textiles arrive at different worlds and often discover surprising backstories because textiles have often been, and still are, a driving force behind radical technological renewal, social change and forward-looking innovation.

All the above aspects lead to textile materials and techniques possessing enormous contemporary potential for art and design-orientated projects. For the very reason that textiles, as an often underestimated, archaic medium, trigger so many mundane associations and pose so many questions on the value of things and activities that socially relevant thematic fields can be handled through them with particular clarity and conciseness. Textile art and culture are, therefore, forms of expression essential to the twenty-first century and create a link between progress and tradition, nature and technology, art and application.

In recent decades an increasing number of institutions have been founded to investigate and promulgate the potential of 'all things textile', to teach crafts skills or to highlight the presentation of this diverse medium.

To take one example, such connections are particularly widespread at the Textiles Zentrum Haslach (Haslach Textile Centre), established in northern Austria. Devoted to all aspects of textiles, the complex inaugurated in a flax-weaving region steeped in tradition known as the Mühlviertel is not just a cultural events venue; it is housed in a former textile factory and comprises along with a weaving museum and a wool factory numerous workshops offering a variety of courses, collaborative projects with universities, limited-edition serial production on modern looms and much more. A high point of the Textiles Zentrum Haslach cultural calendar is an international summer symposium hosted there in July that features a wide range of exhibitions, courses and a widely acclaimed weavers' market. Since 2020 the headquarters of the Europäisches Textilnetzwerk (European Textile Network; ETN) has also been housed in the Textiles Zentrum Haslach. ETN is an international association that links people working in textiles in creative and commercial capacities, researchers, and instructors from many countries worldwide, organises conferences and textile-themed travel and provides regular information on current specialist exhibitions, announcements of invitations to tender, and publications. ETN was founded with the aim of using the power of textiles to bring people together from all points of the compass, East and West, North and South, and making use of the universal language of textiles to design the future.

DE Das Phänomen »Textil« ist uns allen ganz nah und dennoch schwer zu fassen. Es wäre zu kurz gegriffen, das Textile nur als eine Gruppe von Materialien und Fasern zu definieren. Nimmt man das Wort »textil« etwas genauer unter die Lupe, so stellt man fest, dass es sich vom lateinischen Verb *texere* ableitet, was so viel wie „zusammenfügen" bedeutet. Dieser Wortursprung ist auch im Wort »Text« enthalten. So wie ein Text erst durch das kunstvolle Zusammenfügen einzelner Wörter seinen Sinn erhält, so verhält es sich auch mit textilen Flächen: Erst durch das sinnvolle Aneinanderreihen von einzelnen Maschen oder Knoten, durch das kunstvolle Verkreuzen von Fäden oder Verdichten von Fasern entsteht ein kompaktes, aber dennoch flexibles Gefüge. Textilien bauen sich aus vielen kleinen, meist unscheinbaren Einzelteilen auf: von der Faser über den Faden zur Fläche, bis hin zum dreidimensionalen Objekt. Wie in kaum einem anderen Medium kann der Gestaltungsprozess an verschiedensten Punkten beeinflusst werden. Es braucht nicht viel, um beginnen zu können. Textile Strukturen stehen somit am Anfang menschlicher Kulturäußerungen. Es liegt schlichtweg an der Vergänglichkeit des Materials und wohl auch an der meist weiblichen Konnotation dieses Handwerks, dass sich in der Wissenschaft kein »Textilzeitalter« als eine der frühesten Epochen menschlicher Zivilisation etablieren konnte.

Wer sich mit Textilien beschäftigt, wagt den Blick unter die Oberfläche. Textiler:innen sind an den inneren Bauplänen von Dingen interessiert, sie wollen die »Grammatik« textiler Gefüge verstehen und wissen, »was die Welt im Innersten zusammenhält«. Wir leben in einer Zeit, in der wir uns zu einem großen Teil mit dem Bedienen von glatten Oberflächen beschäftigen und verschiedenste digitale Tools zwar virtuos nutzen, ihre Funktionsweise dabei aber oft nicht verstehen. Textilien können aufgrund ihrer haptischen und sinnlichen Qualitäten einen wesentlichen Beitrag leisten, ganzheitliche Wahrnehmung zu fördern und den Dingen wieder auf den Grund zu gehen. Mit den eigenen Händen etwas von der Pike auf zu schaffen ist für viele Menschen nicht nur eine befriedigende Erfahrung, das autonome Gestalten und die »Klugheit der Hände« beeinflussen laut neurologischer Forschungen auch unsere Denkstrukturen. Wer sich mit der Herstellung von Textilien beschäftigt, erlebt die Kraft von Verbindungen und kultiviert die Kunst des Zusammenfügens - eine Erfahrung, die auch für unser zwischenmenschliches Miteinander von hohem Wert ist und als Sinnbild für den Zusammenhalt von Gesellschaften gelesen werden kann.

Textilien führen uns in unterschiedlichste Kulturen und können rund um den Globus als nonverbales Kommunikationsmittel dienen. Die darin versteckten Geschichten handeln von der kreativen Schaffenskraft der Menschen, von lokal verfügbaren Materialien, von kulturellen und individuellen Bedürfnissen und kollektiven Codes. Textilien können als universelle Sprache der Menschheit verstanden werden, denn trotz des raffinierten Variantenreichtums und der Fülle an unterschiedlichen Texturen, die im Laufe der Menschheitsgeschichte entwickelt wurden, lassen sich textile Systeme weltweit auf nur wenige Grundprinzipien herunterbrechen, die in allen Kulturen Anwendung finden: Verdrehen, Verkreuzen, Verschlingen und Verknoten.

Oft sind es Frauengeschichten, die in den Fasern, Fäden und Flächen verborgen sind. Die Erzeugnisse und ihre Herstellerinnen werden einerseits wenig geschätzt und Textilien als beiläufiges Ergebnis des weiblichen Tätigkeitskosmos verstanden. Andererseits handeln auch viele Märchen und Mythen von spinnenden und webenden Frauen, die nicht selten durch ihr Tun über das Schicksal von Menschen entscheiden. Frauen werden in diesen Geschichten nicht zwingend als positive Figuren etabliert, es wird ihnen aber durchaus Handlungsmacht zugewiesen und damit auch die potenzielle Rolle der Frau in den gesellschaftlichen Zusammenhängen deutlich gemacht. Textiles Handwerk, Kult und Religion liegen hier nah beieinander, gemeinsam definieren sie Status und gesellschaftliche Zugehörigkeit. Der Wert von Textilien und die Fähigkeit, diese herzustellen, kann also je nach Kontext extrem changieren.

Da Textilien das menschliche Leben von der Geburt bis zum Tod begleiten, sind sie Träger von verschiedensten Informationen und stiften Identitäten. Sie sind im wahrsten Sinn des Wortes saugfähig und nehmen nicht nur die individuellen Geschichten ihrer Erzeuger:innen in sich auf, sondern haben auch die Fähigkeit, den jeweiligen Zeitgeist zu speichern. Wer sie dekodiert, gelangt in unterschiedliche Welten und entdeckt oft überraschende Hintergründe, denn das Textile war und ist bis heute oft auch treibende Kraft für radikale, technische Erneuerungen, gesellschaftliche Veränderungen und zukunftsweisende Innovationen.

All diese Aspekte führen dazu, dass textile Materialien und Techniken enormes zeitgenössisches Potenzial für künstlerische und designorientiere Projekte in sich bergen. Gerade weil das oft unterschätzte, archaische Medium Textil viele alltägliche Assoziationen auslöst und Fragen zum Wert von Dingen und Tätigkeiten aufwirft, können gesellschaftlich relevante Themenfelder damit besonders gut verhandelt werden. Textile Kunst und Kultur sind somit essenzielle Ausdrucksformen des 21. Jahrhunderts und schaffen Verbindung zwischen Fortschritt und Tradition, Natur und Technik, Kunst und Anwendung.

In den letzten Jahrzehnten haben sich vermehrt Institutionen gebildet, die sich um das Potenzial »des Textilen« bemühen, sich um die Vermittlung handwerklicher Fähigkeiten kümmern oder die Präsentation dieses vielfältigen Mediums in den Fokus rücken.

Im Norden Österreichs hat sich so zum Beispiel das Textile Zentrum Haslach etabliert. Dieses Kulturzentrum in der traditionsreichen Leinenweberregion, dem sogenannten Mühlviertel, ist im Areal einer ehemaligen Textilfabrik untergebracht und beherbergt neben einem Webereimuseum auch eine Wollmanufaktur, zahlreiche Werkstätten, in denen verschiedenste Kurse angeboten werden, Uni-Kooperationen, kleinserielle Produktion auf modernen Webmaschinen und vieles mehr. Höhepunkt ist jährlich im Juli ein internationales Sommersymposium mit zahlreichen Ausstellungen, Kursen und einem weithin bekannten Webermarkt. Seit 2020 ist auch der Sitz des Europäischen Textilnetzwerks ETN im Textilen Zentrum Haslach untergebracht. Diese internationale Vereinigung bringt Textilschaffende, Künstler:innen, Forschende und Lehrende über viele Länder hinweg zusammen, organisiert Konferenzen und Reisen und informiert regelmäßig über aktuelle Ausstellungen, Ausschreibungen und Publikationen. Ziel ist es, die Kraft des Textilen zu nutzen, um Menschen aus Ost und West, Nord und Süd zusammenzuführen und die universelle Sprache des Textilen für die Gestaltung der Zukunft zu nutzen.

WEAVING MUSEUM HASLACH (AT)

TRANSGRESSING TIGHTLY KNIT NETWORKS —
TEXTILE MATTERS.
CONTEMPORARY CREATION IN TEXTILE ART
SILKE GEPPERT

VORSTÖSSE IN DICHTE GEFLECHTE —
TEXTILE MATTERS.
ZEITGENÖSSISCHES SCHAFFEN IN DER
TEXTILKUNST

Working with textile materials as art is on trend. Many artists have discovered textiles as a work material and are advancing traditional techniques such as embroidering, knitting, weaving and macramé in their work. The virtually infinite possibilities textiles afford as work materials evidently motivate creativity and the exploratory urge. The experience of the Covid pandemic ensured textile-related crafts underwent a full-blown boom among the young generation especially. A thirst for the sustainable handling of resources, for the lost knowledge of a traditional craft, for insights into manufacturing chains and a focus on regional production are observable worldwide and are changing training courses and university curricula. A thread perceived as lost is being picked up again everywhere it seems …

Textiles are by their very nature slow objects, objects resulting from a legible manufacturing process. We can see how something has been worked, what materials it is made of. For some years now the fashion and cloth trade has been stretched to its ecological and economic limits – with the key phrase being 'fast fashion' and its consequences.

At the same time, a trend towards textiles is showing up in an array of large exhibitions. Notable in the present connection are the monographic retrospectives on Anni Albers and textile art at the Bauhaus or, for example, Sheila Hicks in Vienna (MAK, 2020/2021), or the groundbreaking *Kunst & Textil* (Art & Textile) exhibition at Kunstmuseum Wolfsburg (2014). *Weaving Abstraction* (2024), an exhibition at The Metropolitan Museum of Art in New York recently demonstrated the close affinities between modern and ancient art from a variety of cultures. Many artistic stances with a focus on textiles were also revealed at the most recent Venice Art Biennale (2024).

Although textile art is becoming ever more relevant at exhibitions and galleries, the subject is still a fringe field at best in cultural studies within German-speaking countries. Standard works on modern or contemporary textile art are still conspicuous by their absence. In 2024 the renowned German magazine Textilkunst ceased publication after fifty years in print. All the more gratifying to note, therefore, that the editor of this book has dedicated so much passion to this topic. Whereas textiles tended to be viewed until the very recent past, and even now, as a craft, as a second skin in the garment industry and as a minor occupation that was reserved for women, both men and women were originally active in the field. Apart from fashionably clothing people, textiles have also – as a third skin – transformed rooms, and on into the eighteenth century precious wall hangings such as tapestries woven in France or the Netherlands formed the backdrop against which the lives of the gentry and nobility were played out.

In both the domestic and the monastic environments, a new image of femininity, embodied morally in the Holy Virgin, who is associated with needlework and weaving, has been consolidated since the Middle Ages. The onset of industrialisation in the nineteenth century saw new jobs, crafts schools and aesthetic trends such as the Arts and Crafts movement emerge as reactions to the roles allocated for so long to the sexes by seeking a new path to design above and beyond the tasks performed by housewives as 'domestic drudgery'. Here, Anni Albers (1899–1994), Yayoi Kusama (*1929) and Dorothea Tanning (1910–2012) established essential female stances in fibre art.

An important cultural aspect is the ancient medium of weaving, which is practised worldwide and has been since humans became sedentary. All aspects of spinning and weaving are encountered in Greco-Roman mythology as well as biblical texts. The loom is particularly significant in Homer: in the Odyssey the instrument is the attribute of Odysseus's faithful wife, Penelope. In the Ovidian Arachne myth, Arachne (English: 'spider') is an accomplished weaver who challenges Athene to a contest at the loom. Angered at a mere mortal's presumption, the goddess transforms Arachne into a spider. Then there are the three Parcae, the Fates, who spin, measure out and cut off the thread of the mortal lifespan. In our present day we are still closely interwoven with our textile tradition when we 'spin a tale', that is, fabricate a tissue of lies, or when we 'lose the thread' of a convoluted explanation or story. The fascination of the tactile appeal and the texture of material allows for association and transformation on multiple planes. The geometry of the lattice first appears at the loom. Knitting, tufting and crocheting are in turn techniques that permit three-dimensional design, describe curves with loops and thus intervene in space.

Fabric exemplifies the idea of abstraction. The orthogonal structure of warp and weft, which corresponds to a grid pattern formed of right angles, literally evokes abstract forms and colour effects. This can also be read as rigidity, as the stringent metaphorical expression of law and order, as a form of incarceration. However, numerous new works in this book show how more flexible structures can be created from it that dissolve the rigidity of fabric and transform the colours specific to it.

DE Die künstlerische Arbeit mit textilen Materialien ist im Trend. Viele Künstler:innen entdecken das Textil als Material für sich und entwickeln traditionelle Techniken wie Sticken, Stricken, Weben und Knüpfen in ihren Arbeiten weiter. Offensichtlich motiviert das textile Material und seine quasi unendlichen gestalterischen Möglichkeiten die Kreativität und den Forschungsdrang. Insbesondere durch die Erfahrung der Pandemie hat textiles Handwerk in der jungen Generation einen regelrechten Boom ausgelöst. Die Sehnsucht nach einem nachhaltigen Umgang mit Ressourcen, nach dem verloren Wissen des traditionellen Handwerks, nach Kenntnissen über Herstellungsketten und der Focus auf regionale Produktionen ist global vorhanden und verändert auch das Profil von Ausbildungen und Universitäten. Überall wird anscheinend der als verloren empfundene Faden wieder aufgenommen …

Textilien sind per se *slow objects*, Gegenstände deren Herstellungsprozess ablesbar bleibt. Wir können sehen, wie etwas verarbeitet wurde, aus welchen Materialien es besteht. Seit einigen Jahren stößt der weltweite Mode- und Textilhandel an seine ökologischen und ökonomischen Grenzen – Stichwort »Fast Fashion« und seine Folgen. Gleichzeitig zeigt sich der Trend zum Textilen in einer ganzen Reihe von großen Ausstellungen. Zu nennen sind hier die monografischen Retrospektiven zu Anni Albers und der Textilkunst am Bauhaus, oder etwa Sheila Hicks in Wien (MAK, 2020/2021), oder die wegbereitende Ausstellung *Kunst & Textil* im Kunstmuseum Wolfsburg (2014). Die Ausstellung *Weaving Abstraction* (2024) im Metropolitan Museum in New York stellte etwa jüngst enge Zusammenhänge zwischen moderner und alter Kunst aus unterschiedlichen Kulturen vor. Viele künstlerische Positionen mit textilem Fokus waren auch auf der letzten Kunst-Biennale in Venedig (2024) zu entdecken.

Obgleich die textile Kunst in Ausstellungen und Galerien immer relevanter wird, ist das Thema in den Kulturwissenschaften im deutschsprachigen Raum noch immer ein Randgebiet. Es fehlen bis heute Überblickswerke zur modernen oder zeitgenössischen Textilkunst und 2024 wurde bedauerlicherweise die renommierte deutsche Zeitschrift Textilkunst nach 50 Jahren eingestellt. Um so erfreulicher, dass sich die Herausgeberin mit viel Herzblut diesem Thema angenommen hat.

Während bis weit in die aktuelle Gegenwart Textilkunst eher als handwerkliches Gewebe, als zweite Haut in der Bekleidung und nachrangiges Betätigungsfeld den Frauen zugeordnet galt, waren ursprünglich beide Geschlechter im textilen Gewerbe tätig. Neben dem modischen Einkleiden von Körpern wurden und waren auch Räume – als dritte Haut des Menschen – durch Textilien transformiert, und bis ins 18. Jahrhundert entfaltete sich vor allem adeliges Leben vor den Kulissen von kostbaren Wandteppichen, wie Tapisserien aus Frankreich oder den Niederlanden.

Im häuslichen und klösterlichen Ambiente wurde seit dem Mittelalter ein neues Bild von Weiblichkeit gefestigt, das mit der handarbeitenden Jungfrau Maria ihre moralische Verkörperung fand. Mit der Industrialisierung im 19. Jahrhundert reagierten neue Arbeitswelten, Kunstgewerbeschulen und Bewegungen wie Arts und Crafts auf lange fixierte Geschlechterrollen, die über den weiblichen »Hausfleiß« hinaus einen neuen Weg in der Gestaltung suchten. Durch Anni Albers (1899–1994), Yayoi Kusama (*1929) oder Dorothea Tanning (1910–2012) werden im 20. Jahrhundert wesentliche weibliche Positionen der Fiber Art begründet.

Ein wichtiger kultureller Aspekt ist die alte und global verbreitete Technik des Webens, das mit dem sesshaften Werden des Menschen begann. So finden sich unendliche Aspekte des Spinnens und Webens in den Mythen, aber auch in den biblischen Texten. Besondere Bedeutung erlangt der Webstuhl bei Homer, in der Odyssee wird er zum markanten Instrument von Odysseus' Gattin Penelope. In Ovids Arachnemythos ist Arachne (dt. »die Spinne«) eine begabte Weberin, die Athene zum Wettstreit am Webstuhl herausfordert. Als sie diesen sehr erfolgreich gewinnt, wird sie von Athene zur Strafe in eine Spinne verwandelt. Dann gibt es die drei Parzen, die den Lebensfaden des Menschen spinnen, bemessen und am Ende abschneiden. In der Gegenwart sind wir, wenn wir Gedanken spinnen oder den Faden verlieren, intensiv mit unserer textilen Tradition verwoben. Die Faszination des taktilen Reizes und der Struktur des Materials erlaubt diesen in viele Richtungen zu assoziieren und zu transformieren. Die Geometrie des Gitters entsteht zuerst am Webstuhl. Stricken, Tuften und Häkeln sind wiederum Techniken, die dreidimensionale Gestaltung ermöglichen, mit Schlingen Kurven beschreiben und damit den Raum erobern.

Das Gewebe birgt in sich die Idee der Abstraktion. Die orthogonale Gewebestruktur von Kette und Schuss, die ihre Entsprechung im rechtwinkeligen Gittermuster findet, provozierte förmlich abstrakte Formen und Farbgestaltungen. Im Textil entspricht die Gewebestruktur von Faden und Schuss dem rechtwinkligen Gittermuster. Dieses kann man als Erstarrung lesen, als strengen Ausdruck von *law and order*, als eine Art von Gefängnis. Zahlreiche neue Arbeiten in diesem Band aber zeigen, wie daraus flexiblere Strukturen gestaltet wurden, die die Strenge des Gewebes und der spezifischen Farbe transformieren.

MASTER FG, AFTER FRANCESCO PRIMATICCIO,
PENELOPE AND HER MAIDS WEAVING, CA. 1545
ENGRAVING ON LAID PAPER

RECTO / VERSO
OR
SORRY, IS THIS THE FRONT?
SABINE FLASCHBERGER

RECTO / VERSO
ODER:
WO IST HIER DIE SCHAUSEITE, BITTE?

·

Entering an exhibition, looking around, getting your bearings, observing your first objects, studying descriptions, recognising the links between works, then suddenly seeing an exhibit from the back. 'Or is that perhaps the front? In any case intriguing. I'll take a closer look!' Visitors to the Textile Manifeste - von Bauhaus bis Soft Sculpture (Textile Manifestos - From Bauhaus to Soft Sculpture) exhibition shown at the Museum für Gestaltung Zürich early in 2025 may have harboured these very thoughts while viewing textile exhibits displayed so that all sides were visible.

The added value of the back

What is the added value of the 'verso' side that is linked inseparably with the 'recto' regardless? The curatorial decision aims at heightening the public's attention to certain points. A person sees something unexpected that first has to be understood and categorised. This process disrupts in a certain sense what might have been systematic progression through the exhibition rooms, forces a detour by making visitors walk all the way round a work for once, and exacts a stop. What has become a heterogeneous tour of the exhibition is supposed to motivate further communication with both the exhibit and the artist who created it.

The reverse opens up unexpected, usually hidden insights, which first of all help to explain the techniques used to make a particular piece. In the case of the artistic jacquard weave, to take one example, the reverse records the motif on the front as a negative mirror image, thus completing the piece as an echo of itself. Often two sides of such a work taken together convey entirely different moods and colour ranges. An effect that never ceases to amaze. Elsewhere the reverse makes clear how the piece was made. In the tufting process the artist uses a tufting gun to shoot her monochrome wool threads through the coarse support fabric from the back. An extremely robust technique, this, because it generates a bang with each thread fired off, which - if you will - underscores the fact that the artist's decision for a specific material thickness, colour and arrangement is unshakeable: 'Bang! Need more yellow here!' Walking around a work allows the viewer to feel more strongly the direct energy that has gone into it and also reveals, among other things, that it is up to the artist to decide whether to make the individual colours on the reverse visible on the front as unmixed colour tones or, on the other hand, to create mixed colours through different thread lengths in the pile.

In part, purely conservation measures are conveyed via the reverse, such as hanging devices or stiffeners that keep the work in the form intended. Thus it may be possible to ascertain how an individual work has been composed, and by whom. It is only here that hidden labels or even signatures or a logo identify authorship. Markers of exhibition history or simply traces of inventory can also be discovered here. Individual artists we asked to show us the reverse of their works were, without exception, only too happy to grant our request.

Case study Lissy Funk (1909-2005)

Le secret (The Secret), a piece of embroidery stitched by Lissy Funk in 1993, is a case in point for studying a specific form of presentation under the aspect of viewing an artwork from all sides. Funk very quickly professionalised her artistic praxis and, while embroidering prestigious wall hangings on commission for public buildings, on which she would sometimes work for several years with the aid of assistants, also participated several times in the Biennale Internationale de la Tapisserie in Lausanne. Le secret is one of the embroideries in small formats, 'minis', which she always completed without assistants.[1] The artist stitched wool, silk, cotton and gold threads on a cotton support and signed her work with her name and date elaborately stitched into the lower right-hand corner. The texture of her embroideries, which varies from fluffy and hairy to rigidly metallic surfaces and distinctive elements jutting out from the support, dominate the markedly architectonic composition of motifs. In places the embroidery support fabric is exposed. The title may refer to the central zone, primed in light blue overlaid with gold threads, which is overarched by the lively sculptural folds of a white cupola resting on golden cornices. The lower third of the embroidery is dominated by coral-red fuzz that is condensed into bands towards the foreground. The lush layout suggests a metaphysical phenomenon but remains undecipherable. To support and protect this treasure executed in such detail, Funk chose to mount it between two sheets of acrylic glass that extend beyond the work on all sides. The reverse reveals small drill holes along the outer contours and the edge of the cornice, through which she sewed her embroidery to the sheet on the back. A second sheet of acrylic glass overlays the work to create a third space in a sculptural gesture. While Funk always planned her large works without frames and wanted to see them - like frescoes - directly on the wall, she has by means of the transparent frame used for the wall hanging here created a transitional zone which moves the embroidery and the wall closer together.

Viewed through the separating sheet of acrylic glass, the reverse of her work is revealed as a rampant tangle of threads. 'The backs are anyway much more beautiful than the fronts,' her husband, the painter Adolf Funk, is said to have constantly commented.[2] What looks precise and under control on the front is here overlaid again and again with the Funk stitch named after her, which secures the red wool fleece with hidden stitches from the reverse but is only visible on the front. Funk's chaotic-looking reverse had the function of enabling her to unpick and change it at any time. Now folded over and tacked to the support with herringbone stitching in fine silk thread, the edges of the support fabric prove that the work is finished, ready for presentation.

With the work shown freely hung, which makes it viewable from both sides, the collected impressions of it form a whole. What better way for an individual work to express its author!

[1] Participation in the 2nd (1962), 4th (1969) and 8th (1977) Biennales. For further information on the artist, see Lissy Funk: A Retrospective, ed. Christa C. Mayer Thruman, exh. cat., Chicago 1988, and Lissy Funk, ed. Fritz Billeter and Rosina Kuhn, Zurich 1999.
[2] Conversation between the author and Rosina Kuhn, daughter of Lissy Funk, Zurich, 17.6.2025.

Eine Ausstellung betreten, sich umsehen, sich orientieren, erste Objekte betrachten, Legenden studieren, Verbindungen zwischen den Arbeiten erkennen und unerwartet plötzlich eine Rückseite sehen. »Oder ist das doch die Schauseite? Auf jeden Fall spannend. Das schaue ich mir näher an!« Solche Gedanken mögen sich Besuchende der Ausstellung *Textile Manifeste - von Bauhaus bis Soft Sculpture*, die zu Beginn des Jahres 2025 im Museum für Gestaltung Zürich gezeigt wurde, in Anbetracht rundum sichtbarer textiler Exponate gemacht haben.

Der Mehrwert der Rückseite
Worin liegt also der Mehrwert der »verso«-Seite, die ja untrennbar mit der Vorderseite verbunden ist? Die kuratorische Entscheidung zielt darauf ab, die Aufmerksamkeit im Publikum punktuell zu erhöhen. Der Mensch sieht etwas Unerwartetes, das erst einmal verstanden und eingeordnet werden muss. Dies stört in gewissem Sinne das womöglich etwas systematische Abschreiten der Säle, lenkt den Schritt zwangsläufig einmal um das Werk herum und fordert einen Stopp ein. Der nunmehr heterogene Gang durch die Ausstellung soll durch die Offenlegung einzelner Rückseiten eine erweiterte Kommunikation mit dem Exponat wie auch mit der Künstlerin anregen.
Die Rückseite öffnet unerwartete, gewöhnlich verborgene Einblicke, die zunächst zur Erschließung der Technik verhelfen. In Falle künstlerischer Jacquardgewebe, etwa, gibt die Rückseite das frontseitige Motiv als Spiegelung im Negativ wieder und komplettiert dieses als Nachhall seiner selbst. Oft vermitteln die beiden Seiten einer Arbeit gänzlich unterschiedliche Stimmungen und Farbspektren. Ein stets aufs Neue verblüffender Effekt. Andernorts verdeutlicht die Rückseite den Prozess der Entstehung. In der Technik des Tuftens schießt die Künstlerin mittels der Tufting-Pistole von der Rückseite her monochrome Wollfäden durch das grobe Trägergewebe. Als äußerst handfeste Technik erzeugt dies mit jedem abgefeuerten Faden einen Knall, der - wenn mal so will - die Entschlossenheit der Künstlerin für die spezifische Materialstärke, Farbe und Anordnung unterstreicht: »Peng! Hierher gehört mehr Gelb!« Die Umrundung des Werkes lässt Betrachtende die direkte Energie stärker spüren, die in die Arbeit eingeflossen ist, und enthüllt unter anderem auch, dass sich der Künstlerin die Wahl stellt, die einzelnen Farben von der Rückseite entweder auf der Schauseite als ungemischte Töne

sichtbar zu machen oder, im Gegensatz dazu, durch unterschiedliche Garnlängen Mischfarben im Flor zu schaffen.
Teils vermitteln sich über die Kehrseite rein konservatorische Maßnahmen, wie Aufhängevorrichtungen oder Verstärkungen, die das Werk in der Form halten. So erschließt sich mitunter die Verfasstheit der einzelnen Arbeit. Allenfalls finden sich hier verborgene Etiketten oder gar Signaturen oder ein Logo der Autorschaft. Auch Marker der Ausstellungsgeschichte oder schlicht die Spuren der Inventarisierung können hier entdeckt werden. Unserer Anfrage an einzelne Künstler:innen, auch die Rückseiten ihrer Werke zeigen zu dürfen, stimmten diese ausnahmslos und freudig zu.

Case Study Lissy Funk (1909–2005)
Am Beispiel der 1993 ausgeführten Handstickerei *Le secret* (Das Geheimnis) von Lissy Funk lässt sich eine spezifische Präsentationsform im Spiegel der Rundum-Betrachtung studieren. In ihrer künstlerischen Praxis hatte sich Funk sehr rasch professionalisiert und neben repräsentativen Auftragsarbeiten für öffentliche Gebäude, an denen sie mit Unterstützung von Assistentinnen teils über mehrere Jahre arbeitete, auch mehrfach an der Biennale Internationale de la Tapisserie in Lausanne teilgenommen. *Le secret* ist Teil ihrer kleinen Formate, den *Minis*, die sie stets allein ausführte. Die Künstlerin setzte Wolle, Seide, Baumwolle und Goldfaden auf einem Trägerstoff aus Baumwolle ein und signierte das Werk in der unteren rechten Ecke mit ihrem kunstvoll eingestickten Namen und der Jahreszahl. Unterschiedliche Strukturen von flauschig-haarigen bis zu metallisch-rigiden Flächen und einige markante Auskragungen dominieren die stark architektonisch bestimmte Motivik. Einzelne Stellen geben den Blick auf den Stickgrund frei. Der Titel mag auf die zentrale hellblau grundierte Zone mit aufliegenden Goldfäden verweisen, die vom lebendigen Faltenwurf einer plastischen weißen Haube überwölbt ist, die auf goldenen Simsen ruht. Das untere Drittel bestimmt ein korallenroter Flaum, der sich in Bändern zum Vordergrund hin verdichtet. Die kostbare Anlage deutet auf ein metaphysisches Phänomen hin, das aber unerschlossen bleibt.
Als Rückhalt und Schutz für das detailreich ausgeführte Kleinod wählte Funk die Montage zwischen zwei Plexiglasscheiben, die rundum über die Arbeit hinausragen. Erst die Kehrseite enthüllt kleine Bohrlöcher entlang der äußeren Konturen und der Kante des Gesimses, durch die sie ihre Sti-

ckerei mit der rückseitigen Scheibe vernäht hat. Eine zweite Plexiglasscheibe überfängt die Arbeit und schafft in einer skulpturalen Geste einen dritten Raum. Während Funk ihre großformatigen Arbeiten stets ohne Rahmen plante und diese - Fresken ähnlich - direkt an der Wand sehen wollte, schafft sie hier mittels des transparenten Rahmens für die Hängung vor einer Wand eine Übergangszone, die Stickerei und Wand einander annähert.
Durch die trennende Scheibe betrachtet, zeigt sich die Rückseite ihrer Arbeit als ungebändigtes Gewirr der Fäden. »Die Rückseiten sind sowieso viel schöner als die Vorderseiten«, soll ihr Ehemann, der Maler Adolf Funk, stets kommentiert haben. Was vorne akkurat und kontrolliert erscheint, ist hier über und über mit dem nach ihr benannten Funk-Stich überfangen, der mit verborgenen Stichen von der Rückseite her etwa das rote Wollvlies fixiert, das lediglich auf der Vorderseite sichtbar ist. Funks chaotisch scheinende Rückseite diente dem Zweck, jederzeit Auftrennungen und Änderungen vornehmen zu können. Die nun umgeschlagenen Ränder des Trägerstoffs, mit feinem Seidenfaden im Hexenstich an den Grund geheftet, belegen, dass die Arbeit abgeschlossen ist, fertig zur Präsentation. Frei hängend gezeigt und von beiden Seiten einsehbar, können die gesammelten Eindrücke nun zusammenfinden. Besser kann ein einzelnes Werk seine Autorin nicht wiedergeben!

[1] Teilnahmen an der 2. Biennale (1962), 4. Biennale (1969), 8. Biennale (1977). Mehr zu Lissy Funk siehe: *Lissy Funk. A Retrospective*, hg. Christa C. Mayer Thruman, Chicago 1988, *Lissy Funk*, hg. Fritz Billeter, Rosina Kuhn, Zürich 1999.
[2] Gespräch der Autorin mit Rosina Kuhn, Tochter von Lissy Funk, Zürich, 17.6.2025.

LISSY FUNK
LE SECRET (DAS GEHEIMNIS), 1993
EMBROIDERY IN SILK, LINEN, COTTON, WOOL,
AND METAL THREAD ON EMBROIDERY CANVAS.
29,5 × 18,5 CM
PLEXIGLAS: 39,5 × 37,5 × 3 CM
FONDATION TOMS PAULI LAUSANNE,
COLLECTION DE L'ÉTAT DE VAUD

COME WEAVE WITH US!   KOMM WEBEN!
CATRIN LORCH

The children wave to the baby and line up in rows two by two. The baby laughs, and the check pattern with its green, pink and purple stripes frames its round head like a veil. But even before they leave, the children have spotted the woman with the poodle behind the garden fence. 'Look,' they call, 'we made those green stripes from your wool.' They spread out one of the baby blankets they have in a bag and hold it up, almost like a banner. The woman places her dog in front of it and takes a photo. Then everyone moves on – two more babies are waiting for their welcome gift that morning.

When I report on what I'm working on in the master class, my classmates look at the photo from that morning: plain weave, tartan pattern without a repeat, various, sometimes unidentifiable materials. The small blanket is also difficult to see; there are too many people in the picture – the preschool group, the parents with the baby behind them, two teachers, the head of the kindergarten and, next to the dog, the Action Weaver. That's me.

For a long time, I had no expression for what I was working on. In our diploma course, we are supposed to define whether we see ourselves as producers in hand weaving, designers or artists. None of the above. Weberei Kai thinks differently; for example, when we stay in the country house of a gallery owner who has ordered a handwoven upholstery fabric for his seating groups and values sustainability. The concept then called for the gallery owner, his youngest son, and his wife to cut open the old covers during the summer holidays, separate the threads, tie them in knots, and wind them onto my spools. So that one thing is clear in the end: the furniture will not be reupholstered.

It was also this gallery owner who introduced me to Travis Meinolf, from whom star painters like Kai Althoff and Peter Doig order something woven when they want to line display cases at London's Whitechapel Gallery or hang their paintings on a massive curtain at the Whitney Biennial in New York. But it wasn't that what interested me about California-based Travis Meinolf, rather his job title: Action Weaver. And that was it.

Travis Meinolf is not unknown in Germany. A decade ago he lived in Berlin, dragging his loom mounted on rollers to Alexanderplatz or Mauerpark to discuss the value of craftsmanship and design with curious onlookers while the shuttle flew back and forth. One of his most famous projects was created at a farmer's market, where, after working among vegetable crates and sausage stands, he left a pile of his precious handwoven fabrics with a note saying that anyone who needed a blanket could take one. But, does one really need a blanket? And can one simply use a fabric made with such skill and an eye calibrated for colours and textures as a blanket?

Back when he was studying industrial design, Travis Meinolf discovered weaving (his grandmother had left him her loom) as a way to maintain control over design, manufacture and sales, out of scepticism about the production cycles of global commodity capitalism. During his art studies at the California College of Art, weaving remained his medium. In his master's thesis, he reflected on the possibility of non-violently changing society by freeing everyday items from the cycles of consumption.

However, the path Travis Meinolf has taken as an Action Weaver is not aimed at producing fabrics or marketing them as works of art in galleries or exhibitions. Rather, it is aimed at encouraging people to take matters into their own hands and to perceive the warp and weft as an experience. For this reason alone, most of his tools are home-made, brightly painted and simple. 'If you want to weave, I want to help you,' reads the website of the weaving school he opened next to a yoga studio in San Anselmo. Travis Meinolf enjoys demonstrating the professional loom there, where an octogenarian from the neighbourhood regularly weaves complicated patterns in warm tones, apparently also working through inner tensions (as his family assures him with relief).

It's not unreasonable to think that the Action Weaver pursues a dual strategy: even if it takes some time before his artistic work has transformed society, attending his 'School of Weaving' very directly enriches the lives of individuals.

We followed his example with Weberei Kai and also founded a school where we help those who want to weave. On the rigid heddle frame,[1] on the floor loom with four or eight shafts,[2] or with band-weaving.[3] We show how it's done – how to make lampshades from strands of cable or a blanket from the many narrow strips that come off the rigid heddle frame. With children at the summer school, we transform the fleece sheared in the morning into a cloth, which we then drape over the naked sheep in the evening. At our all-dayer performances in parks and pedestrian zones, strollers can join in the weaving.

Travis Meinolf has opened up a twenty-first-century role for weaving by systematically applying the idea of relational aesthetics, coined by Nicolas Bourriaud, to hand weaving.[4] This is also timely because, while the combination of art and craft at the Bauhaus in the 1920s is still considered groundbreaking, the art of the time was focused on abstraction and modernism to create templates for the production and marketing cycles of industry. Today, however, the encounter with Socially Engaged Art or Participatory Art is just as groundbreaking for crafts: because they are based on the condition of the existence of relationships and bonds, and their production focuses not only on aesthetic objects but also on the creation of human experiences. In the case of hand weaving, it transforms customers and consumers into actors.

We at Weberei Kai hope that the children with whose blankets, woven from yarn scraps, we welcome newborns in the village will later remember this. Also how we washed the wool together in the sheep pasture. How, along with the half-finished knitting, we also collected stories about why a sweater or a dog coat wasn't finished. That, as teenagers, they will weave their worn T-shirts into curtains or carpets and value the strips of textile they designed themselves more than any logo.

[1] A heddle loom is a simple handloom in which the warp threads are threaded through a reed featuring slots and eyes. By raising and lowering the reed, a shed (opening) for the weft is created. The reed acts as the heald (as seen in large looms) but in a much simplified form. Weaving is done entirely by hand and is particularly suitable for beginners and small-scale artistic textile work.
[2] Shafts are moveable elements in the loom through which each specific warp thread runs. In weaving the shafts are raised or lowered in order to create a shed – the space through which the weft is inserted. The number and combinations of shafts determines the textile's pattern.
[3] Band weaving is a traditional weaving technique used to create narrow bands, in which a small number of warp threads are manipulated in a simple way, for example with a small card or finger weaving technique.
[4] Relational aesthetics describes a set of artistic practices that take collective human relationships and their social contexts as their theoretical and practical departure point rather than establishing an independent and private space.

Die Kinder winken dem Baby zu und stellen sich in Zweierreihen auf. Das Baby lacht und das Karomuster mit den grünen, rosafarbenen und lila Streifen rahmt seinen runden Kopf wie ein Schleier. Schon bevor sie wieder losgehen, haben die Kinder die Frau mit dem Pudel hinter dem Gartenzaun entdeckt. »Schau mal«, rufen sie, »das haben wir aus Deiner Wolle gemacht, die grünen Streifen«. Sie breiten eine der Babydecken, die sie in einer Tasche¡ bei sich haben, aus und halten sie hoch, fast wie ein Transparent. Die Frau stellt ihren Hund davor und macht ein Foto. Dann ziehen alle weiter – noch zwei Babys warten an dem Morgen auf ihr Begrüßungsgeschenk.

Wenn ich in der Meisterklasse berichte, woran ich arbeite, sehen meine Mitschülerinnen auf diesem Foto: Leinwandbindung, Tartanmuster ohne Rapport, verschiedene, teils undefinierbare Materialien. Die kleine Decke ist zudem nicht gut zu erkennen, zu viele Leute auf dem Bild – die Vorschulgruppe, dahinter die Eltern mit dem Baby, zwei Erzieherinnen, die Leiterin des Kindergartens, und neben dem Hund der Action Weaver. Das bin ich.

Lange hatte ich keinen Ausdruck für das, woran ich arbeite. In der Diplom-Ausbildung sollen wir definieren, ob wir uns als Produzenten in der Handweberei sehen, als Designer oder Künstler. Keins von allem. Die Weberei Kai, in der ich mich engagiere, denkt da anders. Beispielsweise wenn wir uns im Country House eines Galeristen einquartieren, der einen handgewebten Bezugsstoff für seine Sitzgruppen bestellt hat und Wert auf Nachhaltigkeit legt. Der Galerist, sein jüngster Sohn und seine Frau wurden in das Projekt umfänglich eingebunden: während der Sommerferien sollten sie die alten Bezüge aufschneiden, die Fäden zertrennen, verknoten und auf meine Spulen aufwickeln. Sie hatten nicht damit gerechnet, dass es so aufwendig würde. Und damit eins am Ende klar ist: noch einmal werden die Möbel nicht bezogen.
Dieser Galerist war es auch, der mich auf Travis Meinolf aufmerksam machte, bei dem Maler-Stars wie Kai Althoff und Peter Doig etwas Gewebtes bestellen, wenn sie Vitrinen in der Londoner Whitechapel Gallery auslegen oder ihre Bilder bei der Whitney Biennale in New York auf einen gewaltigen Vorhang hängen. Doch das war es nicht, das mich an dem in Kalifornien lebenden Travis Meinolf interessierte, sondern seine Berufsbezeichnung: Action Weaver. Das war es – das bin ich.

Travis Meinolf ist in Deutschland nicht unbekannt, in den Zehnerjahren lebte er in Berlin, schleifte seinen auf Rollen montierten Webstuhl auf den Alexanderplatz oder in den Mauerpark, um dort mit Neugierigen über den Wert von Handwerk und Design zu diskutieren, während das Schiffchen hin- und herflog. Eines der bekanntesten Projekte entstand auf einem Wochenmarkt, wo er – nachdem er zwischen Gemüsekisten und Wurstbuden gearbeitet hatte – einen Stapel seiner kostbaren handgewebten Stoffe mit dem Hinweis hinterließ, wer eine Decke brauche, dürfe sich eine nehmen. Aber: Kann man eine Decke brauchen? Und kann man ein mit so viel Geschick und auf Farben und Texturen kalibriertem Auge hergestelltem Gewebe einfach als Decke benutzen?

Schon während seines Studiums im Fach Industrie-Design hat Travis Meinolf das Weben entdeckt (seine Großmutter hatte ihm ihren Webstuhl vererbt) als Möglichkeit, die Kontrolle über Entwurf, Herstellung und Verkauf zu behalten – aus Skepsis gegenüber den Produktions-Zyklen des globalen Waren-Kapitalismus. Im Kunststudium am California College of Art blieb Weben sein Medium. In der Masterarbeit reflektierte er dann über die Möglichkeit, die Gesellschaft gewaltfrei zu ändern, indem man nämlich die Dinge des täglichen Bedarfs aus den Zyklen des Konsums befreit.
Allerdings zielt der Weg, den Travis Meinolf als Action Weaver vorangegangen ist, sowieso nicht auf die Herstellung von Stoffen oder auf deren Vermarktung als Kunstwerk in Galerien oder Ausstellungen. Sondern darauf, Menschen zu ermutigen, selbst zuzugreifen, Kette und Schuss als Erlebnis wahrzunehmen. Schon deswegen sind die meisten seiner Arbeitsgeräte selbstgebaut, bunt lackiert und schlicht gehalten. „Wenn Du weben willst, will ich Dir dabei helfen" steht auf der Internet-Seite der Webschule, die er neben einem Yogastudio in San Anselmo eröffnet hat. Travis Meinolf führt dort gerne den professionellen Webstuhl vor, an dem eine Achtzigjährige aus der Nachbarschaft regelmäßig komplizierte Muster in warmen Tönen webt und dabei offensichtlich auch innere Anspannungen abarbeitet (wie ihm die Familie erleichtert versichert).
Der Gedanke ist nicht abwegig, dass der Action Weaver eine Doppelstrategie fährt: sollte es noch eine Zeitlang dauern, bis sein künstlerisches Werk die Gesellschaft verändert hat, so bereichert der Besuch seiner „School of Weaving" doch sehr unmittelbar das Dasein Einzelner.

Wir sind ihm mit der Weberei Kai gefolgt, haben auch eine Schule gegründet, in der wir denen helfen, die weben wollen. Am Gatterkamm-Rahmen[1], am Webstuhl mit vier oder acht Schäften[2] oder beim Bändchenweben[3]. Wir zeigen, wie es geht – wie man aus Kabelsträngen Lampenschirme macht, oder aus vielen schmalen Streifen vom Gatterkamm-Rahmen eine Decke. Mit den Kindern der Ferienspiele verwandeln wir das am Morgen geschorene Vlies in ein Tuch, das wir abends dem nackten Schaf wieder umlegen. Bei unseren Auftritten in Parks und Fußgängerzonen dürfen Flaneure direkt mitweben.
Travis Meinolf hat der Weberei eine Aufgabe für das 21. Jahrhundert eröffnet, indem er den von Nicolas Bourriaud geprägten Gedanken der Relationalen Ästhetik[4] in aller Konsequenz auf die Handweberei anwendet. Das ist auch deswegen zeitgemäß, weil zwar bis heute die Verbindung von Kunst und Handwerk im Bauhaus der Zwanzigerjahre als wegweisend gilt – nur dass die damals aktuelle Kunst auf Abstraktion und Moderne zielte, um Vorlagen für die Produktions- und Vermarktungszyklen der Industrie zu schaffen. Heute dagegen ist die Begegnung mit Socially Engaged Art oder Participatory Art für das Handwerk genauso wegweisend: Weil sie auf der Bedingung der Existenz von Beziehungen und Bindungen beruhen und bei der Produktion nicht nur auf ästhetische Objekte, sondern auf die Schaffung von menschlichen Erfahrungen konzentriert sind. Im Fall der Handweberei macht sie aus Kunden und Konsumentinnen: Akteure.

Wir in der Weberei Kai hoffen, dass die Kinder, mit deren aus Garnresten gewebten Decken wir im Dorf die Neugeborenen begrüßen, sich später daran erinnern. Auch daran, wie wir auf der Schafweide die Wolle gemeinsam gewaschen haben. Wie wir mit den halbfertigen Strickereien auch Geschichten eingesammelt haben, warum da ein Pullover nicht fertig geworden war oder ein Hundemäntelchen. Dass sie als Teenager ihre abgetragenen T-Shirts zu Vorhängen oder Teppichen verweben und die Streifen, die sie selbst entworfen haben, höher schätzen als irgendein Logo.

[1] Ein Gatterkamm-Rahmen ist ein einfacher Handwebrahmen, bei dem die Kettfäden durch einen Kamm mit Schlitzen oder Löchern geführt werden. Durch Heben und Senken des Kamms entsteht ein Fach für den Schussfaden. Der Gatterkamm übernimmt die Rolle des sogenannten Litzenblatts (wie bei großen Webstühlen), jedoch in stark vereinfachter Form. Das Weben erfolgt vollständig manuell und eignet sich besonders für Einsteiger:innen und künstlerische Textilarbeit im kleinen Format.

[2] Schäfte sind bewegliche Elemente im Webstuhl, durch die jeweils bestimmte Kettfäden laufen. Beim Weben werden die Schäfte gehoben oder gesenkt, um ein sogenanntes Fach zu bilden – den Zwischenraum, durch den der Schussfaden eingeführt wird. Die Anzahl und Kombination der Schäfte bestimmen das Muster des Gewebes.

[3] »Bändchenweben« ist eine traditionelle Webtechnik, mit der schmale Bänder hergestellt werden. Dabei werden wenige Kettfäden auf einfache Weise – beispielsweise mit einem Brettchen oder Fingerwebtechnik – verarbeitet.

[4] »Relationale Ästhetik« meint eine Reihe künstlerischer Praktiken, die als theoretischen und praktischen Ausgangspunkt die Gesamtheit der menschlichen Beziehungen und ihres sozialen Kontextes annehmen, nicht einen unabhängigen und privaten Raum setzen.

CATRIN LORCH AT THE LOOM / WEBEREI KAI

II   FORTY PERSPECTIVES FROM PRACTICES IN TEXTILE   VIERZIG PERSPEKTIVEN AUS DER TEXTILEN PRAXIS

Magdalena Abakanowicz

01 BLACK GARMENT 8 (1977)
270 × 200 CM
WOVEN
SISAL

What is sculpture? With impressive continuity it testifies to man's evolving sense of reality, and fulfils the necessity to express what cannot be verbalized.

EN Magdalena Abakanowicz (1930–2017) endured war and political oppression in her youth – experiences that profoundly affected her work. All her life she used it as a vehicle for addressing the existential issues confronting humanity: identity, vulnerability, collectivity and the individual's relationship to society.

After studying at the Academy of Fine Art in Warsaw, where she specialised in painting and weaving, she soon turned to textile art. She became famous worldwide for sculptures made of jute fibre, wool and other natural materials in large formats. The hanging, curvilinear forms of the group of works she called Abakans challenge perceptions. These works link traditional crafts techniques with a radical sculptural language of forms that infringes the boundaries between textile art and sculpture to liberate textile material from its decorative function. In her oeuvre abstract organic forms fuse with an often bleak, almost mystical, looming presence which had fascinated her since childhood. The very material is steeped in significance: Abakanowicz viewed each fibre as a basic element of all life on earth. She was an artist for whom nerves and sinews, muscles and even the genetic code were the means of expression for a fibroid structure that exists in a profound association with human life and, therefore, also with her own artistic praxis. A rope, for instance, appeared to her like a petrified organism that carries its own history in itself and transfers it to its surroundings.

Despite the restrictive regulations imposed by the Communist regime, she asserted her own artistic freedom through improvisation and experiments with materials, exhibited her works worldwide and taught at several institutions. As a professor at the Academy of Fine Art in Poznań she influenced generations of young artists. Her oeuvre is her legacy as a powerful testimonial to political reflection, human experience and an unceasing search for an artistic idiom distinctively her own – this makes her one of the most important Polish women artists of the twentieth century.

02 ABAKAN RED (1969)
300 × 300 × 350 CM
WOVEN WITH METAL SUPPORT
SISAL

03 ABAKAN YELLOW (1970)
300 × 300 × 50 CM
JACQUARD FABRIC, METAL EYELETS
SISAL, ROPE

04 UNTITLED (1980-1983), DETAIL
400 × 1100 CM
WOVEN IN FIVE PARTS
SISAL

DE Magdalena Abakanowicz (1930–2017) erlebte Krieg und politische Unterdrückung in ihrer Jugend – Erfahrungen, die ihr Werk tief beeinflussten. Sie beschäftigte sich zeitlebens mit zentralen Fragen der menschlichen Existenz: Identität, Verletzlichkeit, Kollektivität und die Beziehung des Individuums zur Gesellschaft.

Nach ihrem Studium an der Akademia Sztuk Pięknych w Warszawie, das sie mit dem Schwerpunkt Malerei und Weberei abschloss, wandte sie sich bald der Textilkunst zu. In den 1960er-Jahren wurde sie mit ihren großformatigen Skulpturen aus Jute, Wolle und anderen Naturmaterialien international bekannt. Mit ihren hängenden, geschwungenen Formen fordern die sogenannten »Abakans« die Wahrnehmung der Betrachter:innen heraus. Diese Werke verbinden traditionelle Handwerkstechniken mit einer radikalen skulpturalen Formensprache, die die Grenze zwischen Textilkunst und Bildhauerei überschreitet und das textile Material aus seiner dekorativen Funktion befreit. In ihrer Arbeit verschmelzen abstrakte organische Formen mit einer oft düsteren, fast mythischen Präsenz, von der sie schon als Kind fasziniert war. Das Material selbst trägt Bedeutung: jede Faser betrachtete Abakanowicz als grundlegendes Element allen Lebens auf der Erde. Für die Künstlerin sind Nervenbahnen, Muskeln und sogar der genetische Code Ausdrucksweisen einer faserigen Struktur, die in einer tiefen Verbindung zu menschlichem Leben und somit auch zu ihrer eigenen gestalterischen Praxis besteht. So erschien ihr ein Seil wie ein versteinerter Organismus, der eine eigene Geschichte in sich birgt und diese an seine Umgebung überträgt. Trotz Reglementierungen durch das kommunistische Regime behauptete sie künstlerische Freiheit durch Improvisation und Materialexperimente, stellte weltweit aus und lehrte an verschiedenen Institutionen. Als Professorin an der Uniwersytet Artystyczny w Poznaniu prägte sie Generationen junger Künstler:innen. Ihr Werk bleibt ein kraftvolles Zeugnis politischer Reflexion, menschlicher Erfahrung sowie einer ständigen Suche nach einer eigenen künstlerischen Sprache – dadurch gehört sie zu den bedeutendsten polnischen Künstlerinnen des 20. Jahrhunderts.

02 03

04

Caroline Achaintre

02

01 M.A.W. (2024)
262 × 180 × 44 CM
HAND TUFTED
WOOL

02 MISSTIQUE (2019)
220 × 167 CM
HAND TUFTED
WOOL

03

03 GUMS (2024)
150 × 300 CM
HAND TUFTED
WOOL

04 ROADRUNNER (2023)
INSTALLATION VIEW,
NEUES MUSEUM NUREMBERG (DE)
350 × 500 CM
HAND TUFTED
WOOL

05 YETI (2021)
247 × 217 CM
HAND TUFTED
WOOL

EN Born in 1969, Caroline Achaintre is known for a mixed-media artistic praxis that encompasses the many materials in which different mediums, such as ceramics, textiles, watercolour and drawing, are realised. Her expressive wall objects made of hand-tufted wool are paradigmatic – hybrid creations that oscillate eerily between the mysterious and the familiar. Employing a conceptual, processual approach, Achaintre creates textures that are the fruit of an intensive investigation of anthropomorphic forms, masks and animistic motifs. Her sources of inspiration are manifold and draw on a fascination for prehistoric art, science fiction films and gothic novels.

Achaintre grew up in Fürth and began her career as an artist by training as an ironsmith, followed by studies in sculpture and metals at Burg Giebichenstein Kunsthochschule in Halle. Through successive scholarships to the Chelsea College of Art and Design (1998–2000) and Goldsmiths College London (2001–2003) she came into contact with textiles for the first time and learnt the technique of tufting. She is still using it in her work because it affords possibilities for achieving a painterly expressiveness with wool as her work material. Her works begin on the drawing board and are then traced on to the support material. The woollen imaginary beings of all sizes created by tufting seem to invade spaces, yet for all their archaic and at the same time futuristic appearance they radiate a feeling of warmth, have an almost a consolatory effect. These are the opposing forces that inform her oeuvre. Achaintre also exploits the tactile quality so characteristic of wool. Just looking at her works activates a physical resonance – as if one already has an inkling of how the material might feel: from fluffy mohair to scratchy fibre, from shaggy fringes to densely trimmed textured surfaces.

Since 2019 Achaintre has held a professorship for painting and textile art at Burg Giebichenstein Kunsthochschule in Halle. In teaching she pursues an interdisciplinary, experimental approach that also draws on her own artistic praxis.

04

05

DE   Die künstlerische Praxis von Caroline Achaintre, geboren 1969, umfasst verschiedene Materialien wie Keramik, Textilien, Aquarell und Zeichnung. Paradigmatisch sind ihre expressiven Wandobjekte aus handgetufteter Wolle – hybride Kreaturen, die zwischen Unheimlichem und Vertrautem changieren. Mit einer konzeptuellen, prozessbasierten Arbeitsweise erschafft Achaintre Texturen, die sich intensiv mit anthropomorphen Formen, Masken und animistischen Motiven auseinandersetzen. Die Inspirationsquellen sind mannigfaltig und bedienen die Faszination für prähistorische Kunst, Science-Fiction-Filme oder Gothic Novels.

Achaintre wuchs in Fürth auf und begann ihre künstlerische Laufbahn mit einer Ausbildung zur Kunstschmiedin und einem anschließenden Studium in Bildhauerei/Metall an der Burg Giebichenstein Kunsthochschule Halle. Durch ein Stipendium am Chelsea College of Art and Design (1998–2000) und am Goldsmiths College London (2001–2003) kam sie anschließend zum ersten Mal mit Textil in Berührung und erlernte die Technik des Tuftings. Diese nutzt sie in ihren Arbeiten nach wie vor, was ihr die Möglichkeit gibt, mit dem Material Wolle einen malerischen Ausdruck zu erzielen. Die Werke entstehen zuerst zeichnerisch und werden anschließend ins Trägermaterial transferiert. Die durch das Tufting entstehenden, wollenen Fantasiewesen in allen Größen scheinen Räume zu erobern – doch trotz ihrer archaischen und futuristischen Erscheinung haben sie eine warme, beinahe tröstliche Ausstrahlung. Diese Gegensätze prägen ihr künstlerisches Schaffen. Dabei nutzt Achaintre auch die charakteristische Haptik von Wolle. Ihre Arbeiten lösen bereits beim bloßen Anblick eine körperliche Resonanz aus – als ahnte man, wie sich das Material anfühlt: vom flauschigen Mohair bis zur kratzigen Faser, von zotteligen Fransen bis zu dicht getrimmten Texturflächen.

Seit 2019 ist Achaintre Professorin für Malerei und Textile Kunst an der Burg Giebichenstein Kunsthochschule Halle. In ihrer Lehre verfolgt sie einen interdisziplinären und experimentellen Ansatz, der auch aus ihrer eigenen künstlerischen Praxis schöpft.

Elfi Baumgartner

01 DAS REICH DES LEGUAN (1991), DETAIL
170 × 90 CM
TAPESTRY IN FREESTYLE GOTHIC WEAVING
TECHNIQUE
WARP: COTTON; WEFT: NEW WOOL

The tapestry lives its own life like a living creature, and it undergoes the same changes to which we are subjected in everyday life. This is completely natural, for it is only alive when the person looks at it.

EN Elfi Baumgartner is an artist who lives in Vienna, and her creative praxis has continued to contribute actively to the survival of one of the most ancient textile genres.

She works in the field of tapestry weaving and since completing her education has concentrated on realising painterly and collage-like designs with textiles as her materials. Born in 1944, Baumgartner studied at what is now the Universität für angewandte Kunst Wien in the Master classes Fashion and Textiles, and Applied Painting and Textiles. She worked on her diploma project under the supervision of Josef Schulz, who was head of tapestry weaving, and Professor Carl Unger in the Master class for painting, a productive formative phase in which she not only learnt crafts skills but also discovered a passion for pictorial weaving. Close affinities with both collage and painting are qualities that make her textiles artworks that look so impressive due to her fascinating handling of glowing colour and fine detail. This is the aspect of her work that Elfi Baumgartner finds exciting: 'painting with wool' has become her signature characteristic and is to this day striking for the delicacy with which the detail is rendered. Even works covering large surfaces are only recognisable as textiles on closer scrutiny. This fluid interdisciplinary aspect makes clear her consummate mastery of colour, material and technique. Her devotion to material and time is undeniable; microscopically minute details fit together to form a coherent whole. Baumgartner's material of choice is pure wool, which she painstakingly dyes herself on the skein[1]. Handled in this way, colour can be perceived on both the visual and the tactile planes. Thus subtle colour gradients that may change over the course of the process are created by layering yarns sixfold. In more recent works she has been increasingly experimenting with other mediums, including oil pastels, watercolours and photographic templates. The resulting images appear in even softer focus, almost blurry, and show how much Baumgartner's signature has changed with the years but without denying its aesthetic provenance.

[1] Skein dyeing: the yarn is dyed in a loop of loose strands before being further processed - not as finished fabric or garments

02 DIPLOMARBEIT (1970)
150 × 200 CM
TAPESTRY IN FREESTYLE GOTHIC WEAVING TECHNIQUE
WARP: COTTON; WEFT: NEW WOOL

03 DER GRÜNE (1975)
135 × 200 CM
TAPESTRY IN FREESTYLE GOTHIC WEAVING TECHNIQUE
WARP: COTTON; WEFT: NEW WOOL

DE Elfi Baumgartner ist eine in Wien lebende Künstlerin, die mit ihrer gestalterischen Praxis bis heute aktiv zum Bestehen einer der ältesten textilen Techniken beiträgt.

Sie arbeitet im Bereich der Tapisserie und beschäftigt sich seit ihrer Ausbildung mit der Verwirklichung von malerischen und collagenartigen Entwürfen mittels textilen Materials. Geboren 1944, studierte Baumgartner an der heutigen Universität für Angewandte Kunst in Wien, in der Meisterklasse für Mode und Textil sowie in der für angewandte Malerei und Textil. Ihre Diplomarbeit entstand bei Josef Schulz, der die Gobelinweberei leitete, unter Professor Carl Unger in der Meisterklasse für Malerei - eine prägende Zeit, in der sie nicht nur das Handwerk lernte, sondern auch ihre Leidenschaft für die Bildweberei entdeckte. Die Nähe zur Collage und zur Malerei lässt die textilen Arbeiten durch ihre faszinierende Farbbrillanz und Feinheit als beeindruckende Kunstwerke erscheinen. Genau dieses Moment reizt Elfi Baumgartner an ihrer Arbeit: Das »Malen mit Wolle« wurde zu ihrem Charakteristikum und besticht bis heute durch Feinheit und Detail. Selbst die großflächigen Arbeiten werden erst bei genauerem Betrachten als textile Flächen erkennbar. In diesem Moment des Übergangs wird deutlich, mit welcher Virtuosität sie Farbe, Material und Technik beherrscht. Die Hingabe zu Materie und Zeit ist unumstritten; mikroskopisch Kleines fügt sich zu einem Ganzen. Baumgartners Material der Wahl ist reine Wolle, welche sie in aufwendigen Prozessen zuvor von Hand am Strang selbst färbt[1]. Auf diese Weise wird die Farbe nicht nur optisch, sondern auch haptisch wahrnehmbar. In unendlicher Farbvielfalt entstehen so durch sechsfach geschichtete Garne subtile Verläufe, die sich im Laufe des Prozesses verändern dürfen.

In ihren neueren Werken experimentiert sie zunehmend mit anderen Medien wie Ölkreiden, Aquarellfarben oder fotografischen Vorlagen. Die Ergebnisse wirken noch weicher, beinahe verschwommen, und zeigen, wie sehr sich Baumgartners künstlerische Handschrift über die Jahre weiterentwickelt hat, ohne ihre ästhetischen Ursprünge zu verlieren.

[1] Am Strang färben: Das Garn wird vor der Weiterverarbeitung in lockeren Strängen am Stück gefärbt - nicht als fertiger Stoff oder Kleidungsstück

02

03

Otti Berger

01 CARPET FOR CHILDREN'S ROOM (1929), DETAIL
185 × 109 CM
MODIFIED LINEN WEAVE
COTTON, MERCERISED COTTON

You have to listen to the secrets of the fabric, follow the sounds of the materials.

Otti Berger (1898–1944) was an influential figure at the Bauhaus, who recognised the potential for industrial processes in textile design early on and made use of it. Born Otilija Ester Berger in Zmajevac in the Austro-Hungarian Empire, she studied at the Royal Academy of Arts and Crafts in Zagreb before going in 1927 for further training to the Dessau Bauhaus. An ear infection left Berger virtually deaf – a highly developed sense of touch and an ability to grasp fabrics with all her senses became a pivotal element of artistic expression for her. She strove not only to understand textile structures technically and rationally but also to develop an intuitive feeling for them.

In 1929 she was co-deputy head with Anni Albers of the weaving studio at the Bauhaus while Gunta Stölzl [→ p. 199] was on maternity leave. Berger pursued a new approach in her own design praxis: she began to abandon the ideal of the artist as an individual, concentrating instead on functional, industrially reproducible textile design.

By addressing the medium in the way she did, she shaped the view of textile design as a modern, functional discipline. In 1930 she completed her training in weaving at the Bauhaus and started her career by gaining experience working in the textile industry.

After the Dessau Bauhaus was shut down in 1932, Berger founded a studio of her own in Berlin. There she collaborated with several industrial firms and had an innovative fabric patented in 1932. Her designs were used in fashion as well as architecture and interior design.

In 1936 she was forbidden to practise her profession because she was Jewish. An attempt to gain a foothold in England failed because of difficulties she had with the language. Finally, she returned to her family in what was then Yugoslavia, where she waited in vain for a US entry visa. She was murdered in Auschwitz in 1944.

Her work was forgotten for a long time. In the meantime she has been rediscovered as an important pioneering exponent of modern textile design and is honoured for her clarity of design, powers of technical innovation and unflagging creative drive.

02 TEXTILE SAMPLE (CA. 1935)
14 × 23 CM
WOVEN
COTTON

03 TEXTILES SAMPLE 55.115.1 (MID 1930S),
DETAIL
24 × 9.5 CM
PEACOCK EYE PATTERN
COTTON

04 TEXTILE 1 (BETWEEN 1919–1933)
43 × 37 CM
WOVEN
CELLOPHANE, COTTON

02

03

04

DE Otti Berger (1898–1944) war eine prägende Gestalt am Bauhaus, die bereits früh das Potenzial industrieller Verfahrensweisen für Textilgestaltung erkannte und nutzte.

Geboren als Otilija Ester Berger in Zmajevac im damaligen Österreich-Ungarn studierte sie an der Kunstakademie in Zagreb, bevor sie sich 1927 am Dessauer Bauhaus einschrieb. Aufgrund einer Gehörerkrankung war Berger nahezu taub – ihr ausgeprägtes Tastempfinden und ihre Fähigkeit, Stoffe mit allen Sinnen zu erfassen, wurden zum zentralen Element ihres künstlerischen Ausdrucks. Sie versuchte, textile Strukturen nicht nur technisch und rational zu begreifen, sondern auch intuitiv zu erspüren.

1929 vertrat sie gemeinsam mit Anni Albers kommissarisch die Leitung des Webereiateliers am Bauhaus während des Mutterschutzes von Gunta Stölzl [→ S. 199]. In ihrer eigenen gestalterischen Praxis verfolgte sie einen neuen Ansatz: Sie wandte sich zunehmend vom Ideal der individuellen Künstler:innenhandschrift ab und konzentrierte sich stattdessen auf funktionales, industriell reproduzierbares Textildesign. Damit prägte sie das Verständnis von Textilgestaltung als moderne, funktionale Disziplin. 1930 erlangte sie ihren Abschluss in der Weberei am Bauhaus und sammelte anschließend erste Erfahrungen in der Industrie.

Nach der Auflösung des Dessauer Bauhauses 1932 gründete Berger ein eigenes Atelier in Berlin, arbeitete mit verschiedenen Industrieunternehmen zusammen und ließ 1932 ein innovatives Gewebe patentieren. Ihre Entwürfe fanden Anwendung in der Mode sowie in der Architektur und Innenarchitektur. 1936 wurde ihr als Jüdin die Berufsausübung in Deutschland verboten. Ein Versuch, in England Fuß zu fassen, scheiterte an sprachlichen Hürden. Schließlich kehrte sie zu ihrer Familie ins damalige Jugoslawien zurück, wo sie vergeblich auf ein US-Visum wartete. 1944 wurde sie im KZ Auschwitz ermordet.

Lange Zeit war ihr Werk weitgehend vergessen, zwischenzeitlich wurde sie jedoch als eine bedeutende Pionierin des modernen Textildesigns wiederentdeckt und wird seitdem für ihre gestalterische Klarheit, technische Innovationskraft und ihren unermüdlichen Gestaltungswillen geschätzt.

Emma Dahlqvist

01 UNDER REGNBÅGEN / UNDER THE RAINBOW
(2023)
120 × 140 CM
LASER CUT, WOVEN
BIRCH, TULLE

Through textiles I feel connected to previous generations;
for example, when I knit, I feel the presence of my grandmother, who taught me. There's something quite philosophical
about textiles that touches me on a deep level.

EN Born in 1987, Emma Dahlqvist is an artist whose works are interdisciplinary, combining art and design. She unites traditional crafts techniques with digital technologies in order to recontextualise material properties. Her oeuvre centres on birch bark, a traditional and natural material for weaving and braiding that she translates into a contemporary context by deploying a variety of processes such as weaving, laser cutting and origami. Fusing organic and recycled materials, she creates sustainable textile objects, thus exploring the boundaries between applied arts design and fine art. Consummate craftsmanship always forms the basis of her aesthetic praxis and is the keystone of each of her works.

After taking a bachelor's degree in design at the Högskolan för konst och design (HDK-Valand) in Gothenburg in 2012, she received a master's degree in textile design from the Textilhögskolan in Borås in 2015. Emma Dahlqvist has an affective relationship with textiles. To her, fabric is something for which almost everyone has a personal affinity – from the first moment of life, wrapped in a blanket, to death. Dahlqvist feels textiles have a philosophical profundity that appeals to everyone on the emotional plane.

Nonetheless, her material of choice is still birch bark. She appreciates its versatility – bark can be both stable and durable as well as soft and ductile. This particular material property enables Dahlqvist to explore the boundary between wood and cloth in a playful spirit and redefine it.

Emma Dahlqvist now lives and works in Östersund. She shares a studio with four other women artists who are exponents of different disciplines. The collective space not only serves their own production needs but is also used for exhibitions, showing films and hosting lectures.

Alongside her work in art she is also an author: in her publications, *Näver* (2019) on sewing, and *Fläta* (2022) on weaving, she reflects on the traditional techniques of Nordic basket weaving and their relevance in the contemporary discourse.

02 BIRCH DRAGON (2023)
140 × 240 CM
LASER CUT, WOVEN
BIRCH, TULLE

03 GRID (2022)
120 × 170 CM
WOVEN
BIRCH BARK

02

DE Emma Dahlqvist, geboren 1987, ist eine interdisziplinär arbeitende Designerin und Künstlerin. Sie verbindet traditionelle Handwerkstechniken mit digitalen Technologien, um die Eigenschaften von Materialien neu zu kontextualisieren. Im Zentrum ihres Schaffens steht die Birkenrinde - ein traditionelles und natürliches Flechtmaterial, das sie mittels unterschiedlicher Verfahren wie Weben, Laser-Cut und Origami in einen zeitgenössischen Kontext überführt. Durch die Fusion von organischen und recycelten Materialien erschafft sie nachhaltige textile Objekte und lotet dabei die Grenzen zwischen angewandter Gestaltung und freier Kunst aus. Das handwerkliche Können bildet stets das Fundament ihrer ästhetischen Praxis und ist der Grundbaustein jeder ihrer Arbeiten.

Nach einem Bachelor in Design an der HDK in Göteborg 2012 absolvierte sie 2015 ihren Master in Textildesign an der Swedish School of Textiles in Borås. Emma Dahlqvist steht in einem affektiven Verhältnis zum Textil. Für sie ist das Material etwas, zu dem nahezu jeder Mensch eine persönliche Beziehung hat - vom ersten Moment des Lebens, eingehüllt in eine Decke, bis in den Tod. Für Dahlqvist haben Textilien eine philosophische Tiefe, die alle Menschen emotional stark anspricht.

Ihr bevorzugtes Material bleibt dennoch die Birkenrinde. Sie schätzt deren Vielseitigkeit - die Rinde kann sowohl stabil und haltbar, aber auch weich und biegsam sein. Diese besondere Materialeigenschaft erlaubt Dahlqvist, die Grenze zwischen Holz und Textil spielerisch zu erkunden und neu zu definieren.

Heute lebt und arbeitet Emma Dahlqvist in Östersund. Ihr Atelier teilt sie mit vier anderen Künstlerinnen aus verschiedenen Disziplinen. Der Raum dient nicht nur der eigenen Produktion, sondern wird auch für Ausstellungen, Filmvorführungen und Vorträge genutzt.

Neben ihrer künstlerischen Tätigkeit ist sie auch Autorin: In ihren Publikationen *Näver* (2019; dt. »Nähen«) und *Fläta* (2022; dt. »Flechten«) reflektiert sie über traditionelle Techniken des nordischen Korbflechtens und deren Relevanz in zeitgenössischen Diskursen.

03

02

Sofie Dawo

01 UNTITLED (1979)
140 × 115 CM
FREESTYLE WEAVING TECHNIQUE WITH KNOTTED
EFFECT YARN
COTTON, WOOL, POLYETHYLENE

02 UNTITLED (1969)
68.5 × 68.5 CM
PLAIN WOVEN BASE WITH INSERTED FRINGES
COTTON, WAXED LINEN

EN The recipient of multiple awards, Sofie Dawo (1926–2010) was a textile artist, designer and teacher whose work continues to inspire numerous designers. After completing her studies at the then Staatliche Schule für Kunst und Handwerk in Saarbrücken, where she specialised in textile design, she increasingly shifted her focus to freelance artistic praxis – although she had initially worked for industry on a commission basis. In the pioneering spirit and with a huge appetite for experimentation, in the 1960s she began to develop an autonomous textile idiom that was deliberately distanced from functional and industrial applications.

At a time when textiles were usually consigned to design contexts, Dawo was already addressing the issue of where textile art belonged outside those conventions. She rejected the principles of Bauhaus Modernism, which so often aimed at reproducibility and practical applications, and created works that are distinguished by radical subjectivity and a processual approach to production.

She worked intuitively and directly at her loom, often without preparatory sketches. Her works emerged in a lively dialogue with the material: texture, resistance and structure determined artistic expression. Dawo did not see weaving as a purely technical process but rather as a medium that she transformed into an artistic praxis that intervened in space. From the textile surface she developed relief-like, sculptural objects – often incorporating such unconventional work materials as nylon, jute or plastic.

In choosing this approach, she deliberately transgressed the set of rules applied to weaving: knots, tears, exposed threads or loosely textured structures generate new visual force fields. Usually colour reductive, her works divert the focus of attention to form, density and material properties through the deliberate eschewal of colour.

Apart from her work as an artist, Sofie Dawo was actively engaged for more than three decades in teaching textile design at a variety of art academies and education centres in Hesse. From 1968 to 1986 she was a member of the Deutscher Werkbund – her entire oeuvre exemplifies the emancipation of textile art as an autonomous art discipline.

03 UNTITLED (UNDATED)
87 × 25 CM
PLAIN WEAVE WITH FLOATING, BROCADED WEFT
SYNTHETIC FIBRE

04 UNTITLED (1975)
170 × 78 CM
PLAIN WEAVE WITH WARP AND WEFT FLOATS,
VARYING WARP AND WEFT DENSITY
COTTON, WOOL

DE Sofie Dawo (1926–2010) war eine vielfach ausgezeichnete Textilkünstlerin, Designerin und Pädagogin, deren Werk bis heute zahlreiche Gestalter:innen inspiriert. Nach ihrem Studium an der Staatlichen Schule für Kunst und Handwerk in Saarbrücken, das sie im Fach Textiles Gestalten absolvierte, wandte sie sich – nach anfänglichen Designaufträgen für die Industrie – zunehmend der freien künstlerischen Praxis zu. Mit Pioniergeist und Lust am Experiment entwickelte sie ab den 1960er-Jahren eine autonome textile Sprache, die sich bewusst von funktionalen und industriellen Anwendungen distanzierte.

In einer Zeit, in der Textilien meist einer gestalterischen Zweckbindung unterlagen, stellte Dawo die Frage, wie sich textile Kunst jenseits dieser Konventionen verorten lässt. Sie wandte sich von den Prinzipien der Bauhaus-Moderne ab, die häufig auf Wiederholbarkeit und Gebrauchsfunktion zielten, und schuf Werke, die sich durch radikale Subjektivität und prozesshafte Entstehung auszeichnen.

Oft ohne vorbereitende Skizzen arbeitete sie intuitiv und unmittelbar am Webstuhl. Ihre Werke entstanden im lebendigen Dialog mit dem Material: Textur, Widerstand und Struktur bestimmten den künstlerischen Ausdruck. Dawo erkannte im Weben kein rein technisches Verfahren, sondern ein Medium, das sie zur raumgreifenden künstlerischen Praxis transformierte. Aus der Fläche entwickelte sie reliefartige, plastische Objekte – häufig unter Einbezug unkonventioneller Werkstoffe wie Nylon, Jute oder Kunststoff.

Dabei durchbrach sie gezielt die Ordnung des Gewebes: Knoten, Risse, offene Fäden oder locker gesetzte Strukturen erzeugen neue visuelle Spannungsfelder. Ihre meist farbreduzierten Arbeiten lenken durch den bewussten Verzicht auf Farbe den Fokus auf Form, Dichte und Materialität.

Neben ihrer künstlerischen Arbeit war Sofie Dawo über drei Jahrzehnte in der Lehre an unterschiedlichen Kunsthochschulen und Bildungszentren in Hessen im Bereich Textilgestaltung tätig. Von 1968 bis 1986 war sie Mitglied im Deutschen Werkbund – ihr gesamtes Werk steht beispielhaft für die Emanzipation der Textilkunst als eigenständige künstlerische Disziplin.

04

03

Lucienne Day

01 LAPIS CURTAIN FABRIC (1953)
SCREEN PRINTED
COTTON

I wanted the work I was doing to be seen by people and used by people. They were starved of interesting things for their homes during the war years, either textiles or furniture.

EN Lucienne Day (1917–2010) was one of the most important textile designers in Britain. Her innovative, colourful and timeless fabric patterns were acclaimed worldwide and exerted a paramount influence on the development of modern textile design after the Second World War. Day's insistence that her designs be accessible to the public at large was particularly remarkable. Breaking down the boundaries between art and mass production and concomitant collaboration with the textile industry ensured that her fabrics were affordable for far more people – especially during the post-war years. Lucienne Day was interested in art as far back as her youth and was encouraged by a teacher to study the subject. At the Croydon School of Art and in London at the Royal College of Art, she initially experimented with different media before going on to discover her passion for textiles. Her works are characterised by geometric forms and organic motifs that are inspired by both nature and the abstract European painting of her time. She usually created designs in gouache on paper, and the fabrics were then industrially produced.

The Second World War era and the post-war years were very challenging for Lucienne Day as a designer. She was working as an instructor and freelancer designer long before the term 'designer' had come into common usage, a circumstance that made it difficult for her to earn the recognition she deserved for her work. Her free, lively designs proved a challenge to the manufacturers she worked with in their development of new techniques and materials. *Calyx* (1951), which is probably the best known of all her patterns, is still an icon of twentieth-century textile design. *Calyx* was presented at the Festival of Britain, a national exhibition and trade fair hosted in the summer of that year in London, and received multiple awards. Lucienne Day's influence went far beyond textiles: she also designed wallpapers and ceramics, with which she made a substantial contribution to popularising the Mid-Century Modern style. She has remained a groundbreaking figure in the field of design.

02 MAGNETIC FURNISHING FABRIC (1957)
DETAIL
ROLLER PRINTED
COTTON

03 SPECTATORS FURNISHING FABRIC (1953)
DETAIL
SCREEN PRINTED
COTTON

DE Lucienne Day (1917–2010) war eine der bedeutendsten britischen Textildesignerinnen. Ihre innovativen, farbenfrohen und zeitlosen Stoffmuster erlangten international große Anerkennung und prägten maßgeblich die Entwicklung des modernen Textildesigns nach dem Zweiten Weltkrieg. Besonders bemerkenswert war Days Anspruch auf Zugänglichkeit ihrer Designs für eine breite Bevölkerungsschicht. Der Transfer zwischen Kunst und Massenproduktion sowie eine damit verbundene Zusammenarbeit mit der Textilindustrie führte dazu, dass ihre Stoffe für eine größere Zahl von Menschen erschwinglich wurden – besonders in der Nachkriegszeit. Lucienne Day interessierte sich bereits als Jugendliche für Kunst, ein Lehrer ermutigte sie schließlich zum entsprechenden Studium. An der Croydon School of Art sowie in London am Royal College of Art experimentierte sie zunächst mit verschiedenen Materialien und entdeckte dadurch ihre Leidenschaft für Textilien. Ihre Arbeiten zeichnen sich durch geometrische Formen und organische Motive aus, die von der Natur ebenso inspiriert sind wie von der abstrakten europäischen Malerei ihrer

Zeit. Ihre Entwürfe entstanden meist zuerst mit Gouache auf Papier und wurden anschließend industriell produziert.

Die Zeit des Zweiten Weltkriegs und die anschließenden Jahre waren für Lucienne Day als Designerin sehr herausfordernd. Sie arbeitete als Dozentin und freie Gestalterin, als der Berufsbegriff »Designer:in« kaum geläufig war, was es ihr erschwerte, Anerkennung für ihre Arbeit zu finden. Ihre freien und lebendigen Designs forderten die Manufakturen, mit denen sie zusammenarbeitete, heraus, neue Techniken und Materialien für die Umsetzung zu entwickeln. Ihr wohl bekanntestes Muster, *Calyx* von 1951, steht bis heute ikonisch für Textildesign im 20. Jahrhundert. Der Entwurf wurde noch im gleichen Jahr beim Festival of Britain, einer Art nationaler Leistungsschau in London, präsentiert und mehrfach ausgezeichnet. Lucienne Days Einfluss reicht weit über Textilien hinaus: Sie entwarf auch Tapeten und Keramiken, womit sie wesentlich zur Popularisierung des Mid-Century-Modern-Stils beitrug. Bis heute bleibt sie eine richtungsweisende Figur für die Disziplin des Designs.

02

03

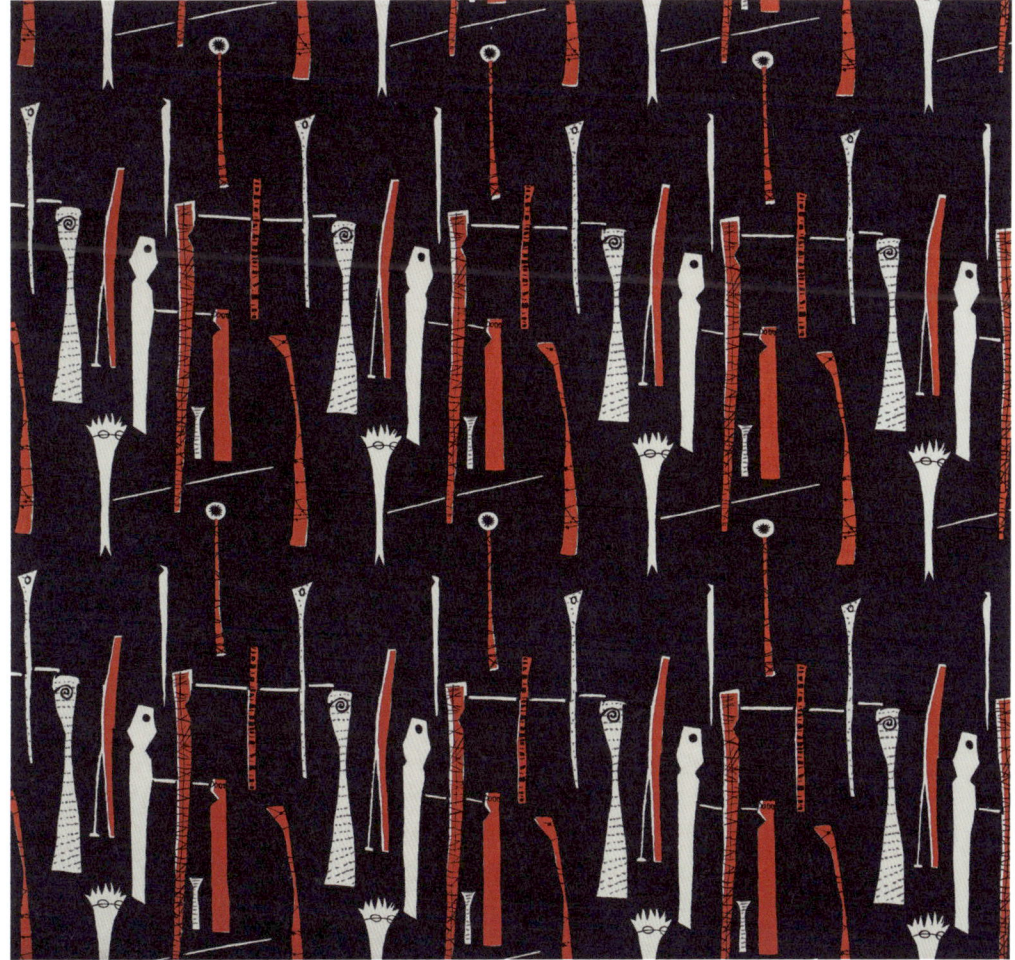

Pauline van Dongen
initiator of heliotex

02

01 SOLAR SHIRT (2015)
VARIOUS SIZES
THIN FILM SOLAR CELLS, TEXTILE

02 HELIOTEX COLOUR TEST (2024)
VARIOUS SIZES
COLLAGE
MIXED MEDIA

EN The work by Pauline van Dongen, born in 1986, combines design, technology and social responsibility, a symbiosis that invites us to rethink the relationship between human beings, materials and the environment. After taking a master's degree in fashion design at ArtEZ University of Arts in Arnhem, she founded a design studio of her own in 2010 and began to pursue a growing interest in smart textiles, expanding her knowledge of them by collaborating with research facilities and businesses in the field of renewable energy. Pauline van Dongen experiments with materials and is guided by the properties of any she happens to be working on – for example, solar energy, which she views as cultural material, or the living ductility of natural fibres.

In 2019 she completed a PhD at the Technische Universiteit Eindhoven to ensure her vision of fashion as a dynamic and protean medium was grounded in science. Over the years her focus has shifted from wearable technology to architectonic applications, where overarching themes such as care, the environment and energy have priority.

Cities are seeking new solutions for reducing heat stress in public spaces whereas festivals are interested in lightweight constructions that provide shade as well as grid-independent energy. This is where the heliotex project comes in, which develops solar-active textiles to provide sustainable energy for spaces and at the same time create atmospheric immersive experiences.

Heliotex integrates solar cells in a flexible, palpably tactile material that is suitable for temporary architectonic installations such as pavilions. This approach to design is not exclusively based on technical performance but also represents an aesthetic intention to create a special atmosphere, something that functions in its immediate surroundings, feels good to the touch and provides added value on manifold levels. Alongside her practical work Van Dongen imparts her knowledge in a range of lectures and podcasts with the goal of making the sources of inspiration she draws on and the insights she has gained in the process accessible to a broader public.

03 DEPLOYABLE HELIOTEX SAMPLE (2024)
50 × 50 CM
WOVEN
ORGANIC PHOTOVOLTAIC CELLS,
TEXTILE TAPING

04 SOLAR SHIRT (2015), DETAIL
VARIOUS SIZES
THIN FILM SOLAR CELLS, TEXTILE

05 HELIOTEX SOLAR TEXTILE (2022), DETAIL
50 × 200 CM
WOVEN
ORGANIC PHOTOVOLTAIC CELLS,
RECYCLED POLYESTER

DE Die Arbeit von Pauline van Dongen, geboren 1986, führt Design, Technologie und gesellschaftliche Verantwortung zusammen - eine Symbiose, die einlädt, das Verhältnis zwischen Mensch, Material und Umwelt neu zu denken. Nach ihrem Masterabschluss in Modedesign an der ArtEZ University of the Arts Arnhem gründete sie 2010 ihr eigenes Designstudio und entwickelte ein immer größeres Interesse für Smart Textiles, die sie durch interdisziplinäre Zusammenarbeit mit Forschungseinrichtungen und Unternehmen aus dem Bereich der erneuerbaren Energien vertiefte. Van Dongen experimentiert mit Materialien und lässt sich vom Charakter des Werkstoffs leiten - exemplarisch stehen hier Solarenergie, die von ihr als kulturelles Material begriffen wird, oder die lebendige Formbarkeit natürlicher Fasern. 2019 schloss sie mit ihrem PhD an der Eindhoven University of Technology ab, um ihre Vision von Mode als dynamisches und wandelbares Medium wissenschaftlich zu fundieren. Ihr Fokus verschob sich über die Jahre von tragbarer Technologie hin zu architektonischen Anwendungen, in denen Themen wie Fürsorge,

Umwelt und Energie im Mittelpunkt stehen. Städte suchen nach neuen Lösungen, um Hitzebelastungen im öffentlichen Raum zu reduzieren, während Festivals an leichten Konstruktionen interessiert sind, die sowohl Schatten spenden als auch netzunabhängig Energie liefern. Hier setzt das Projekt heliotex an, das solaraktive Textilien erarbeitet, um Räume mit nachhaltiger Energie zu versorgen und zugleich atmosphärische Erlebniswelten zu schaffen.

Heliotex integriert Solarzellen in ein flexibles, fühlbares Material, das sich für temporäre architektonische Installationen wie Pavillons eignet. Der gestalterische Anspruch bezieht sich nicht ausschließlich auf technische Leistung, sondern auch auf das ästhetische Bestreben, eine besondere Atmosphäre zu schaffen - etwas, das im unmittelbaren Umfeld funktioniert, sich gut anfühlt und auf vielfältige Weise Mehrwert bietet. Neben ihrer praktischen Arbeit teilt van Dongen ihr Wissen in diversen Vorträgen und Podcasts, mit der Ambition, ihre Inspirationen und Erkenntnisse einem breiten Publikum zugänglich zu machen.

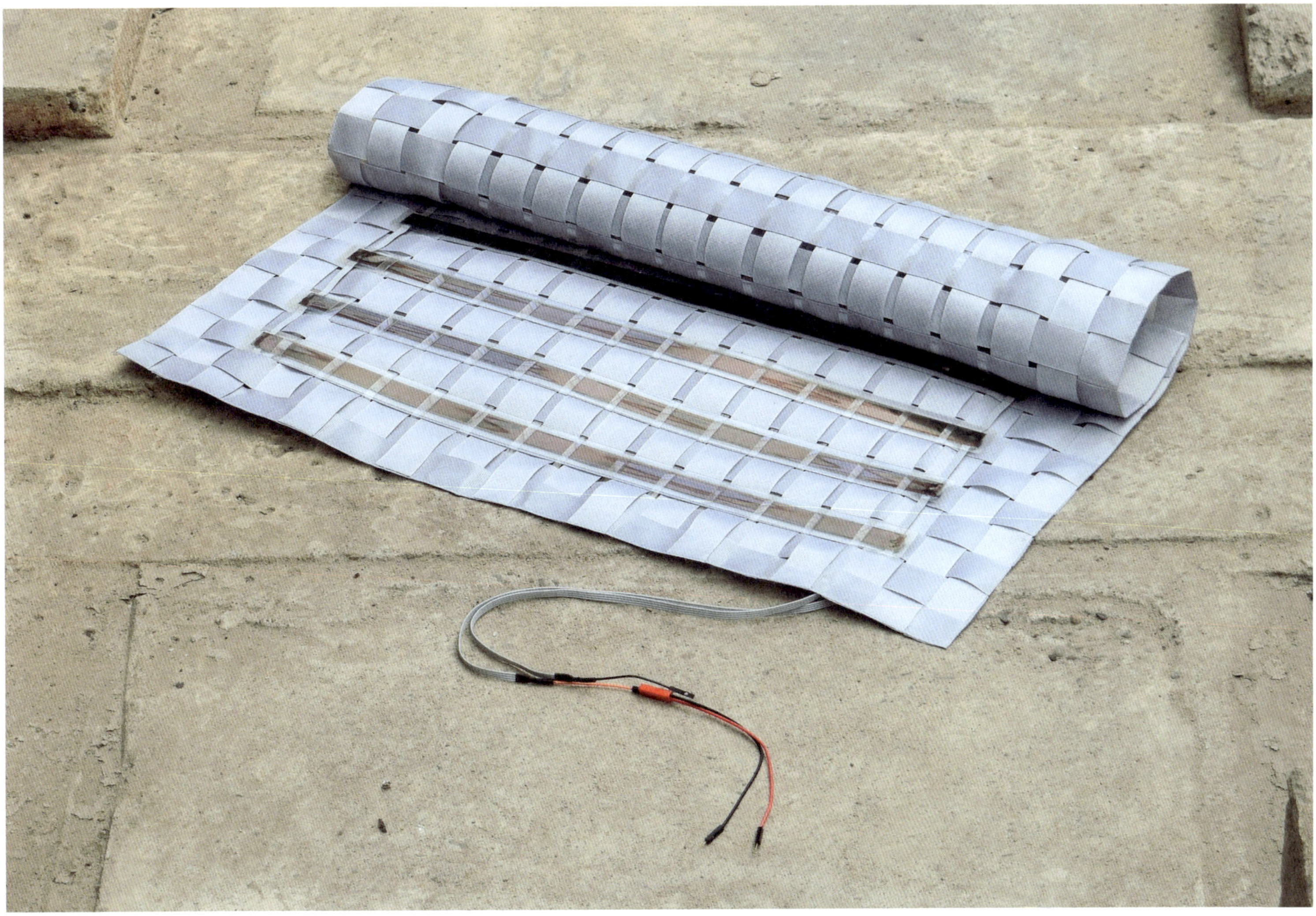

03

04

05

Annette Douglas

01 MONO-TONI UND MULTI-TONI (2014)
ACOUSTIC CURTAINS FOR MUSIC ROOMS AND
LECTURE HALLS, ZHDK, TONI-AREAL,
ZURICH (CH)
340 × 620 CM
WOVEN
TREVIRA CS (FLAME RETARDANT)

I think I get the 'research gene' from my family. Even back when I was studying, I found this mix of design and development exciting.

Annette Douglas is versatile and expert in a wide range of textile techniques as a designer and visionary developer. Her skills and years of experience in her chosen field enable her to perfect designs realised at the interface of aesthetics, technological innovation and sheer skill. Born in 1971, she studied textile design at the Schweizerische Textilfachschule and at the Hochschule für Gestaltung in Basel. She attributes being endowed with the 'research gene' to her family, which has been rooted in the textile industry for four generations. The close affinity between design and engineering has been an enduring fascination - an interest that she professionalised with in-depth further training in project management for research and development at the Hochschule Luzern. Since 1999 she has headed her own business, Annette Douglas Textiles, which launched as a public limited company in 2011. Drawing on a small, highly qualified team, she realises textile projects focused on design, architecture, interior design and acoustics.

By 2004 she was exploring the interaction between textiles and acoustics - at the time still relatively uncharted territory, which has continued to gain in importance. She compares her creative process to a funnel: at first filled with diverse impulses, it gradually condenses into clearly defined, focused concepts.

Her Swiss studio is in Wettingen, where it is housed in a historic spinning mill. This is where she develops her textile solutions for optimising spatial acoustics, for instance - comparable to the way perforated acoustic ceiling panels function, which absorb sound through the friction produced by the oscillation of longitudinal sound waves at the edges of the holes.

She procures her materials chiefly through the ranges manufactured by trusted partner industries yet is always open to new sources of inspiration. What counts for her is collaboration with reliable producers who unite top quality with ecological responsibility.

Douglas used to work towards that aim at her own loom but nowadays by means of specialised software that translates the demands she makes of design to the digital sphere.

02 ACOUSTIC NEEDLEWORK (2014)
ACOUSTIC WALL WITH ARTIST BEAT ZODERER,
MUSIC HALL, RHEINAU MONASTERY
900 × 1200 CM
WOVEN, EMBROIDERED
TREVIRA CS (FLAME RETARDANT)

03 ACOUSTIC NEEDLEWORK (2014), DETAIL
ACOUSTIC WALL WITH ARTIST BEAT ZODERER
900 × 1200 CM
WOVEN, EMBROIDERED
TREVIRA CS (FLAME RETARDANT)

04 ACOUSTIC NEEDLEWORK (2014), DETAIL
ACOUSTIC WALL WITH ARTIST BEAT ZODERER
900 × 1200 CM
WOVEN, EMBROIDERED
TREVIRA CS (FLAME RETARDANT)

03

04
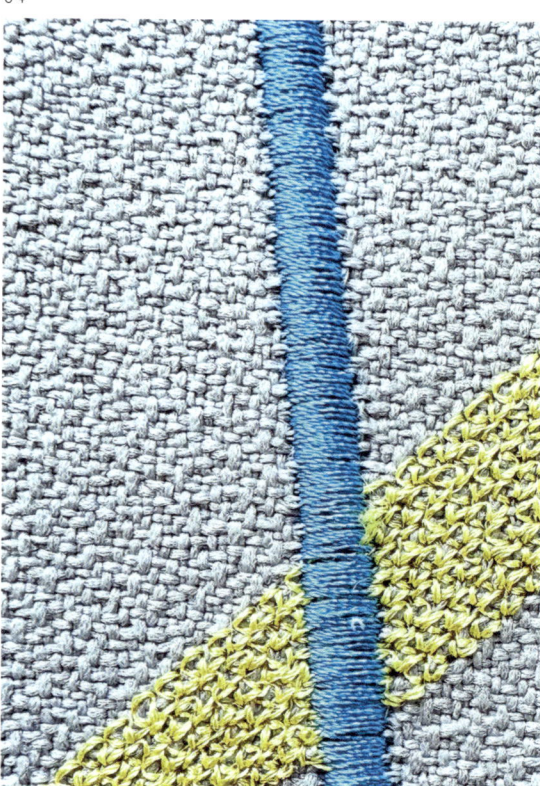

02

DE Als Designerin und visionäre Entwicklerin verfügt Annette Douglas über eine weitreichende Expertise in einer Vielzahl textiler Techniken. Diese Kenntnisse und eine langjährige Erfahrung in ihrem Metier befähigen sie dazu, Gestaltungen an der Schnittstelle von Ästhetik, technologischer Innovation und Kompetenz in der gestalterischen Umsetzung zur Perfektion zu bringen. 1971 geboren, studierte sie Textildesign an der Schweizerischen Textilfachschule in Wattwil sowie an der Hochschule für Gestaltung in Basel. Das »Forscher-Gen« schreibt sie ihrer Familie zu, die seit vier Generationen in der Textilindustrie verwurzelt ist. Die enge Verbindung zwischen Gestaltung und Engineering fasziniert sie nachhaltig – ein Interesse, das sie durch eine vertiefende Weiterbildung im Projektmanagement für Forschung & Entwicklung an der Hochschule Luzern (HSLU) weiter professionalisierte.

Seit 1999 führt sie das Unternehmen Annette Douglas Textiles, das seit 2011 als Aktiengesellschaft firmiert. Mit einem kleinen, hochqualifizierten Team realisiert sie textile Projekte mit Schwerpunkt auf Design, Architektur, Innenraumgestaltung und Akustik. Bereits 2004 begann sie, sich mit dem Zusammenspiel von Textil und Akustik auseinanderzusetzen – damals noch ein kaum erschlossenes Feld, das bis heute zunehmend an Bedeutung gewonnen hat. Ihren kreativen Prozess vergleicht sie mit einem Trichter: Anfangs gefüllt mit vielfältigen Impulsen, findet allmählich eine Verdichtung in klar definierte, fokussierte Konzepte statt.

Ihr Atelier liegt in Wettingen (CH), in einem historischen Spinnereigebäude. Hier entwickelt sie beispielsweiße ihre textilen Lösungen zur Optimierung der Raumakustik – vergleichbar mit der Funktionsweise perforierter Akustikdecken, bei denen Schall durch Reibung an den Lochrändern absorbiert wird.

Die Materialien bezieht sie vorrangig aus dem Sortiment bewährter Industriepartner:innen, bleibt jedoch stets offen für neue Anregungen. Entscheidend ist für sie die Kooperation mit verlässlichen Produzent:innen, die höchste Qualität und ökologische Verantwortung verbinden.

Früher arbeitete sie dafür am eigenen Webstuhl, heute mittels spezialisierter Software, die Douglas' Anspruch an gestalterischen Ausdruck in eine digitale Sphäre überträgt.

Mae Engelgeer

01 EMBUED BLUE (2023)
45 × 220 CM
JACQUARD
WOOL, COTTON

I was always more intrigued by creating fabric as a thing in itself than in experimenting with form.

02

02 CHROMA TRACES (2023)
125 × 96 CM
WOVEN
IGUSA STRAW, COTTON, WOOD

03 DIM (2020)
200 × 130 CM
JACQUARD
WASHI, MIXED MATERIALS

04 ISHOKU PERSPECTIVE (2022)
180 × 85 CM
WOVEN
IGUSA STRAW, COTTON

EN   Born in 1982, Mae Engelgeer discovered a love for textiles in childhood. At school she took a course in textiles rather than the classic drawing class, and from then on spent most of her time in studios. Between 2000 and 2004 she studied fashion design, specialising in textiles, at the Amsterdam Fashion Institute and, after taking a bachelor's degree in textile design, worked for two years in the fashion industry. During that time, however, she grew to realise how much she missed the creative, direct involvement with materials. With the desire for a more in-depth study of art, she took a master's degree from the renowned Sandberg Instituut in Amsterdam under the auspices of the Gerrit Rietveld Academie master's programme (2006-2009). Working with Jacquard weaving during her master's marked a turning point in her development as a designer: as a result, her aesthetic-conceptual praxis centres on weaving - preferably on large machine looms or in collaboration with traditional crafts workshops. Her material of choice is wool, which she sees as the epitome of textile tactility. A signature feature of her work is the recurrent use of a subtly pervasive shade of pink that lends the pieces an atmospheric quality.

The artist now works from Kyoto, where she is currently based while still having her studio space in Amsterdam. Whereas works are prepared and collected for international galleries at her Dutch studio, she collaborates with artisans in Japan on interdisciplinary projects in the contrasting field of textiles and other media while gaining access to centuries-old archives.

A processual, intuitive approach to textile materials informs Engelgeer's oeuvre. In spatial installations and object-like works she transforms traditional techniques and cultural codes into contemporary poetic narratives. Subtle shifts in colour, scale and material iconography are key aspects.

She is currently realising her hitherto most extensive project: Abstract Notes, a site-specific wall hanging that covers 600 square metres for the Tivoli Vredenburg music complex in the Netherlands.

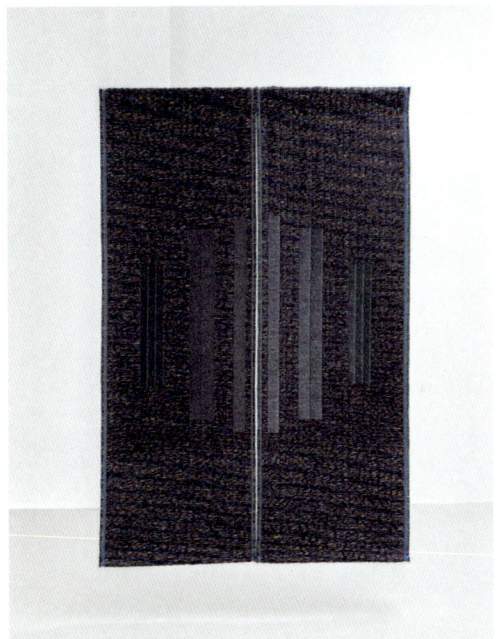

03

04

DE Schon im Kindesalter entdeckte die 1982 geborene Mae Engelgeer ihre Affinität zu Textilien. Während der Schulzeit belegte sie statt klassischem Zeichenunterricht das Fach Textil und verbrachte fortan einen Großteil ihrer Zeit im Atelier. Zwischen 2000 und 2004 absolvierte sie ein Studium im Fachbereich Modedesign mit Schwerpunkt Textil am Fashion Institute in Amsterdam und arbeitete anschließend zwei Jahre in der Modeindustrie. In dieser Zeit wurde ihr jedoch bewusst, wie sehr ihr die kreative, unmittelbare Auseinandersetzung mit Materialien fehlte. Mit dem Wunsch nach einer vertiefenden künstlerischen Auseinandersetzung absolvierte sie am renommierten Sandberg Institute, dem Masterprogramm der Gerrit Rietveld Academie, ihre Ausbildung in Angewandter Kunst (2006-2009).

Die Beschäftigung mit der Jacquardtechnik während ihres Masterstudiums markierte einen Wendepunkt in ihrer gestalterischen Entwicklung: so steht das Weben – bevorzugt auf großformatigen Maschinenwebstühlen oder in Kollaboration mit traditionellen Handwerksbetrieben – im Zentrum ihrer künstlerisch-konzeptuellen Praxis. Ihr bevorzugtes Material ist Wolle, die sie als Inbegriff textiler Haptik versteht. Charakteristisch für ihr Werk ist die wiederkehrende Verwendung eines subtilen Rosétons, der den Werken eine atmosphärische Qualität verleiht.

Die Künstlerin arbeitet von Kyoto aus, wo sie derzeit lebt. Sie hat ihr Atelier in Amsterdam aber behalten, dort werden ihre Werke für die Präsentation in internationale Galerien zusammengestellt und aufbereitet. In Japan hingegen arbeitet sie mit Kunsthandwerkern an interdisziplinären Projekten im Spannungsfeld von Textilien und anderen Materialien zusammen, dabei erhält sie Zugang zu jahrhundertealten Archiven.

Engelgeers Werk ist geprägt von einer prozessualen, intuitiven Herangehensweise an textiles Material. In raumbezogenen Installationen und objekthaften Arbeiten transformiert sie traditionelle Techniken und kulturelle Codes zu zeitgenössischen, poetischen Narrativen. Aktuell realisiert sie mit Abstract Notes ihr bislang umfangreichstes Projekt – ein 600 m² umfassendes, ortsspezifisches Wandtextil für das Musikzentrum Tivoli Vredenburg in den Niederlanden.

01 AYANA (2012)
30 × 20 CM
WRAPPED WITH WIRE
FEATHERS, ANTIQUE STAMENS FOR ARTIFICIAL
FLOWERS, SILK THREAD

02 FORMEN DER NATUR (2019)
40 × 15 CM
BRAIDED
WHEAT STRAW, SILK THREAD

Christiane Englsberger

EN Born in 1970, Christiane Englsberger devotes herself to the traditional Swiss medium of straw-weaving, a craft that has been virtually forgotten. Self-taught, she gained access to this delicate craft through a fortuitous present of small works in straw. Originally trained as a business administrator, Englsberger intensively research how to acquire the unusual skills required for working the material, a knowledge of the tools and weaving techniques used for it - a process marked by intuitive curiosity, methodical precision and assured handling of design. Since 2000 she has been freelancing under the label Soy Como Soy ('I am what I am') as a self-employed artist in the field of designer accessories, with a focus on millinery and brooches.

In her studio in the district of Passau, Lower Bavaria, she practices an almost meditative form of work. Seclusion empowers her to engage in a silent dialogue with her material. Straw - most of it ancient cereals such as tall wheatgrass or rye - assumes the role of a silent yet dominant interlocutor. Englsberger still procures her supplies of it from France and Switzerland but is planning to cultivate her own straw - as a consistent approach to the motives underlying her work: origin, resource and rhythm.

Englsberger's work is characterised by an exciting interplay of tradition and innovation. She pushes the boundaries of her material with precision and great tactile sensitivity. The tools she uses reveal both historical connections and modifications: rose forks for shaping floral elements, hand-carved splinters of bone for splitting fibres or the vernacular tool known as a Schnürlirädli (straw spinner) for making the finest braided straw.

Each of her works is a one-off piece made meticulously by hand in an exacting process that takes days. Particularly sophisticated works may take weeks. Monotonous repetition, serial movement, contemplation - all that is part of her creative process and aesthetic statement.

03 EWELINA (2012)
185 × 35 CM
KNOTTED
FEATHERS, STEEL WIRE, PLEATED CRINOLINE

04 FORMEN DER NATUR (2023)
25 × 20 CM
BRAIDED
WHEAT STRAW

05 FORMEN DER NATUR (2024)
25 × 25 CM
BRAIDED
NATURAL AND DYED WHEAT STRAW

DE Die 1970 geborene Christiane Englsberger widmet sich mit der traditionellen Schweizer Strohflechttechnik einer nahezu vergessenen Handwerkskunst. Die Autodidaktin fand über eine zufällige Schenkung kleiner Stroharbeiten Zugang zu diesem filigranen Metier.

Ursprünglich zur Industriekauffrau ausgebildet, eignete sich Engelsberger das rare Wissen um Materialverhalten, Werkzeuge und Flechttechniken in intensiver Eigenrecherche an - ein Prozess, der von intuitiver Neugier, methodischer Genauigkeit und gestalterischer Souveränität geprägt ist. Seit dem Jahr 2000 arbeitet sie unter dem Label Soy Como Soy (dt. »Ich bin wie ich bin«) als freie Künstlerin im Bereich kunsthandwerklicher Accessoires - mit einem Fokus auf Kopfschmuck und Broschen.

In ihrem Atelier im niederbayerischen Landkreis Passau kultiviert sie eine nahezu meditative Form des Arbeitens. Diese Zurückgezogenheit ermöglicht ihr einen stillen Dialog mit dem Material. Das Stroh - meist alte Sorten wie hochwüchsiger Weizen oder Roggen - übernimmt dabei die Rolle einer stillen, aber bestimmenden Partnerin. Engelsberger bezieht es derzeit noch aus Frankreich und der Schweiz, plant jedoch, künftig selbst Stroh anzubauen - als konsequente Annäherung an ihre Arbeitsmotive: Ursprung, Ressource und Rhythmus.

Engelsbergers Werk ist geprägt von einem spannungsreichen Wechselspiel zwischen Tradition und Innovation. Mit Präzision und großer haptischer Sensibilität experimentiert sie mit Materialgrenzen. Ihre Werkzeuge weisen sowohl historische Bezüge als auch Modifikationen auf: Rosengabeln zur Formung floraler Elemente, handgeschnitzte Knochensplitter zur Faserdifferenzierung oder das sogenannte »Schnürlirädli« zur Herstellung feinster Kordeln.

Jede ihrer Arbeiten ist ein Unikat, das in tagelanger und dabei gleichzeitig minutiöser Handarbeit gefertigt wird. Besonders komplexe Arbeiten entstehen über mehrere Wochen hinweg. Die monotone Wiederholung, die serielle Bewegung, die Kontemplation - all das ist Teil des schöpferischen Prozesses und der ästhetischen Aussage.

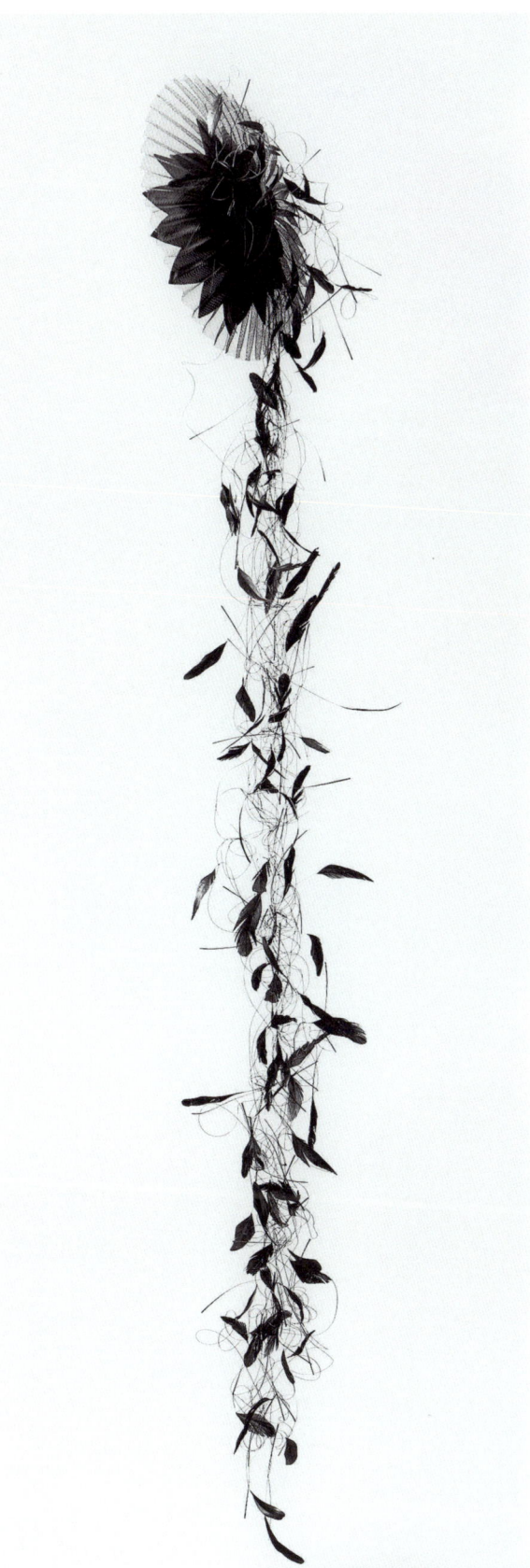

03

04

05

02

01 SAMPLE RESEARCH (2018)
50 × 20 CM
3D KNITTED PLISSÉ
MONOFILAMENT, GLASS BEADS, CHENILLE
YARN, LUREX, HAND DYED

02 JOHANNA (2015)
80 × 50 CM
3D KNITTED
MONOFILAMENT, GLASS BEADS, LYCRA

Cécile Feilchenfeldt

Cécile Feilchenfeldt is one of the most fascinating artists working today in experimental and artisanal knitting techniques. She develops unique textile creations for fields ranging from haute couture to the automotive industry. Born in 1973, she went to Switzerland as a young adult to study textile design at the Zürcher Hochschule der Künste. While still a student she acquired her first hand-operated knitting machine and extended her knowledge of knitting techniques. On finishing her studies she was awarded the Micheline and Jean-Jacques Brunschwig Prize for Applied Arts and founded her studio in Paris, where she still lives and works. Her works in textiles are distinguished by her profound understanding of techniques and materials – and above all by her focus and acute power of observation. They exact so much skill and are so time-consuming that they cannot be industrially produced. Hence they are realised in the studio on about ten semi-automatic domestic knitting machines by Cécile Feilchenfeldt and her team in close collaboration with their clientele.

Feilchenfeldt views herself more as a researcher or surface designer than as a classic textile designer. She relishes the mathematical element of knitting, which she has perfected over the years, an approach to technique that enables her and her team to work spontaneously and at the same time creatively. Being prepared to a certain extent to take risks is an essential part of the process: if a thread tears, an entire work might have been in vain. An analogue approach to work is a trademark of Feilchenfeldt's. Each row of knitting is comparable to a line designed by hand, in which she incorporates beads, feathers or other materials. Her chief concern is to continue researching, taking volumes to the limit and creating mobile sculptures. Chance and time are her constant companions.

Alongside works done on commission, she develops innovative techniques and combinations of materials. Feilchenfeldt deliberately distances herself from prevailing trends in fashion in order to make room for new ideas.

03 SAMPLE RESEARCH (2016)
70 × 50 CM
KNITWEAVE
FOAM RUBBER, LYCRA

04 SAMPLE RESEARCH (2016)
80 × 40 CM
3D KNITTED
MONOFILAMENT, PLASTIC TUBING, LYCRA

05 JOHANNA (2015)
80 × 35 CM
3D KNITTED PLISSÉ
MONOFILAMENT, GLASS BEADS

03

04

05

DE Cécile Feilchenfeldt gehört zu den faszinierendsten Strickkünstlerinnen der Gegenwart. Sie entwickelt für den Bereich der Haute Couture bis hin zur Automobilindustrie handwerklich einzigartige Textilien. Geboren 1973, ging sie als junge Erwachsene in die Schweiz, um Textildesign an der Zürcher Hochschule der Künste zu studieren. Noch während ihres Studiums erwarb sie ihre erste eigene Handstrickmaschine und vertiefte ihre Kenntnisse über die Technik des Strickens. Nach ihrem Abschluss gewann sie den Prix Micheline et Jean-Jacques Brunschwig und gründete Anfang 2000 ihr Studio in Paris, wo sie bis heute lebt und arbeitet. Ihre textilen Arbeiten zeichnen sich durch ein tiefes Verständnis für Technik, Materialien – und vor allem durch Konzentration und eine genaue Beobachtungsgabe aus. Sie sind so aufwendig, dass sie nicht industriell umgesctzt werden können. Daher werden sie an ca. zehn halbautomatischen Handstrickmaschinen von Cécile Feilchenfeldt und ihrem Team in enger Zusammenarbeit mit den Auftraggeber:innen im Atelier realisiert.

Feilchenfeldt sieht sich selbst eher als Forscherin oder Oberflächendesignerin, denn als klassische Textildesignerin. Sie schätzt das mathematische Element des Strickens, was sie über die Jahre perfektioniert hat, wobei ihr die Technik ein spontanes und gleichzeitig kreatives Arbeiten ermöglicht. Eine gewisse Risikobereitschaft ist dabei unerlässlich: Reißt der Faden, kann die gesamte Arbeit schnell umsonst gewesen sein. Die analoge Arbeitsweise ist ein Markenzeichen von Feilchenfeldt. Jede Reihe im Strick wird, vergleichbar mit einer Linie, von Hand gestaltet, wobei sie Perlen, Federn oder andere Materialien einarbeitet. Es geht ihr darum, kontinuierlich weiter zu forschen, Volumen auszureizen und bewegte Skulpturen zu erschaffen. Der Zufall und die Zeit sind dabei stetige Begleiter.
Neben den Auftragsarbeiten werden innovative Techniken und Materialkombinationen entwickelt. Dabei löst sich Feilchenfeldt bewusst von aktuellen Modetrends, um Raum für neue Ideen zu schaffen.

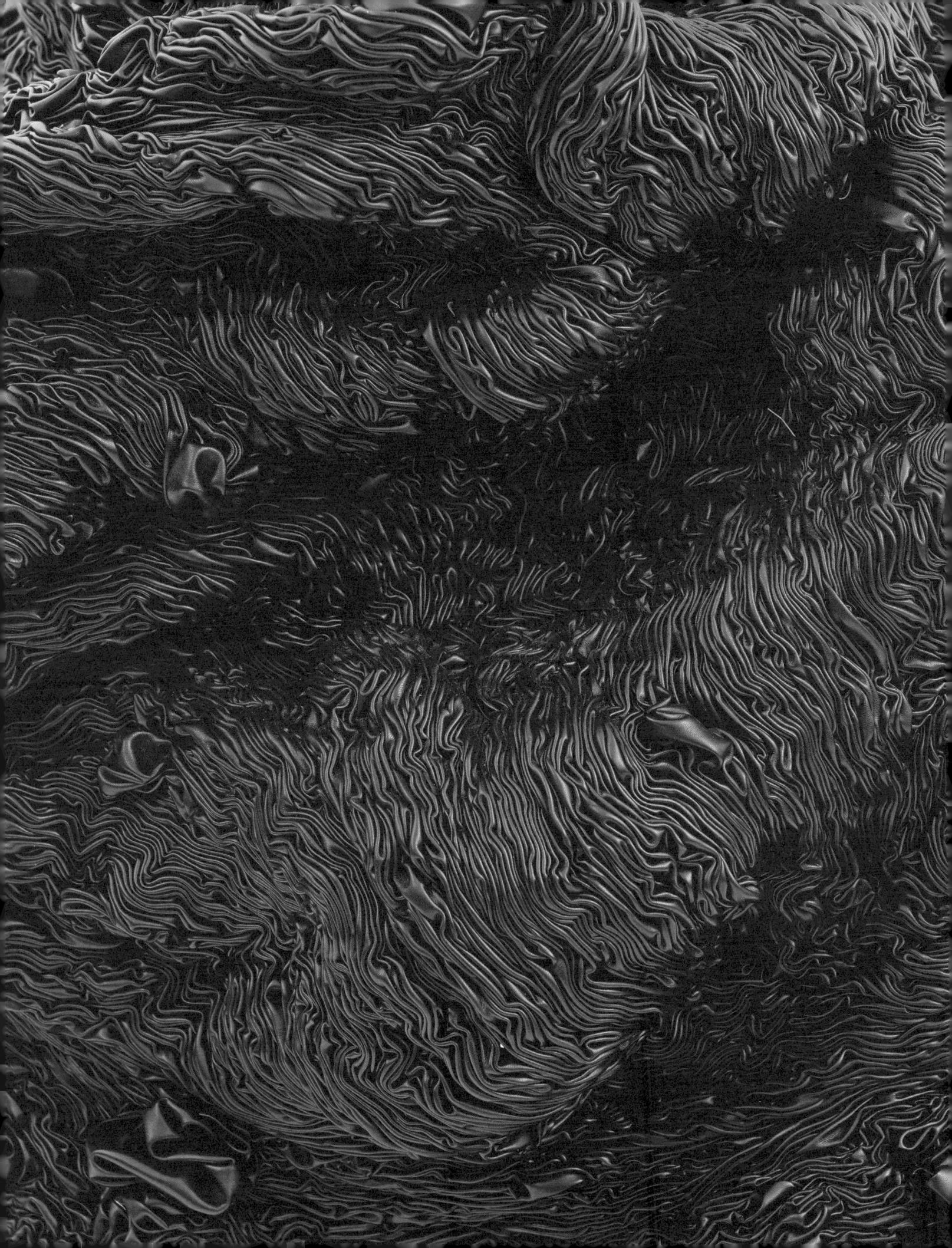

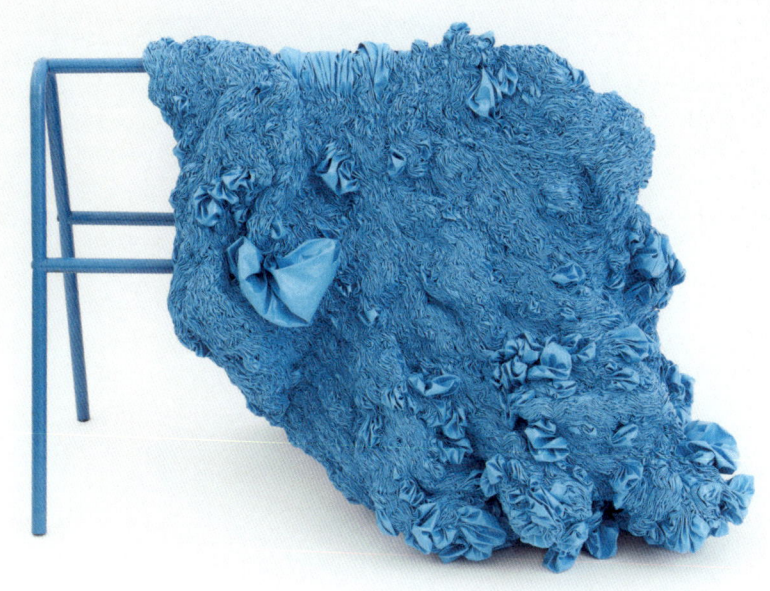

02

01 LA VAGUE (2020-2022), DETAIL
HAND STITCHED
FAUX LEATHER, STEEL

02 IMPULSE (CYAN) (2021-2022)
74 × 93 × 78 CM
HAND STITCHED, PAINTED STEEL
VINYL

¹⁰⁷ Hanne Friis

EN Born in 1972, the Norwegian artist Hanne Friis has specialised in working in sculpture with textiles as her material. The outcome has been what are called her 'soft sculptures', which redefine the field of classic sculpture. She started out studying painting and sculpture at Kunstakademiet in Trondheim, and from there it was only logical that she would turn to textiles.

Using the techniques of sewing, folding and draping she developed herself, Friis transforms soft fabrics into dense structures that proliferate and have an organic feel while at the same time possessing a solid presence and developing material ambivalence.

A theme central to her work is the interplay of materiality, form and process. Her sculptures grow gradually and intuitively, often for months on end – during which she is in direct, physically intensive contact with the material. Doing manual work of this kind is for Friis a contemplative, almost ritual act. The physical dimension lends her works a performative quality and emphasises their temporal profundity. At the same time, her handling of textiles can be read as a tacit feminist gesture: a deliberate revaluation of techniques that traditionally have feminine connotations but are transformed into powerfully sculptural forms of expression. The choice of material and colour is essential to the impact her works make. Friis works with natural materials, also, however, with remnants from the garment industry. This in turn results in colour gradients and textures that reinforce the organic aspect of her works. Her palette ranges from earthy, subdued tones to luminous pigments of synthetic origin. The natural environment serves as her chief source of inspiration – not only in respect of form but also for sustainably handling resources. Thus her works open up a force field between beauty and unease, control and transformation – and invite viewers to be swept up in this process.

03 MAP VI (2022)
150 × 55 × 18 CM
HAND STITCHED
UPCYCLED SILK SCARVES FROM HOLZWEILER,
NYLON THREAD

04 MEMBRANE (2023–2024)
370 × 200 × 44 CM
HAND DYED, HAND SEWN
NYLON ORGANZA

05 LA VAGUE (2020–2022)
98 × 78 × 75 CM
HAND STITCHED
FAUX LEATHER, STEEL

03

04

05

DE Die norwegische Künstlerin Hanne Friis, geboren 1972, hat sich auf das skulpturale Arbeiten mit textilen Materialien spezialisiert. Auf diese Weise entstehen ihre sogenannten »Soft-Sculptures«, die den Bereich der klassischen Bildhauerei neu definieren. Ausgangspunkt ist ihr Studium der Malerei und Bildhauerei an der Akademie der Bildenden Künste in Trondheim, welches sie zu einer konsequenten Hinwendung zum Textilen führte.

Durch eigens entwickelte Näh-, Falt- und Drapiertechniken verwandelt Friis weiche Stoffe in dichte, wuchernde Strukturen, die organisch anmuten, zugleich massive Präsenz behaupten und dabei eine materielle Zweideutigkeit entfalten.

Ein zentrales Thema ihrer Arbeit ist das Zusammenspiel von Materialität, Form und Prozess. Ihre Skulpturen wachsen langsam und intuitiv, oft über Monate hinweg im direkten, körperlich intensiven Kontakt mit dem Material. Dieses manuelle Arbeiten ist für Friis ein meditativer, beinahe ritueller Akt. Die körperliche Dimension verleiht ihren Werken eine performative Qualität und betont deren zeitliche Tiefe. Gleichzeitig lässt sich ihr Umgang mit Textil als stille feministische Geste lesen: eine bewusste Aufwertung traditionell weiblich konnotierter Techniken, die zu kraftvollen, skulpturalen Ausdrucksformen transformiert werden. Material- und Farbauswahl sind essenziell für die Wirkung ihrer Werke. Friis arbeitet mit natürlichen Stoffen, aber auch mit Abfällen der Bekleidungsindustrie. Dadurch entstehen malerische Farbverläufe und Texturen, die das organische Moment ihrer Arbeiten verstärken. Ihre Farbpalette reicht von erdigen, gedämpften Tönen bis hin zu leuchtenden Pigmenten synthetischer Herkunft. Die Natur dient ihr als zentrale Inspirationsquelle - nicht nur formal, sondern auch im nachhaltigen Umgang mit Ressourcen. So eröffnen ihre Werke ein Spannungsfeld zwischen Schönheit und Unbehagen, Kontrolle und Transformation - und laden Betrachter:innen dazu ein, sich in diesen Prozess mit hineinnehmen zu lassen.

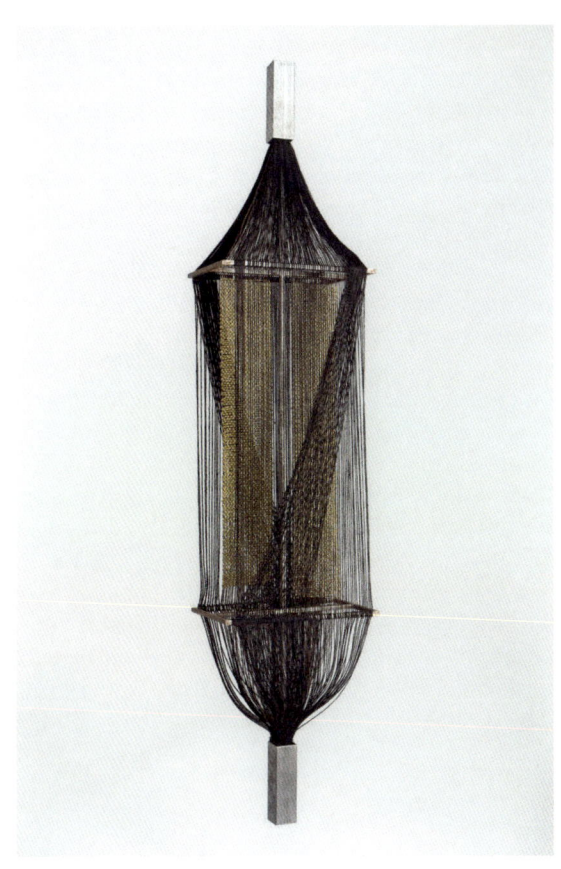

02

01 TEXTILE ELEMENTS IN SPACE (1970/72)   02 KLEINE SÄULE (1967)
VARIABLE DIMENSIONS   85 × 18 × 11 CM
TENSION WOUND   COUCHED CORD, METAL
LINEN, SILK, WOOL, METAL   LINEN, METAL THREAD, GOLD LUREX THREAD

¹¹¹ Elsi Giauque

Elsi Giauque (1900–1989) was a groundbreaking Swiss artist in textiles whose oeuvre ranges from 1920s decorative arts to the textile spatial art in the fine-arts sector of later decades. Born Berta Elsa Kleinpeter, she began training as a crafts teacher at the Frauenfachschule Zürich. So talented was she both as a craftswoman and designer that she transferred in 1918 to the Kunstgewerbeschule Zürich, where her instructors included Sophie Taeuber-Arp. Her teacher's avant-gardist design concepts shaped Giauque's early geometric woven and cross-stitch tapestries as well as her designer bead accessories and printed fabrics.

While training at the Kunstgewerbeschule, Giauque discovered a second passion: puppet theatre. She collaborated on various performances and founded a venue of her own, which she headed until 1943.

Through Johannes Itten, director of the Kunstgewerbeschule Zürich and a former Bauhaus Master, she received an appointment that she held from 1944 until 1966 to teach textile design in parallel with her own design practice. Her approach to teaching was memorably innovative. In the 1950s she began to emancipate herself from schemata she had formerly used in tapestry design and developed her own textile works from rhythmically articulated structures. Her suspended mobile thread objects transformed space to generate a poetic interplay of light, colour and movement in which the thread – as a textile line – plays a dominant role. Her works reveal abstract natural forms or symbolic signs and conduct a dialogue with both space and the constructive art of her time. Radiating an impressive lightness, the dynamic of her works and the impact they make recalls kinetic art to some extent. Giauque created textile tributes to various distinguished artists and took part regularly in international textile art biennales. Until her death in 1989 she remained unflaggingly active as an artist. She revolutionised classic tapestry design and set new standards by creating textile works that are not merely decorative but shape space.

03 ELEFANT (1970)
200 × 180 CM
HIGH-WARP LOOM, TENSION WOUND
WOOL, SILK, GILDED THREAD, SILVER THREAD

04 ELÉMENT SPATIAL (1979)
TWENTY PARTS, EACH 90 × 95 × 0.6 CM
TENSION WOUND
LINEN, SILK, WOOL, METAL

03

04

DE   Elsi Giauque (1900–1989) war eine wegweisende Schweizer Textilkünstlerin, deren Œuvre von der angewandten Kunst der 1920er-Jahre bis zur freien textilen Raumkunst der späteren Jahrzehnte reicht. Geboren als Berta Elsa Kleinpeter, begann sie ihre Ausbildung zur Handarbeitslehrerin an der Frauenfachschule Zürich. Aufgrund ihres handwerklichen und gestalterischen Talents wechselte sie 1918 an die Züricher Kunstgewerbeschule, wo sie unter anderem von Sophie Taeuber-Arp unterrichtet wurde. Deren avantgardistischen gestalterischen Konzepte prägten Giauques frühe geometrische Web- und Kreuzstichteppiche ebenso wie von ihr gestaltete Perlenaccessoires oder bedruckten Stoffe.

Im Rahmen der Ausbildung entdeckte sie ihre zweite Leidenschaft: das Marionettentheater. Sie wirkte an unterschiedlichen Aufführungen mit und gründete ihre eigene Spielstätte, die sie bis 1943 leitete. Durch Johannes Itten, Direktor der Zürcher Kunstgewerbeschule und vormaliger Bauhausmeister, erhält sie anschließend von 1944 bis 1966 einen Lehrauftrag für Textiles Gestalten, welchen sie mit innovativem Unterricht prägt, den sie parallel zu ihrer eigenen gestalterischen Praxis ausübte. Ab den 1950er-Jahren emanzipierte sie sich von bisherigen gestalterischen Schemata im Bereich der Bildteppiche und entwickelte ihre eigenen textilen Werke aus rhythmisch gegliederten Strukturen. Ihre hängenden, beweglichen Fadenobjekte verwandelten den Raum und erzeugen ein poetisches Zusammenspiel aus Licht, Farbe und Bewegung, in denen der Faden - als textile Linie - eine zentrale Rolle spielt. Ihre Werke zeigen abstrahierte Naturformen oder symbolhafte Zeichen und stehen im Dialog mit dem Raum sowie der konstruktiven Kunst ihrer Zeit. Ihre Werke strahlen eine beeindruckende Leichtigkeit aus, deren Dynamik und Wirkung teils an kinetische Kunst erinnert. Giauque schuf textile Hommagen an verschiedene Künstler:innenpersönlichkeiten und nahm regelmäßig an internationalen Textilkunst-Biennalen teil.

Bis zu ihrem Tod im Jahr 1989 blieb sie künstlerisch unermüdlich aktiv. Sie revolutionierte die klassische Tapisserie und setzte neue Maßstäbe, indem sie textile Werke schuf, die nicht nur dekorativ, sondern raumprägend wirken.

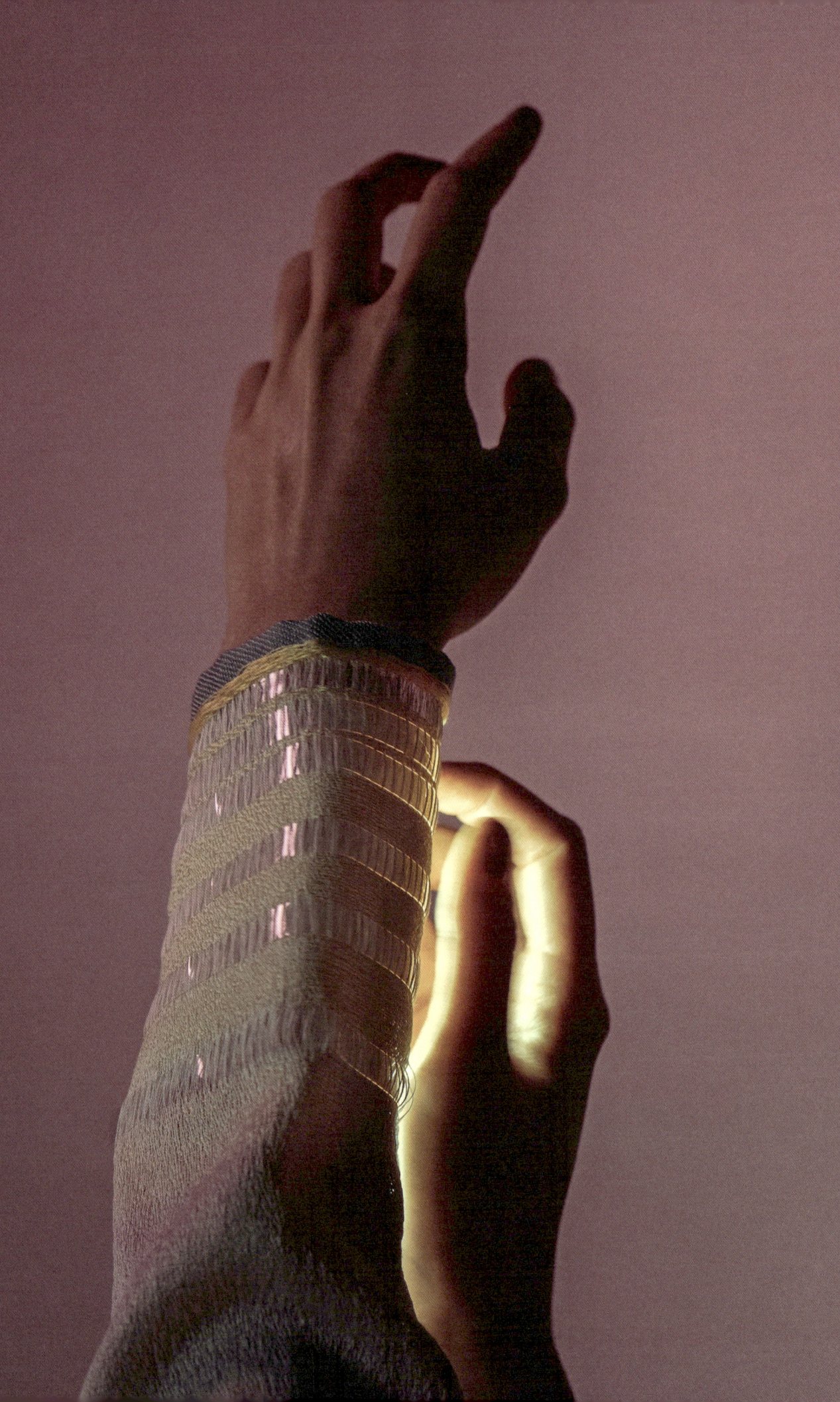

I'm fascinated by the beauty of textiles, their extreme relevance in our daily lives and their constant interaction with the human body.

01 LIGHT TISSUE — LIGHT GARMENT (2021)
50 × 50 CM
JACQUARD
COTTON YARNS, CMC OPTICAL WAVEGUIDES

Sofía Guridi

EN   Born in 1990, Sofía Guridi employs a transdisciplinary approach to her work by linking design, material science and textile knowledge. She does so because she is concerned with developing new textile materials systems that are experienceable as both ecologically sustainable and interactive.

A childhood spent in Latin America sensitised her to handmade textiles and an appreciation for cultural diversity, influences that still inform her future-orientated approach: the interplay of traditional crafts, biomaterial innovation and digital technologies. Design studies at the Pontificia Universidad Católica in Chile was followed by a master's degree in contemporary design from Aalto University in Finland and participation in the international Fabricademy programme at the Waag Society Amsterdam, which specialises in research into innovative textile technologies. Weaving is at the core of Guridi's design praxis, which enables her to integrate experimental materials such as conductive bioplastics or cellulose optical fibres in complex fabric structures. The investigation of electronic textiles especially is closely linked to ecological issues in her approach. Guridi is currently working towards a doctorate

within the Bioinnovation Centre at Aalto University. She is collaborating closely with internationally known scientists and designers, always pursuing an experimental, open-ended approach to her research. In analogy with her transdisciplinary approach to design, she links material and design knowledge to create concrete scenarios of future everyday culture. Concomitantly with her research she teaches courses on biomaterials, e-textiles and experimental design at international universities. With her theoretical and practical work, she boldly ventures into speculative space – where research, design and sustainable visions fuse.

Project description to accompany the pictures:
To meet challenges with respect to material applications and refuse management, Sofía Guridi studies wood-derived cellulose, to take one example, as a light-conducting material for developing bio-based smart textiles. The textile sensors and light factors resulting from this research present with novel experimental patterns and exemplify the contribution that knowledge of textile design can make to basic research in materials science.

02 LIGHT TISSUE – CMC IN GEL STATE
(2021)
5 CM
CARBOXYMETHYL CELLULOSE GEL
CARBOXYMETHYL CELLULOSE

03 LIGHT TISSUE – LIGHT POCKETS (2021),
DETAIL
15 × 15 CM
JACQUARD
COTTON YARNS, CMC OPTICAL WAVEGUIDES

04 LIGHT TISSUE – TEXTILE SAMPLE (2021)
7 × 5 CM
JACQUARD
COTTON YARNS, CMC OPTICAL WAVEGUIDES

02

03

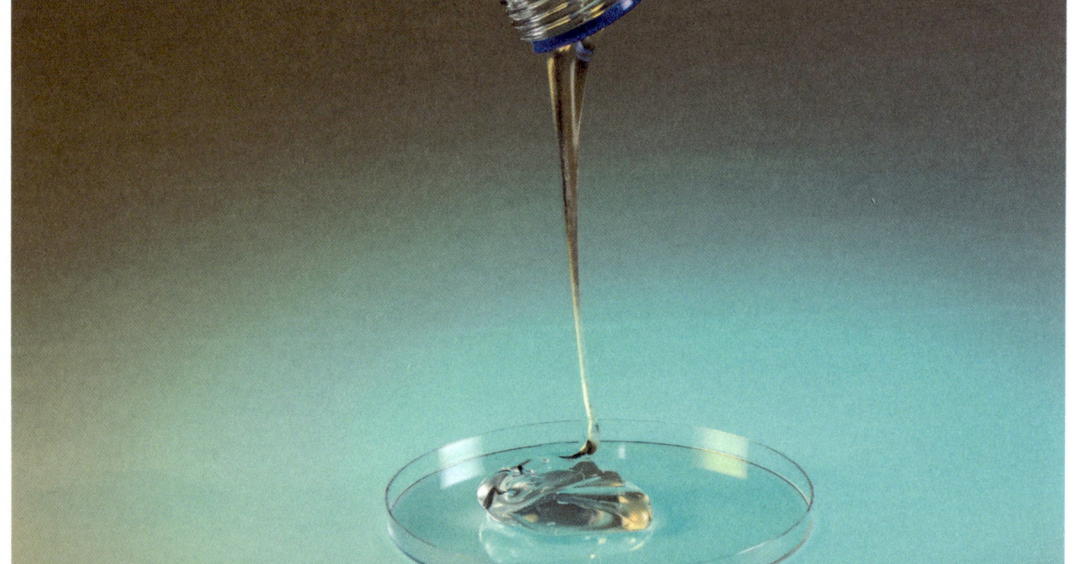

DE Sofía Guridi, geboren 1990, arbeitet transdisziplinär, indem sie Design mit Materialwissenschaft und Kenntnissen aus dem textilen Bereich verbindet. Dabei geht es ihr um die Entwicklung neuer textiler Materialsysteme, die sowohl ökologisch tragfähig als auch interaktiv zu erleben sind.

Ihre Kindheit in Lateinamerika sensibilisierte sie für handgefertigte Textilien und kulturelle Vielfalt – Einflüsse, die bis heute ihren zukunftsorientierten Ansatz prägen: das Zusammenspiel von traditionellem Handwerk, biomateriellen Innovationen und digitalen Technologien.

Auf ihr Designstudium an der Universidad Católica de Chile folgte ein Master in Contemporary Design an der Aalto University in Finnland, sowie die Teilnahme am internationalen Programm Fabricademy an der Waag Society Amsterdam, das auf die Forschung an innovativen Textiltechnologien spezialisiert ist. Weben bildet den Kern von Guridis gestalterischer Praxis, was ihr erlaubt, experimentelle Materialien wie leitfähige Biokunststoffe oder optische Fasern aus Zellulose in komplexe Stoffstrukturen zu integrieren. Insbesondere die Auseinandersetzung mit elektronischen Textilien steht in einer engen Verbindung zu ökologischen Fragestellungen. Derzeit promoviert Guridi an der Aalto University im Rahmen des Bioinnovation Centers zum Thema Sustainable Computational Fabrics. Sie arbeitet eng mit internationalen Wissenschaftler:innen und Designer:innen zusammen, wobei sie stets einen experimentellen, offenen Forschungsansatz verfolgt. Analog zu ihrem transdisziplinären Gestaltungsansatz verbindet sie Material- und Gestaltungskenntnisse, um konkrete Szenarien zukünftiger Alltagskultur zu entwerfen. Parallel zu ihrer Forschung lehrt sie an internationalen Hochschulen zu Biomaterialien, E-Textiles und experimenteller Gestaltung. Sie bewegt sich mit ihrer theoretischen und praktischen Arbeit bewusst im spekulativen Raum – dort, wo Forschung, Gestaltung und nachhaltige Visionen fusionieren.

Projektbeschreibung zu den Bildern:
Um Herausforderungen im Hinblick auf Materialeinsatz und Abfallmanagement zu begegnen untersucht Sofía Guridi beispielsweise synthetisierte holzbasierte Zellulose als lichtleitendes Material für die Entwicklung biobasierter Smart Textiles. Die daraus entstandenen textilen Sensoren und Lichtfaktoren präsentieren neuartige, experimentelle Muster und zeigen beispielhaft, welchen Beitrag textilgestalterisches Wissen zu einer materialwissenschaftlichen Grundlagenforschung leisten kann.

04

More is more.

01 SWANI DRESS IN RUDI (SILVER SLIVER, SS2025)
ONE SIZE
DIGITAL PRINT, SHIBORI PLISSÉ
RECYCLED POLYESTER CREPE

Julia Heuer

EN Since 2018 the textile and fashion designer Julia Heuer has been designing clothes under the label of that name with a distinctive focus on the extraordinary handling of surfaces – including prints she develops herself and materials ingeniously pleated by hand. Her designs are distinguished by glowing colour and expressive, often eccentric motifs. Born in 1982, she completed her studies in textile design at the Staatliche Akademie der Bildenden Künste Stuttgart in 2009. While still a student, she was producing works that moved seamlessly between design and fine art, already attesting to high aesthetic standards and consummate craftsmanship.

After working in the garment industry for several years, Heuer opted for self-employment and founded a studio in Paris. Characteristic of her creations are colourful, imaginative prints that are the result of analogue processing in their initial stages and often reveal folkloric overtones. In conjunction with the Japanese arashi shibori[1] technique they form the basis of sculptural silhouettes of her designs that, despite their expressive contours, are light and comfortable to wear. Her work centres on the aim of preserving traditional textile techniques and at the same time translating them into a contemporary design context.

Fascinating patterns and exquisitely worked pleats lend her designs a visual dynamic and a remarkable formal diversity that effortlessly adapts to different body forms. All prototypes are created in her Paris studio in close collaboration with her team, and all stages of production take place exclusively in France. To ensure that justice was done to the elaborate process of hand pleating, Heuer also founded a production centre in Estonia, where an all-women team works exclusively for the Julia Heuer label. Julia Heuer herself is firmly established in the international fashion scene as a textile designer, yet the creative focus of her work is always aimed at designing textile surfaces and patterns as art.

[1] Shibori is a traditional Japanese resist-dyeing technique in which the material is variously fixed, folded and pressed, creating characteristic patterns. The best-known variants include arashi shibori, itajime shibori and kanoko shibori.

02 EKKE SKIRT AND LINN TOP IN MURIEL,
LEE TOP IN ROSE (FURRY GEMS, AW2024)
ONE SIZE
DIGITAL PRINT, CRYSTAL PLISSÉ
RECYCLED POLYESTER CREPE, RECYCLED
POLYESTER CHIFFON

03 PAX DRESS IN ELIAS (FURRY GEMS, AW24)
ONE SIZE
DIGITAL PRINT, SHIBORI PLISSÉ
RECYCLED POLYESTER CREPE

04 KARLOTTA TOP AND MAX SKIRT IN SVEN,
LEE TOP IN LILLIE (SILVER SLIVER, SS25)
ONE SIZE
DIGITAL PRINT, SHIBORI PLISSÉ
RECYCLED POLYESTER CREPE, RECYCLED
POLYESTER CHIFFON

DE Die Textil- und Modedesignerin Julia Heuer entwirft seit 2018 unter ihrem gleichnamigen Label Bekleidung mit einem unverwechselbaren Fokus auf außergewöhnlichen Oberflächenbearbeitungen – darunter selbst entwickelte Drucke und kunstvoll von Hand gearbeitete Plissees. Ihre Entwürfe zeichnen sich durch leuchtende Farben und ausdrucksstarke, oft exzentrische Motive aus. Geboren 1982, schloss sie 2009 ihr Studium in Textildesign an der Staatlichen Akademie der Bildenden Künste Stuttgart ab. Schon während ihrer Ausbildung bewegten sich ihre Arbeiten an der Schnittstelle zur freien Kunst und zeugten von einem hohen ästhetischen wie handwerklichen Anspruch.

Nach mehrjähriger Tätigkeit in der Industrie entschied sich Heuer für die Selbstständigkeit und gründete ihr Atelier in Paris. Charakteristisch für ihre Kreationen sind farbenfrohe, fantasievolle Drucke, die zunächst analog entstehen und oft folkloristische Anklänge tragen. In Verbindung mit der japanischen Arashi-Shibori-Technik[1] bilden sie die Basis für die skulpturalen Silhouetten ihrer Entwürfe, die trotz ihrer expressiven Formen leicht und komfortabel zu tragen sind. Im Zentrum ihres Schaffens steht der Anspruch, traditionelle textile Techniken zu bewahren und zugleich in einen zeitgenössischen gestalterischen Kontext zu überführen.

Die faszinierenden Muster und fein gearbeiteten Plissees verleihen ihren Entwürfen eine visuelle Dynamik und eine besondere Formvielfalt, die sich mühelos verschiedenen Körperformen anpasst. Alle Prototypen entstehen im Pariser Atelier in enger Zusammenarbeit mit ihrem Team, während die Produktion ausschließlich in Frankreich erfolgt. Um dem aufwendigen Prozess der Handplissierung gerecht zu werden, gründete Heuer zudem eine eigene Produktionsstätte in Estland, in der ein ausschließlich weibliches Team exklusiv für ihr Label arbeitet. Julia Heuer ist als Textildesignerin in der internationalen Modebranche etabliert – doch bleibt der kreative Fokus ihrer Arbeit stets auf die künstlerische Gestaltung textiler Oberflächen und Muster gerichtet.

[1] Shibori ist eine traditionelle japanische Färbetechnik, bei der Stoffe durch verschiedene Abbindungs-, Falt- und Pressmethoden reserviert werden und dadurch charakteristische Muster erhalten. Zu den bekanntesten Varianten gehören Arashi Shibori, Itajime Shibori und Kanoko Shibori.

03

04

02

121 JULIA HEUER

Quilting represents care, memory and resilience. It's about piecing together fragments – sometimes damaged or discarded – to make something whole again.

01 EDGES IN CONVERSATION (2022), DETAIL
61 × 61 CM
HAND-STITCHED APPLIQUÉ, LINEN REMNANTS

Rebekah Johnston

EN The way the artist Rebekah Johnston, born 1981, works is intuitive and tends to be processual; she often begins without a predetermined goal and arrives at understanding her works through the process by which they are made. She works with techniques such as quilting[1] and the Japanese boro method[2]. In her hands, this open-ended approach symbolises care and resilience: a new configuration emerges from scraps: sewing becomes a meditative gesture that is grounding, and the finished textile stores quiet strata of time. After studying contemporary textile practice at Cardiff Metropolitan University (2005), she trained as an art teacher, a profession she practised for fourteen years. In the meantime she is again working primarily as an artist in the textile sector and has chosen sustainability as her central theme; Johnston works with used household fabrics, personal clothing and remnants from small factories that are naturally dyed with vegetal substances such as avocado peels, tea or sumac leaves from her own garden. In her studio - once a lace factory, in Nottingham - a community centre is now housed. Here she finds the exchange of ideas that is essential to her practice and regularly participates in workshops, exhibitions and collective projects.

Textiles fascinate Johnston because of their tactile and emotional qualities, which she alters through creative and sustainable reprocessing. Sewing is a sensual and at the same time meditative practice - an act of remembrance and repair. During the Covid pandemic she began to show via digital channels how sewing by hand helped her to deal with anxieties, and a series of tutorials and an ongoing exchange of ideas with her followers developed from there.

Johnston draws inspiration from mundane observations and social issues. Her works are distinguished by emotional depth, the slowness of sewing by hand and a genuine investigation of themes such as memory, care and a concept of home.

[1] Quilting: an old crafts technique in which several layers of cloth - as a rule a quilt top, fleece batting and backing - are linked with each other through backstitch seams. This can be done by hand or machine.
[2] Japanese boro method: boro is a traditional Japanese technique used for mending in which scraps of cloth, often from old clothes, are sewn on to other fabrics to mend or reinforce them. It almost counts as a textile form of remembering - every seam, every patch tells a story of, for example, care, renewal or quiet beauty. It is employed deliberately as a symbol of modesty, sustainability and respect for materials.

02 BETWEEN SHADOWS (2021)
45 × 50 CM
HAND-STITCHED APPLIQUÉ
LINEN REMNANTS

03 MIDCENTURY QUILT AND CUSHION (2024)
QUILT 75 × 75 CM
CUSHION 48 × 48 CM
HAND-STITCHED APPLIQUÉ AND PATCHWORK
PLANT-DYED DEADSTOCK, LINEN REMNANTS

04 REMNANTS (2022), DETAIL
56 × 120 CM
HAND-STITCHED APPLIQUÉ AND PATCHWORK
LINEN REMNANTS

DE Die Arbeitsweise der 1981 geborenen Künstlerin ist intuitiv und prozessorientiert - häufig beginnt sie ohne festgelegtes Ziel und begreift ihre Werke durch den Prozess ihrer Entstehung. Sie arbeitet mit Techniken wie Quilting[1] und der japanischen Boro-Methode[2]. Dieser ergebnisoffene Zugang steht in ihrer Arbeit sinnbildlich für Fürsorge und Widerstandskraft: Aus Fragmenten entsteht ein neues Gebilde: das Nähen wird zur meditativen, erdenden Geste und das fertige Textil speichert stille Schichten von Zeit. Nach ihrem Studium in Contemporary Textile Practice an der Cardiff Metropolitan University (2005) absolvierte sie eine Ausbildung zur Kunstlehrerin, ein Beruf, den sie über 14 Jahre hinweg ausübte. Mittlerweile arbeitet sie wieder hauptberuflich im Bereich der textilen Kunst und setzt Nachhaltigkeit als zentrales Thema; Johnston arbeitet mit gebrauchten Haushaltsstoffen, persönlichen Kleidungsstücken und Schnittresten kleiner Manufakturen, welche mit pflanzlichen Substanzen wie Avocadoschalen, Tee- oder Sumachblättern aus dem eigenen Garten natürlich gefärbt werden. In ihrem Atelier - einer ehemaligen Spitzenfabrik in Nottingham - ist heute ein Gemeinschaftszentrum untergebracht. Hier findet sie den für ihre Praxis essenziellen Austausch und beteiligt sich regelmäßig an Workshops, Ausstellungen und kollaborativen Projekten. Textilien faszinieren Johnston aufgrund ihrer taktilen und emotionalen Qualität, die sie durch kreative und nachhaltige Wiederaufbereitung verändert. Das Nähen ist eine sinnliche, zugleich reflexive Praxis - ein Akt des Erinnerns und Reparierens. Während der Coronapandemie begann sie, über digitale Kanäle zu zeigen, wie das Handsticken ihr half, mit Ängsten umzugehen, woraus sich eine Reihe von Tutorials und ein fortlaufender Austausch mit ihrem Publikum entwickelte.

Johnston lässt sich durch Alltagsbeobachtungen und gesellschaftliche Fragestellungen inspirieren. Ihre Arbeiten zeichnen sich durch emotionale Tiefe, handgestickte Langsamkeit und eine unverstellte Auseinandersetzung mit Themen wie Erinnerung, Fürsorge und einem Begriff von Heimat aus.

[1] Quilting: Von »Quilten«; ist eine alte Handwerkstechnik, bei der mehrere Stofflagen - in der Regel Quilt-Top, Vlies und eine Rückseite - durch Steppnähte miteinander verbunden werden. Dies kann von Hand oder maschinell erfolgen.
[2] Japanische Boro-Methode: Boro ist eine traditionelle japanische Flicktechnik, bei der Stoffstücke, oft aus alten Kleidungsstücken, auf andere Stoffe genäht werden, um diese zu reparieren oder zu verstärken. Es zählt beinahe als eine textile Form des Erinnerns - jede Naht, jeder Flicken erzählt eine Geschichte von beispielsweise Sorgfalt, Erneuerung oder stiller Schönheit. Es wird bewusst als ein Symbol für Bescheidenheit, Nachhaltigkeit und Respekt vor Materialien eingesetzt.

02

04

03

02

01 UNDERTONE VIEW, FROM THE SERIES
WOVEN WINDOWS (2020)
96 × 82 CM
WOVEN ON A DIGITAL JACQUARD LOOM
PAPER, LINEN, COTTON, MIXED YARNS,
POWDER-COATED METAL FRAMES

02 WOVEN BRICK (2019)
INTERLACE EXHIBITION AT LAFAYETTE
ANTICIPATIONS, PARIS
57 × 20 × 40 CM
HANDWOVEN ON FOUR LOOMS CUT AND
JOINED TOGETHER TO FORM A NEW MACHINE
LINEN, COTTON, MIXED YARNS

Hella Jongerius

EN Hella Jongerius is known for her research-based approach to her art and for constantly raising the issue of the connection between overconsumption and quality. She lends her industrially manufactured objects particular depth with the help of additive artisanal touches – imperfection, sensitivity and character. Born in 1963, she is one of the world's leading women designers, teaches on a regular basis and gives lectures worldwide. After completing her studies in industrial design at the Design Academy Eindhoven in 1993, she joined Droog, a Dutch design collective whose playful and subjective formal idiom provided a counterpoint to elitist 1980s design. That year she founded a studio of her own, Jongeriuslab, in which she still works on collaborative commissions from a clientele consisting of major manufacturing corporations and where she also works on projects of her own and develops objects for exhibition. Her works are held by internationally important museum collections, and in 2024 Jongerius's archives were taken over by the Vitra Design Museum.

Fluctuating between completion and process, her works are nonetheless recognisably part of a greater whole – with a past and an open future. Unsurprisingly, Jongerius not only emphasises the value of process but also invites viewers and users to take part in it. She positions herself intersectionally in the cultural field of contrast between aesthetics, philosophy, ethics and ecology by exploring urgent social issues via her work. At an early stage of her career, she was already refusing to align herself with market-driven demand; instead, she mapped out her own agenda: how can design act as the force mediating between human beings and the world? She is still investigating this issue through sound research and studies relating to materials and colour, such as her experiments with pigments, light effects and ageing processes. The results of these are sophisticated research projects and iconic industrial products.

03 WOVEN BRICK (2019)
INTERLACE EXHIBITION AT LAFAYETTE
ANTICIPATIONS, PARIS
57 × 20 × 40 CM
HANDWOVEN ON FOUR LOOMS CUT AND JOINED
TOGETHER TO FORM A NEW MACHINE
LINEN, COTTON, MIXED YARNS

04 UNFOLDABLE CUBES (2021)
WOVEN COSMOS EXHIBITION AT GROPIUS BAU,
BERLIN
50 × 30 × 10 CM
WOVEN ON A DIGITAL JACQUARD LOOM
PAPER, LINEN, COTTON, MIXED YARNS

05 LOOM ROOM (2023), DETAIL
COMMISSIONED BY THE TECHNICAL UNIVERSITY
EINDHOVEN (NL)
900 CM HIGH
SITE-SPECIFIC INSTALLATION, 3D HANDWOVEN
CONSTRUCTION
PAPER, LINEN, COTTON, MIXED MATERIALS

03

04

05

DE Hella Jongerius ist bekannt für ihren forschungsbasierten Ansatz und dafür, stets die Frage nach dem Zusammenhang zwischen überflüssigem Konsum und Qualität in den Raum zu werfen. Dabei verleiht sie industriell gefertigten Objekten mit Hilfe von additivem Handwerk durch Imperfektion, Sensibilität und Charakter eine besondere Tiefe. Geboren 1963, zählt sie zu den weltweit führenden Designerinnen, lehrt regelmäßig und hält international Vorträge. Nach ihrem Abschluss in Industriedesign an der Design Academy Eindhoven im Jahr 1993 schloss sie sich dem niederländischen Designkollektiv Droog an, das mit spielerischer und subjektiver Formensprache einen Kontrapunkt zum elitären Design der 1980er-Jahre setzte. Im selben Jahr gründete sie ihr eigenes Studio Jongeriuslab, in dem bis heute Aufträge in Kooperation mit großen Industriekunden entstehen, in dessen Rahmen sie aber auch freie Themen bearbeitet und ausstellungsbasierte Objekte entwickelt. Ihre Werke befinden sich in den Sammlungen international bedeutender Museen und im Jahr 2024 wurde Jongerius' Archiv vom Vitra Design Museum übernommen.

Ihre Arbeiten oszillieren zwischen Fertigstellung und Prozess: Sie wirken abgeschlossen, lassen aber gleichzeitig erkennen, dass sie Teil eines größeren Ganzen sind - mit einer Vergangenheit und offener Zukunft. So betont Jongerius nicht nur den Wert des Prozesses, sondern lädt Betrachter:innen und Nutzer:innen ein, daran teilzuhaben. Sie bewegt sich im kulturellen Spannungsfeld zwischen Ästhetik, Philosophie, Ethik und Ökologie, indem sie über ihre Arbeit drängende gesellschaftliche Fragen thematisiert. Bereits früh in ihrer Karriere lehnte sie es ab, sich an marktgetriebenen Anforderungen zu orientieren, stattdessen formulierte sie ihre eigene Agenda: Wie kann Design als vermittelnde Kraft zwischen Mensch und Welt agieren? Diese Frage untersucht sie bis heute durch fundierte Recherche und material- und farbbezogene Untersuchungen wie beispielsweise ihre Experimente mit Pigmenten, Lichtwirkungen und Alterungsprozessen. Daraus sind vielschichtige Forschungsprojekte und ikonische Industrieprodukte entstanden.

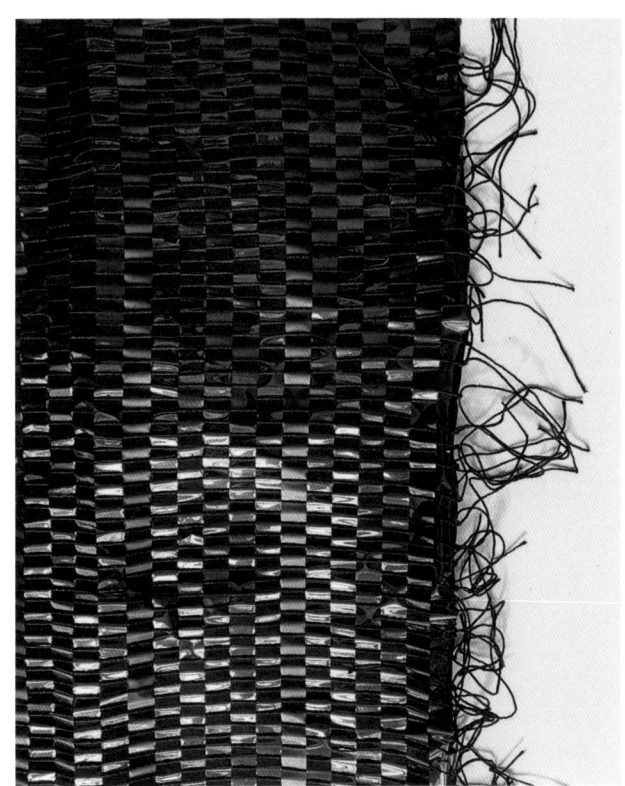

02

01 TECHNO PLASTIC
(.SHIFTED BODIES, 2024)
ONE SIZE
SCREEN PRINTED BY HAND
COTTON-POLYURETHANE

02 STRIPES AND CHECKS (2024), DETAIL
190 × 95 CM
HANDWOVEN IN 6 PARTS ON A FRAME
VHS TAPE

Stephanie Kahnau

EN The author of this book, Stephanie Kahnau, is herself a practitioner of textile art. In 2012 she took a diploma in textile design at the Staatliche Akademie der Bildenden Künste Stuttgart. One focus of her design praxis, clothing, is distinguished above all by the textile material and the handling of its surface as determining factors. Hence the material with its given properties is crucial to the pattern and cut, which are kept simple – you could say it is what shapes the body and gives it form. Deliberately deployed colours and textures provide additional expression through a wide range of traditional and contemporary textile techniques such as silkscreen printing, shibori dyeing[1] or experimental weaving on a handloom, all of which, when used for a particular purpose to create a desired effect, in part experimentally with open-ended results, steer the design process.

Born in 1986, Kahnau was exposed to textiles as materials at an early age through the tape-weaving factory and label-printing facility founded by her great-great-great-grandfather and has been fascinated with them ever since.

Alongside apparel for specific uses, Kahnau is also developing art objects that allude to functional usability but, on closer scrutiny, disappoint expectations of that kind. They mislead viewers by teasing the imagination, implying functional interconnectivity, only to break with it again. They are part of everyday living only in the sense that they seem like foreign bodies within it. Kahnau develops her textile works in her Munich studio. The production route could not be shorter; her one-offs can be bought in the adjoining outlet for local design, the HIER- Store. This concept not only makes her independent in producing; it positions her label outside mass production. To make her clothes Kahnau resorts to using scraps of high-quality materials left over from overproduction by large clothing companies. Since 2014 she has also taught regularly at a number of universities.

[1] For an explanation, see p. 120.

[1] For an explanation, see p. 120.

03 DEEP SEA, BABY
(.CAPSULE COLLECTION, 2023),
SCARF DETAIL
135 × 135 CM (SCARF DETAIL)
SILK-SCREEN PRINTED BY HAND,
ETCH PRINTING SILK

04 OBJEKT III, STUDIES ON SURFACE AND
DEPTH — TEXTILE TECHNIQUES AND BODILY
APPEARANCES (2021)
50 × 115 × 20 CM
KAPOK, BLACK VELVET, PROJECTION

05 .SEARCHING FOR BELONGING, TOO. (2023)
VARIOUS SIZES
SCREEN PRINTED BY HAND, HAND STITCHED
COTTON, SILK, WOOL, RECYCLED POLYESTER

03

04

05

DE   Die Autorin dieses Buches, Stephanie Kahnau, kommt selbst aus der Praxis und absolvierte 2012 ihr Diplom in Textildesign an der Staatliche Akademie der Bildenden Künste in Stuttgart. Ein besonderer Schwerpunkt ihrer gestalterischen Praxis, die Bekleidung, zeichnet sich insbesondere dadurch aus, dass vor allem das textile Material sowie dessen Oberflächenbehandlung formbestimmend sind. Das Material mit seinen gegebenen Charakteristika ist daher ausschlaggebend für die schlicht gehaltene Schnittform – man könnte sagen, es formt den Körper und verleiht ihm Gestalt. Bewusst eingesetzte Farben und Strukturen geben zusätzlich Ausdruck – durch diverse traditionelle wie zeitgenössische textile Techniken wie dem Siebdruck, Shiborifärbungen[1] oder dem experimentellen Weben am Handwebrahmen, welche zielgesetzt, teils experimentell mit offenem Ausgang den gestalterischen Prozess leiten.

Geboren 1986, kam Kahnau früh in der durch ihren Ur-Ur-Urgroßvater gegründeten Bandweberei und Etikettendruckerei mit dem Material Textil in Berührung und war von da an fasziniert. Neben der anwendungsorientierten Bekleidung entwickelt Kahnau auch künstlerische Objekte, die auf funktionale Nutzbarkeit anspielen, aber bei näherer Betrachtung mit dieser Erwartungshaltung brechen. Sie verleiten die betrachtende Person zu einem Spiel mit der Einbildungskraft, indem sie Funktionszusammenhänge suggerieren und damit zu gleich wieder brechen. Damit sind sie gewissermaßen Teil unserer Alltagswelt sowie sie darin als Fremdkörper erscheinen. Kahnau entwickelt ihre textilen Arbeiten in ihrem Münchner Atelier. Ihre Produktionswege könnten nicht kürzer sein; in ihrem direkt angrenzenden Ladengeschäft für lokales Design, dem HIER- Store, sind die Unikate erhältlich. Durch dieses Konzept ist sie nicht nur unabhängig in ihrer Produktion, es positioniert ihr Label jenseits der Massenproduktion. Für die Herstellung ihrer Kleidung greift Kahnau auf hochwertige Restmaterialien zurück, die durch die Überproduktion der Großkonzerne ungenutzt bleiben. Seit 2014 ist sie außerdem regelmäßig an verschiedenen Universitäten in der Lehre tätig.

[1] Erläuterung, vgl. S. 120.

Through ordinary materials, I sense the passage of time and transformation.

01 UNTITLED (2019)
295 × 200 CM
WOVEN
WILD SILK, COTTON, STEEL

Soojin Kang

EN Soojin Kang, born in 1978, studied Fashion Prints (BA, 2006) and Textile Futures (MA, 2009) at Central Saint Martins College in London. The work she produces as an artist is informed by the sensitive handling of themes associated with material, memory and space. Her point of departure is the conflictual relationship between the organic softness of natural fibres such as raw silk, linen or jute and the rough hardness of industrially produced working materials such as concrete or cement. Profoundly intrigued by unconventional possibilities and endowed with a finely honed feeling for social and autobiographical referencing, Kang has consistently used - at first in fashion design, later in the mass-produced furnishings sector - a diverse repertory of crafts techniques. Her approach to finding form is shaped by an interest in tactile impact. Weaving, knotting, wrapping and dyeing produce fragile, complex structures that enter on a tacit yet intense exchange with solid elements, thus lending the material expanded semantic significance.

Kang views the textile gesture as an act of remembrance. Each woven detail is linked with events in her biography, a process that not only reproduces time but also embodies it in the design of the material. Her sculptures are reminiscent of rampantly proliferating configurations or canker on diseased trees. They reflect internal and external transformation processes - triggered by injury, illness or age-related decline. In vivid contrast to those possibilities for expression in textiles, concrete represents a ductile material that awaits design like a bobbin of unwoven yarn. Air bubbles, tears and traces left in the material refer to the process of working, thus for their part preserving time. Her sculptures look archaic -manmade yet alien. Abstract when viewed from a distance, they reveal formal borrowings from skin, hair and sinew on close scrutiny.
Kang is currently living and working on an old farm in Kulmbach. There she enters into an unmediated dialogue with her rural surroundings, the pervasive quiet and the materials she is working.

02 HEAD (2020)
30 × 40 × 40 CM
WOVEN
METAL ARMATURE, RAW SILK

03 UNTITLED (2019)
50 × 20 × 20 CM
WOVEN
METAL ARMATURE, SILK, COTTON,
JUTE, HEMP

04 UNTITLED (2023), DETAIL
70 × 30 × 20 CM
WOVEN, MOULDED
RAW SILK, METAL, CEMENT

DE Soojin Kang, geboren 1978, studierte Fashion Prints (BA, 2006) und Textile Futures (MA, 2009) am Central Saint Martins College in London. Ihre künstlerische Arbeit ist geprägt von einem sensiblen Umgang mit den Themen Material, Erinnerung und Raum. Ausgangspunkt ist das Spannungsverhältnis zwischen der organischen Weichheit natürlicher Fasern wie Rohseide, Leinen oder Jute und der rohen Härte industrieller Werkstoffe wie Beton oder Zement. Mit einer tiefen Faszination für unkonventionellen Möglichkeiten und einem feinen Gespür für gesellschaftliche wie autobiografische Bezüge nutzt Kang - zunächst im Modedesign, später im Bereich maßgefertigter Möbel - konsequent ein vielfältiges Repertoire handwerklicher Techniken. Ihr Zugang zur Formfindung ist dabei von einem Interesse an der haptischen Wirkung geprägt. Durch Weben, Knoten, Wickeln und Färben entstehen fragile, vielschichtige Strukturen, die mit massiven Elementen in einen stillen, aber intensiven Dialog treten und dem Material so eine erweiterte Bedeutung verleihen.
Die textile Geste versteht Kang als Akt der Erinnerung. Jedes gewebte Detail ist verbunden mit ihren

biografischen Momenten - ein Prozess, der Zeit nicht nur abbildet, sondern in der Gestaltung des Materials auch verkörpert. Ihre Skulpturen erinnern an wuchernde Gebilde oder Baumgeschwülste. Sie reflektieren Prozesse innerer und äußerer Transformation - die durch Verletzung, Krankheit oder Vergehen ausgelöst wurden. Im Gegensatz zu diesen textilen Ausdrucksmöglichkeiten steht Beton als formbares Material, das wie eine Spule ungewobenen Garns auf seine Gestaltung wartet. Luftblasen, Risse und Spuren im Material verweisen auf den Prozess der Verarbeitung und bewahren so ihrerseits die Zeit. Ihre Skulpturen erscheinen archaisch - menschengemacht, aber fremd. Aus der Ferne abstrakt, offenbaren sie aus der Nähe betrachtet formale Anleihen an Haut, Haar, Sehnen.
Aktuell lebt und arbeitet Kang in Kulmbach auf einem ehemaligen Bauernhof. Dort tritt in einen unmittelbaren Dialog mit der ländlichen Umgebung, der Stille und den Materialien.

02

03

04

01 ELECTRIC MOVE (2022)
50 × 20 × 5 CM
WOVEN
HORSEHAIR, COTTON, PINS

Textiles tell unique stories through time and cultures. They can be full of symbolic meanings. There is so much history in textiles; I'm continuously learning more and more about them.

EN Marianne Kemp, artist and designer, has been weaving for more than twenty years and devotes herself in her praxis chiefly to a single unusual material: horsehair.

Born in 1976, Kemp has been passionate about textiles as a medium since childhood, an affinity that led her to study fashion design as a first approach. She took her bachelor's degree in textile design at the Koninklijke Academie van Beeldende Kunsten in The Hague and then specialised in sustainable design in a Master of Arts in Design for the Environment at the Chelsea College of Art and Design in London.

Her studies aroused in her a fascination with textures and structures that has informed her work and her signature as an artist ever since. The handloom has become Marianne Kemp's primary tool, which she uses both for meticulously precise work and for free experimentation. The elemental structure of weaving and woven fabric consisting of warp and weft forms the stable scaffolding for each work – the backbone of her works, as it were. Nonetheless she blurs the boundaries of traditional weaving techniques with those she has developed herself for the purpose of allowing characteristic textures to emerge that might be disturbing in appearance. The focus is always on process, the constant repetition of a hand movement and the creation of a textured form. Marianne Kemp pushes the boundaries of material and technique, a stance that she also passes on in her teaching. Apart from horsehair with its contradictory material properties - fragility but firmness, transparency yet structure – she works other natural materials such as cotton, wool and linen as well as Korean hanji paper and even gold lurex. Since 2001 Kemp's works have been created in a collective studio in Zutphen. These pieces have manifold functions and uses: some of her works are hung on walls as expressive tapestries while others mutate into textile sculptures or are transformed into wearable objects.

02 SUNNY SPELLS (2024)
220 × 200 × 10 CM
WOVEN
HORSEHAIR, COTTON, PINS

03 DEW (2024)
120 × 250 × 10 CM
WOVEN
HORSEHAIR, COTTON, PINS

02

03

Die Künstlerin und Designerin Marianne Kemp webt seit über 20 Jahren und widmet sich in ihrer Praxis primär einem ungewöhnlichen Material: Rosshaar.

Das Medium Textil begeisterte die 1976 geborene Kemp schon seit ihrer Kindheit, was sie zunächst dazu veranlasste, Modedesign zu studieren. Ihren Bachelor in Textildesign absolvierte sie an der Koninklijke Academie van Beeldende Kunsten in Den Haag und spezialisierte sich anschließend auf nachhaltige Gestaltung im Rahmen des Studiengangs Master of Arts in Design for the Environment am Chelsea College of Art and Design in London.

Dieses Studium weckte ihre Faszination für Texturen und Strukturen, die ihr Werk seither durchziehen und ihre künstlerische Handschrift prägen. Der Handwebstuhl wird zu Marianne Kemps zentralem Werkzeug - sowohl für akribische Präzisionsarbeit als auch für freies Experimentieren. Die Grundstruktur des Webens, bestehend aus Kette und Schuss, bildet das stabile Gerüst jeder Arbeit - sozusagen das Rückgrat ihrer Werke. Trotzdem löst sie mit eigens entwickelten Techniken und ungewöhnlichen Farbkombinationen die Grenzen traditioneller Webtechniken bewusst auf und lässt charakteristische Oberflächen entstehen, die durch ihr Erscheinen irritieren dürfen. Immer im Fokus steht der Prozess, die stetige Wiederholung eines Handgriffs sowie das Erschaffen einer texturierten Form. Marianne Kemp reizt die Möglichkeiten von Material und Technik aus - eine Haltung, die sie auch in ihrer Lehrtätigkeit weitergibt. Neben der Gegensätzlichkeit des Rosshaars - fragil und zugleich fest, transparent und doch strukturiert -, verarbeitet sie weitere natürliche Materialien wie Baumwolle, Wolle, Leinen sowie koreanisches Hanji-Papier und Goldlurex. Seit 2001 entstehen Kemps Arbeiten in einer Ateliergemeinschaft in Zutphen. Die Einsatzbereiche sind dabei vielfältig: manche ihrer Werke werden als expressive Wandteppiche gehängt, andere verwandeln sich in textile Skulpturen oder werden zu tragbaren Gegenständen verarbeitet.

01 SCARF (2024), DETAIL
104 × 104 CM
SILK-SCREEN
SILK TWILL

Inspiration is often a journey ... but it also simply comes
when it comes – drawn from what has been stored within.

EN The textile visual worlds created by designer and artist Sonnhild Kestler, born 1963, are complex. Her works unite archaic and contemporary forms, folkloric and artistic elements, and ornamental poetry with graphic clarity. What at first glance might seem decorative turns out to be a profound meditation on cultural imagery - an expression of design that is understood worldwide.

It was clear to Kestler from an early age that she wanted to realise her own ideas, and do so independently and with self-determination as her goal. After taking a diploma at the specialist textile class at the Schule für Gestaltung Zürich, she founded a silk-screen printing workshop of her own. She still produces her prints herself and develops her analogue patterns independently, which guarantees her artistic freedom.

Kestler's cloths and fabrics are the result of intensive study of the sensuous qualities of materials. Inspiration is, for her, a complex process, a blend of subjects that are of personal interest to her and observations of her surroundings. She has retained particularly strong and lasting impressions from her travels through India, where past, present, shiny surfaces and precarious social realities collide. Details are what has lodged in her memory to later find their way associatively into her compositions.

Her designs, usually collage-like configurations made of paper, often evoke figurative associations - beings on a sliding scale between animal and human or floral hybrids. Kestler's works are informed by interstitiality, the in-between, playing on polysemy and formal friction. Everything is juxtaposed on an equal footing; there is no centre, no weighting. This additive approach is premised on a fundamental openness to material and the process of working it. Instead of the classic repeating pattern, which is a static design, her motifs create textile imagery, visual worlds that make the impact of atmospheric narratives.

Collaborating with the people who commission work from her complements the work she does by choice as an artist but without taking precedence over it. Working on her own, she creates textile wall designs, fabrics for furnishings, and carpets - always in a dialogue with space and function.

02 PILLOW (2023)
50 × 50 CM
WOVEN
COTTON

03 STOOL COLLABORATION WITH GREGO ARCHITEKTUR, UC-04 (2022)
Ø 50 × 40 CM
WOVEN
COTTON

04 ELIS (2022)
120 × 83 CM
HAND SPUN, HAND KNOTTED
TIBETAN WOOL

DE Die textilen Bildwelten der Designerin und Künstlerin Sonnhild Kestler (*1963) sind vielschichtig. Ihre Arbeiten verbinden archaische und zeitgenössische Formen, folkloristische und künstlerische Elemente, ornamentale Poesie mit grafischer Klarheit. Was auf den ersten Blick dekorativ erscheinen mag, entpuppt sich als tiefgründige Reflexion über kulturelle Bildsprachen - ein gestalterischer Ausdruck, der weltweit verstanden wird.

Für Kestler war früh klar, dass sie ihre eigenen Ideen verwirklichen möchte - unabhängig und selbstbestimmt. Nach dem Diplom an der Textilfachklasse der Schule für Gestaltung Zürich gründete sie eine eigene Siebdruckwerkstatt. Bis heute produziert sie ihre Drucke selbst und entwickelt ihre analogen Muster eigenständig, was ihr gestalterische Freiheit garantiert.

Kestlers Tücher und Stoffe entstehen aus einer intensiven Auseinandersetzung mit der Sinnlichkeit des Stoffs. Inspiration ist für sie ein komplexer Prozess - eine Mischung aus persönlichen Themen und der Beobachtung ihrer Umwelt. Besonders starke Eindrücke hinterließen ihre Reisen durch Indien, wo Vergangenheit und Gegenwart, glänzende Oberflächen und prekäre soziale Wirklichkeiten aufeinandertreffen. Es sind Details, die sich im Gedächtnis festsetzen und später assoziativ Eingang in ihre Kompositionen finden.

Die Entwürfe, meist zuerst collagenartige Gebilde aus Papier, rufen oft figurative Assoziationen hervor; Wesen zwischen Tier und Mensch oder florale Hybride. Kestlers Arbeiten leben vom Dazwischen, vom Spiel mit Mehrdeutigkeit und formaler Reibung. Alles steht gleichwertig nebeneinander, es gibt kein Zentrum, keine Gewichtung. Diese additive Herangehensweise impliziert eine grundlegende Offenheit gegenüber dem Material und dem Prozess der Verarbeitung. Statt dem klassischem Rapport, einem statischen Muster, bilden die Motive textile Bildwelten, die wie atmosphärische Erzählungen wirken. Die Zusammenarbeit mit Auftraggeber:innen ergänzt ihre freie künstlerische Arbeit ohne sie zu dominieren. Dabei entstehen textile Wandgestaltungen, Möbelstoffe oder Teppiche - immer im Dialog mit Raum und Funktion.

02

04

03

01 SHIFT - LOCK (2023)
200 × 130 × 4.5 CM
JACQUARD ON CANVAS STRETCHER
POLYESTER

I love working with textiles – especially because of the community, which shows how shared knowledge has kept these techniques alive across generations.

EN In her work Constanza Camila Kramer Garfias, who was born in 1988, concentrates on a critical examination of textiles as a signifier of cultural, material and political values. The themes that are central to her work are her German-Chilean roots and the textile legacy of indigenous communities, most notably that of the Mapuche, who to this today are actively engaged in opposing the colonisation of their life spaces. Several terms spent studying philosophy at Ludwig-Maximilians-Universität München and Kramer Garfias's interest in post-colonial theory inform her artistic praxis and lend her work conceptual depth.

An early fascination with textile fabrics led her to study conceptual textile design at Burg Giebichenstein Kunsthochschule in Halle. Her diploma project - supervised by Professor Caroline Achaintre [→ p. 63] - reveals she was already subverting the status quo of positions occupied by textile design in art and reflecting on their aesthetic and societal dimensions. On study trips abroad, for instance to Japan, she has deepened her knowledge of traditional techniques such as plant-based dyeing processes and widened the intercultural insight into materiality and textile-related practices that she has striven to retain in her own work.

Kramer Garfias lives and works in Munich. Her exhibits in large formats are often planned with the aid of digital weaving software and are then realised at a Jacquard weaving mill in Italy. However, she views these precisely produced textiles as source materials rather than end states: she alters them, deconstructing and supplementing them manually, or recontextualises them - for instance, by means of additional painting, retroactive tufting or the deliberate violation of conventional colour and texture normes through a range of interventions in the material.

Her work is informed by the tensions thus generated between machine-made perfection and manual intervention. In realising her ideas, she subverts perceptions of textiles, thus lending seemingly familiar structures fresh creative significance.

02 AUTOBAHN 3 (2022)
140 × 147 CM
JACQUARD, METAL EYELETS
POLYESTER

03 AUTOBAHN REPEAT / UNTIL (2023)
224 × 142 CM
JACQUARD, METAL RODS
POLYESTER

DE Das Werk von Constanza Camila Kramer Garfias, geboren 1988, konzentriert sich auf die kritische Auseinandersetzung mit Textilien als kulturelle, materielle und politische Bedeutungsträger. Zentrale Themen ihrer Arbeit sind ihre deutsch-chilenischen Wurzeln sowie das textile Erbe indigener Gemeinschaften, insbesondere jenes der Mapuche, die sich der Kolonialisierung ihrer Lebensräume bis heute aktiv widersetzen. Einige Semester des Philosophiestudiums an der Ludwig-Maximilians-Universität München sowie Kramer Garfias' Interesse an postkolonialen Theorien durchdringen ihre künstlerische Praxis und verleihen ihnen konzeptuelle Tiefe.

Ihre frühe Faszination für textile Materialien führte sie zum Studium Conceptual Textile Design an der Burg Giebichenstein Kunsthochschule Halle. Bereits in ihrer Abschlussarbeit - betreut von Prof. Caroline Achaintre [→ S. 63] - hinterfragte sie die Stellung textilgestalterischer Positionen in der Kunst und reflektierte deren ästhetische wie gesellschaftliche Dimensionen. Auf Studienreisen, etwa nach Japan, vertiefte sie ihr Wissen über traditionelle Techniken wie pflanzenbasierte Färbeverfahren und erweiterte ihren interkulturellen Blick auf Materialität und textile Praktiken, die sie in ihrer eigenen Arbeit zu bewahren versucht.

Kramer Garfias lebt und arbeitet heute in München. Ihre großformatigen Exponate entstehen häufig zuerst mithilfe digitaler Webprogramme und werden anschließend in einer Jacquardweberei in Italien realisiert. Diese präzise produzierten Textilien begreift sie jedoch nicht als Endpunkt, sondern als Ausgangsmaterial: sie verändert, dekonstruiert und ergänzt diese manuell oder führt sie in neue Kontexte über - etwa durch zusätzliches Bemalen, nachträgliches Tufting oder durch das bewusste Aufbrechen der gewohnten Farb- und Strukturcodes durch unterschiedliche Eingriffe in das Material.

Ihr Werk ist geprägt von einem Spannungsverhältnis zwischen maschineller Perfektion und handwerklicher Intervention. Dabei hinterfragt sie die Wahrnehmung des Textilen und verleiht scheinbar vertrauten Strukturen neue gestalterische Bedeutung.

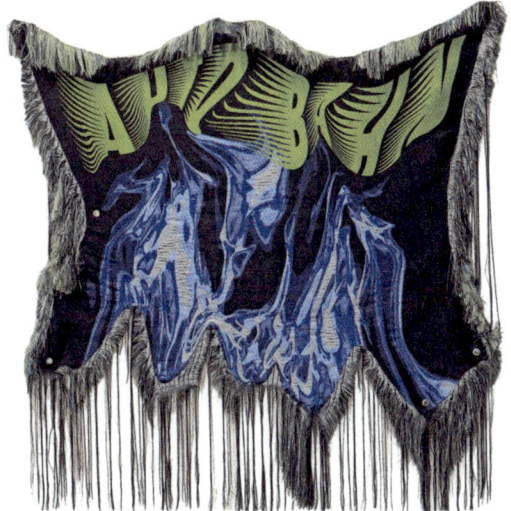

02

03

01 CALL IT ANGEL EARTH (2023)
300 × 300 × 300 CM
TUFTED, EMBROIDERED, WOOD-CARVED,
GLASS-BLOWN
WOOL, WOOD, GLASS

My practice started from a need to pull myself out of a dark place and to create the visual and emotional surroundings I wanted to live in.

Alfhild Külper creates gentleness through colour, form and material as well as textile techniques, thus designing a counter-world to an environment that is growing ever more digital. Born in 1982, she worked for ten years in the fashion industry after completing her studies in design at the Central Saint Martins College of Art and Design in London. Külper gradually developed a need to detach herself from working as a fashion designer and to create a tactile life world. The transition from fashion to art was not so much due to a disappointment with the work as such, rather more the result of a general disillusionment in regard to global developments as well as the consequences of personal health challenges. Nevertheless, her profound love for the magic of the fashion industry has stayed with her and continues to inform her artistic practice to this day. Her yearning for something soft that was both physical and emotional became the leitmotif of her artistic praxis. In her work Alfhild Külper gradually unites consummate craftsmanship with psychic and physical wellbeing. This feeling of secure snugness and warmth is what she also wants to convey to other people. Külper applies a wide range of traditional textile techniques as well as techniques she has developed herself. She is constantly in search of new possibilities for enlarging the medium of textiles.

Working with wool she procures from remainders left over from textile production is characteristic of her design praxis. This material is distinguished by natural softness yet also provides her with an opportunity for working in three dimensions. Wool is an accommodating material; its consistency and texture tolerate any unevenness so that wearing a woollen fabric can feel like an embrace.

On the basis of her training, Külper has experienced the interface between art and design as particularly rewarding. Her works grow from textile objects into sculptural installations that are spatial interventions. Since 2021 Alfhild Külper has pursued a fulfilling career as a textile artist. Working from her Amsterdam studio, she presents her works at international galleries, including venues in New York, Brussels and Amsterdam.

02 WE CREATE OUR OWN LIGHT (2023)
150 × 200 CM
TUFTING, EMBROIDERY
WOOL

03 THE WAY OUT CAN BE UP (2024)
TAPESTRY
275 × 180 CM
FELTED, EMBROIDERED
WOOL

04 BLOOM OF CONNECTION (2024)
90 × 70 CM
TUFTING, EMBROIDERY
WOOL

02

03

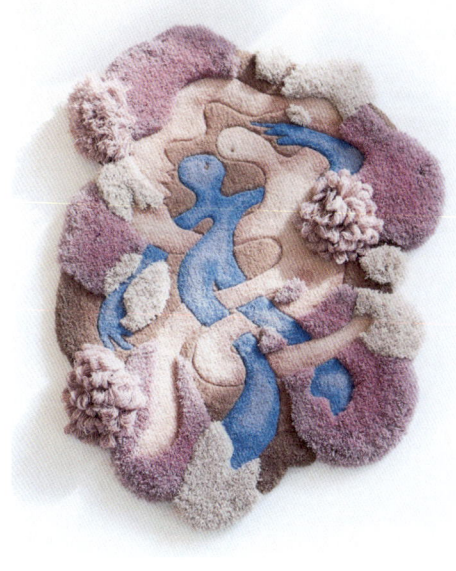

04

DE   Alfhild Külper erschafft Sanftheit durch Farbe, Form und Material sowie textilen Techniken und entwirft somit ein Gegenstück zu einer immer digitaler werdenden Umwelt. Geboren 1982, hat sie nach ihrem Modedesign-Studium am Central Saint Martins College of Art and Design in London zehn Jahre in der Modeindustrie gearbeitet. Doch nach und nach entwickelte Külper das Bedürfnis, sich aus der Tätigkeit als Modedesignerin zu lösen und eine taktile Lebenswelt zu schaffen. Der Übergang von der Mode zur Kunst war weniger eine Enttäuschung über die Arbeit an sich, sondern vielmehr das Ergebnis einer allgemeinen Desillusionierung im Hinblick auf globale Entwicklungen sowie Konsequenz persönlicher gesundheitlicher Herausforderungen. Dennoch ist ihre tiefe Liebe für die Magie der Modeindustrie stets geblieben und prägt auch heute noch ihre künstlerische Praxis. Diese Sehnsucht nach etwas körperlich und emotional Weichem wurde zum Leitmotiv ihrer künstlerischen Praxis. In ihrer Arbeit verbindet Alfhild Külper handwerkliches Können mit psychischem und physischem Wohlbefinden. Dieses Gefühl der Geborgenheit und Wärme will sie auch auf andere Menschen zu übertragen. Külper verwendet eine Vielzahl traditioneller sowie selbst entwickelter textiler Techniken. Sie ist stets auf der Suche nach neuen Möglichkeiten, das textile Medium zu erweitern.

Charakteristisch für ihre gestalterische Praxis ist die Arbeit mit Wolle, die sie aus Restbeständen der Textilindustrie bezieht. Das Material zeichnet sich durch eine natürliche Weichheit aus und bietet trotzdem die Möglichkeit, dreidimensional zu arbeiten. Wolle ist anpassungsfähig, ihre Beschaffenheit verzeiht kleine Unebenheiten und adaptiert Körperwärme, sodass sich das Tragen eines Wolltextils wie eine Umarmung anfühlen kann.

Basierend auf ihrer Ausbildung hat Külper die Schnittstelle zwischen Kunst und Design als besonders bereichernd erlebt. Ihre Arbeiten wachsen von textilen Objekten zu skulpturalen, raumübergreifenden Installationen. Seit 2021 verwirklicht sich Alfhild Külper hauptberuflich als Textilkünstlerin. Sie arbeitet in ihrem Atelier in Amsterdam und präsentiert ihre Werke in internationalen Galerien, unter anderem in New York, Brüssel und Amsterdam.

01 TISSAGE DE VERRE (2024)
30 × 15 CM
WOVEN
GLASS FILAMENT,
SILVER-PLATED METAL THREAD

Craftsmanship is a space of innovation. Unlike industrial processes, hand weaving offers total freedom: everything can be imagined, tested, created – guided by the hand rather than the machine.

02

EN   Born in 1987, Aurélia Leblanc took a master's degree in textile design at the Académie royale des Beaux-Arts in Brussels. During the five years she studied there she acquired a profound knowledge of textile techniques – weaving in particular, which soon emerged in her work as the revelation of a pivotal means of personal expression. Weaving is a medium that allows her to tell stories through materiality, structure and contrasts. In addition to its narrative potential, weaving also contains emotional depth and a tactile language that is leading Leblanc to explore an ever broadening range of possibilities for expression. For Leblanc crafts is a locus of innovation. Unlike industrial processes, weaving by hand gives her unlimited scope for testing the boundaries of artistic freedom: there is nothing that cannot be thought up, tried out and realised – visions become reality through work being done by hand rather than being machine-made. Since 2024 her studio has been located in Pantin, where she carries out work on commission while also realising experimental projects of her own.

For more than a decade Aurélia Leblanc has worked at the interface of haute couture, interior design and fashion, always without strictly demarcating the boundaries between art and design. As she sees it, the two fields are engaged in a constructive dialogue: the artistic urge is grounded by the technical demands of design – and vice versa.
Her artistic praxis centres on investigating and testing rare and unusual combinations of materials, such as horsehair with brass, or denim with ceramic beads. Her research in design is based on a quest to discover the relationship between tensile properties and the harmonious interplay of disparate elements. Since 2017 she has collaborated with Lucile Viaud on woven glass – a soft, flexible fabric made of glass filaments notable for a strikingly distinctive material aesthetic.
For this innovative linkage of two crafts that traditionally might seem incompatible, the collaborators were presented with the Liliane Bettencourt Dialogues Award by the French Bettencourt Schueller Foundation.

03   04

DE   Aurélia Leblanc wurde 1987 geboren und absolvierte 2015 ihren Masterabschluss in Textildesign an der Académie royale des Beaux-Arts in Brüssel. Im Verlauf ihres fünfjährigen Studiums erwarb sie ein profundes Verständnis für textile Techniken – insbesondere für das Weben, das sich in ihrer Arbeit rasch als persönliche Offenbarung eines zentralen Ausdrucksmittels herauskristallisierte. Dieses Medium erlaubt ihr, Geschichten durch Materialität, Struktur und Kontraste zu erzählen. Die Weberei birgt neben dem erzählerischen Potenzial auch eine emotionale Tiefe und eine taktile Sprache, die Leblanc zu immer neuen Ausdrucksmöglichkeiten führt. Für Leblanc ist Handwerk ein Ort der Innovation. Anders als industrielle Prozesse ermöglicht das manuelle Weben ein uneingeschränktes Austesten von gestalterischer Freiheit: Alles kann erdacht, erprobt und verwirklicht werden – geführt von der Hand, nicht von der Maschine. Seit 2024 ist ihr Atelier in Pantin ansässig, wo sie sowohl Auftragsarbeiten als auch eigene Forschungsprojekte umsetzt.

Seit über einem Jahrzehnt bewegt sich Aurélia Leblanc an der Schnittstelle von Haute Couture, Interior Design und Mode – stets ohne eine strikte Trennung zwischen Kunst und Design zu ziehen. Beide Bereiche stehen für sie in einem lebendigen Dialog: Der künstlerische Impuls wird durch technische Gestaltung geerdet – und umgekehrt.

Im Zentrum ihrer künstlerischen Praxis steht die Auseinandersetzung mit seltenen und ungewöhnlichen Materialien, wie etwa Kombinationen von Pferdehaar mit Messing oder von Denim mit Keramikperlen. Die Suche nach Spannungsverhältnissen und harmonischem Zusammenspiel unterschiedlichster Elemente bildet das Fundament ihrer gestalterischen Forschung. Seit 2017 entwickelt sie gemeinsam mit Lucile Viaud gewebtes Glas – ein weiches, flexibles Textil aus Glasfilamenten mit einer ganz besonderen Materialästhetik.

Für diese innovative Verbindung zweier traditionell scheinbar gegensätzlicher Handwerke wurde das Duo 2023 mit dem Dialogues-Preis der französischen Fondation Bettencourt Schueller ausgezeichnet.

02

01 THE REST WILL BE FAMILIAR TO YOU
(2021)
INSTALLATION AND PERFORMANCE
MACHINE AS DEPICTED: 120 × 180 × 40 CM
KNITTED PIECE: 450 × 75 CM
MACHINE MANIPULATED, KNITTED
DOMESTIC KNITTING MACHINE, DIGITAL
PUNCHCARD, YARN

02 DAS FLOSS DER MEDUSA (2024)
PAVILLON 333, MÜNCHEN
1200 × 1200 × 500 CM (INSTALLATION)
7000 × 75 CM (KNITTED PIECE)
MACHINE KNITTED, 80-H PERFORMANCE
COTTON, POLYESTER YARN

EN Karen Modrei's oeuvre is an interdisciplinary blend of textile art, sound experiments and performative process. Her works centre on machines that are at once tools and musical instruments and on making what is inaudible visible. The knitting machine is pivotal for her artistic research – not as a nostalgic piece of equipment but as a medium for expression. Modrei, born 1992, first trained as a bespoke tailor, then took a bachelor's degree in architecture at the Bauhaus-Universität Weimar. She followed up her studies in architecture with a master's degree in textile art at Konstfack in Stockholm. The result of this interdisciplinary combination is an idiosyncratic handling of materials, machines and narration. Textile practices appear here to be a form of thinking – the kind of thinking that, if you will, sews, unravels seams and joins them again. What makes Modrei's work distinctive is her intellectual stance: she does not view textiles as mere fabric: they are movement, resonance, resistance. Her machines do not work in time with the beat of industrial perfection but operate in rhythms of their own: slow, deliberate and sometimes querulous. To work in this way, she intervenes in the manually set patterning of the knitting machine by means of punchcards and manipulates them. She expands the technology available by adding a component she has developed herself that translates acoustic signals into binary codes and ultimately into knitting patterns. Thus the machine receives a 'body extension' that enables her to design the pattern of a piece of knitting autonomously and in unmediated interaction with her surroundings. In this way Modrei opens up her processes to participation in them – the aim is always the exchange of ideas as well as highlighting awareness of political and social issues. At a time when high-paced living, replaceability and superficiality prevail, Karen Modrei provides with her work resistance as an art form in which fabrics are written on and machines speak. Her work represents an invitation to listen more attentively – and not to take the surface for the whole.

03 DAS FLOSS DER MEDUSA (2024)
INSTALLATION: 1200 × 1200 × 500 CM
KNITTED PIECE: 7000 × 75 CM
MACHINE KNITTED, PERFORMANCE
COTTON, POLYESTER YARN

04 DAS FLOSS DER MEDUSA (2024)
7000 × 75 CM
MACHINE KNITTED
COTTON, POLYESTER YARN

05 DAS FLOSS DER MEDUSA (2024)
INSTALLATION: 1200 × 1200 × 500 CM
KNITTED PIECE: 7000 × 75 CM
MACHINE KNITTED, PERFORMANCE
COTTON, POLYESTER YARN

03

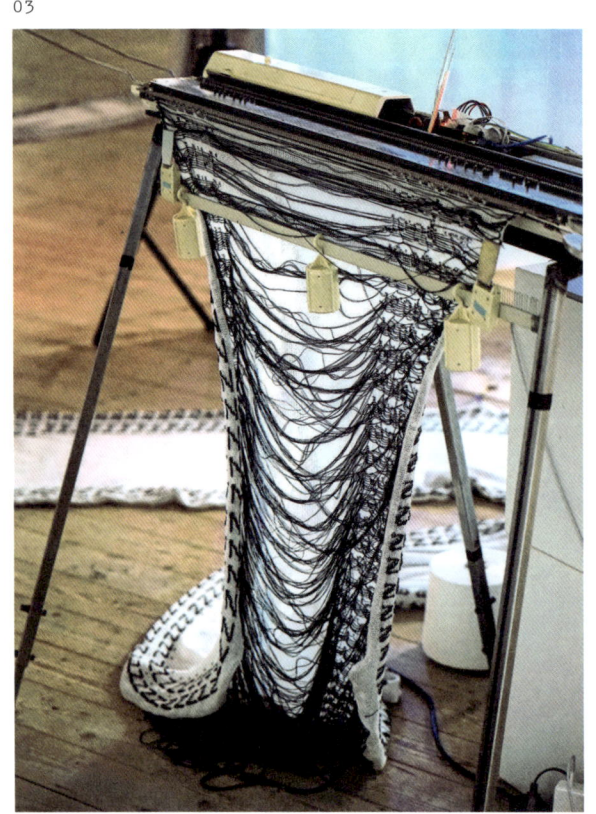

04

05

DE   Das Werk von Karen Modrei oszilliert zwischen Textilkunst, Klangexperiment und einem performativen Prozess. Ihre Arbeiten kreisen um Maschinen, die zugleich Werkzeug und Instrument sind, und um das Sichtbarmachen des Ungehörten. Die Strickmaschine steht dabei im Zentrum ihrer künstlerischen Forschung – nicht als nostalgisches Gerät, sondern als Medium des Ausdrucks. Modrei, geboren 1992, schloss zuerst eine Ausbildung als Maßschneiderin ab und absolvierte anschließend ihren Bachelor in Architektur an der Bauhaus-Universität Weimar. Im Anschluss folgte ein Master in Textilkunst an der Konstfack - University of Arts, Crafts and Design in Stockholm. Aus dieser Kombination entsteht ein eigenwilliger Umgang mit Material, Maschine und Narration. Textile Praktiken erscheinen hier als eine Form des Denkens – ein Denken, das, wenn man so will, näht, auftrennt und wieder verbindet. Was Modreis Arbeit auszeichnet, ist ihre Haltung: für sie ist Textil nicht bloß Stoff – es ist Bewegung, Resonanz, Widerstand. Ihre Maschinen arbeiten nicht im Takt industrieller Perfektion, sondern in eigenen Rhythmen: langsam, bewusst und manchmal hadernd. Dafür greift sie in die manuelle Mustersteuerung der Strickmaschine mittels Lochkarten ein und manipuliert diese. Sie erweitert die vorhandene Technik, durch ein eigens entwickeltes Bauteil das akustische Signale in binäre Codes und schließlich in Strickmuster übersetzt. Dadurch erhält die Maschine eine „körperliche Erweiterung", die es ihr ermöglicht, das Muster des Strickstücks autonom und in direkter Interaktion mit ihrer Umgebung zu gestalten. So öffnet Modrei ihre Prozesse für Beteiligung – im Zentrum stehen dabei stets der Austausch sowie die Sensibilisierung für politische und soziale Themen. In einer Zeit, in der Schnelligkeit, Ersetzbarkeit und Äußerlichkeiten vorherrschen, bietet Karen Modrei mit ihrer Arbeit eine widerständige Kunstform, in der auf Stoffen geschrieben und mit Maschinen gesprochen wird. Ihr Werk lädt dabei ein, genauer zuzuhören – und die Oberfläche nicht für das Ganze zu halten.

02

163 Emilie Palle Holm

01 ORIORI (2023)
102 × 30 × 30 CM
JACQUARD
LINEN, ELASTANE, COTTON, POLYESTER, WOOL

02 ORIORI/LENTICULAR WOVEN PANEL (2023),
DETAIL
90 × 150 × 15 CM
JACQUARD
LINEN, ELASTANE, COTTON, POLYESTER

EN Born in 1994, Emilie Palle Holm specialised in digital Jacquard weaving and focuses in her work on overcoming the two-dimensional character of woven fabrics. By tying form-altering mechanisms directly into the weaving process, she explores the hidden potential of the loom to develop textile sculptures that gradually assume a three-dimensional quality – without cutting from a pattern, without sewing seams, without waste. Material and form emerge synchronously, through weaving alone, a process which introduces the additional perspective of ecological sustainability to aesthetic praxis.

Her signature as a designer was formatively shaped by her BFA studies at Designskolen Kolding and MFA at the Textilhögskolan in Borås, where she graduated in 2023. Since then she has been working in a studio collective in Copenhagen. Her methodical and exploratory approach is deliberately poised at the interface of design and art.

Fascinated by the systematic structure of the loom, she unites rationality and intuition. The weaving process is defined as an art medium that allows for experimentation above and beyond technical process. Holm's works challenge prevailing notions of aesthetics, functionality and technology and in an increasingly digitalised world represent an invitation to engage sensorily and physically with textiles.

Since Jacquard weaving can only be carried out by very large and expensive machines, Holm also works in addition to her studio activity with such specialised facilities as TextielLab in Tilburg. It is here, as well as in other workshops, that her sophisticated sculptural works see the light of day - at the interface of crafts, technology and art.

Emilie Palle Holm views the medium of textiles as something dynamic, mutable. Her praxis subverts not only traditional formats but also the role of textiles in contemporary design – always with the aim of opening up new spaces for the expressive powers of design.

03 ORIORI (2023)
50 × 45 × 25 CM
JACQUARD
LINEN, ELASTANE, COTTON, POLYESTER

04 ORIORI (2023), VERSION 1
60 × 35 × 35 CM
JACQUARD
LINEN, ELASTANE, COTTON, POLYESTER

05 ORIORI (2023), VERSION 2
60 × 35 × 35 CM
JACQUARD
LINEN, ELASTANE, COTTON, POLYESTER

03

04

05

DE Emilie Palle Holm, geboren 1994, hat sich auf die digitale Jacquard-Weberei spezialisiert und setzt den zentralen Fokus ihrer Arbeit auf das Überwinden der Zweidimensionalität gewebter Textilien. Durch das Einbinden formverändernder Mechanismen in den unmittelbaren Webprozess erforscht sie die verborgenen Potenziale des Webstuhls und entwickelt textile Skulpturen, die nach und nach eine Dreidimensionalität entfalten – ohne Zuschnitt, ohne Nähte, ohne Abfall. Material und Form entstehen gleichzeitig, allein durch das Weben, was die zusätzliche Perspektive einer ökologischen Nachhaltigkeit in die ästhetische Praxis einbringt.

Ihre gestalterische Handschrift ist stark durch ihr Studium an der Design School Kolding (BFA) sowie der Swedish School of Textiles in Borås (MFA) geprägt, das sie 2023 abschloss. Seitdem arbeitet sie in einer Ateliergemeinschaft in Kopenhagen. Ihr methodischer wie forschender Zugang bewegt sich bewusst an der Schnittstelle zwischen Design und Kunst.

Fasziniert vom systematischen Aufbau des Webstuhls vereint sie Rationalität mit Intuition. Der Webprozess wird über das technische Verfahren hinaus als künstlerisches Medium verstanden, das Experimente zulässt.

Holms Werke fordern gängige Vorstellungen von Ästhetik, Funktionalität und Technik heraus – und laden in einer zunehmend digitalen Welt zur sinnlichen, physischen Auseinandersetzung mit Textilien ein.

Da die Jacquard-Weberei nur durch sehr große und kostspielige Maschinen ausgeführt werden kann, arbeitet Holm zusätzlich zu ihrer Tätigkeit im Atelier derzeit in spezialisierten Einrichtungen wie beispielsweise dem TextielLab in Tilburg. Dort, aber auch in anderen Werkstätten, entstehen ihre komplexen, skulpturalen Werke – an der Schnittstelle von Handwerk, Technologie und Kunst.

Emilie Palle Holm versteht das textile Medium als etwas Dynamisches, Wandelbares. Ihre Praxis hinterfragt nicht nur traditionelle Formate, sondern auch die Rolle des Textils in zeitgenössischer Gestaltung – stets mit dem Ziel, neue Räume für gestalterische Ausdruckskraft zu eröffnen.

01 EUCALYPTUS I (2023), DETAIL
33 × 58 CM
EMBROIDERED USING LUNÉVILLE HOOK
AND NEEDLE
SILK, GOLD METALLIC THREAD, RAYON,
PEARLS, BRASS, HANDMADE PISTILS

02 MILLEPORA (2022)
31 × 41 CM
EMBROIDERED USING LUNÉVILLE HOOK
AND NEEDLE
SILK, GOLD METALLIC THREAD, RAYON, BEADS

02

EN Zoé Pignolet, born 1988, is a freelance textile artist and embroidery designer. Her works are the expression of a dreamy, poetically heightened nature that invites contemplative observation. Plant forms and changing light moods – nature is an inexhaustible source of inspiration for her. With delicate embroidery she transforms the fleeting moment into exquisite textile sculptures, linking a traditional craft with a contemporary sensitive eye. She studied at the École Supérieure des Arts Appliqués Duperré in Paris, where she took a Brevet de Technicien Supérieur (the equivalent of a two-year higher education diploma) in textiles, materials and environmental studies, and later complemented this with a Diplôme des Métiers d'Art in embroidery, as well as a bachelor's degree in fashion. She completed her education by spending a year studying at the Escola Massana in Barcelona.

After gaining professional experience by working for several years in a Paris haute couture studio, she has pursued her own praxis in art by freelancing as a self-employed designer and artist since 2021. Her work centres on the Lunéville technique[1] – a traditional French needlework method that enables precise, rhythmic embroidery stitching. Deploying meticulous craftsmanship, Pignolet enhances fine silk fabrics by embroidering them with beads, sequins and threads. She prefers natural materials that produce a particularly sensuous effect with light, transparency and tactility. She chooses to procure her tools and materials from specialist shops or small French workshops. Pignolet's signature as an artist is the quiet poetry of her works. Her embroideries are delicate, organic, dreamy, and at the same time hint at mysterious depths. Positioned at the interface where art, crafts and design meet, her intersectional works possess a special fineness: they enhance nature without imitating it, and open up spaces for tranquillity, wonder and subtle perception.

[1] Lunéville: a historic embroidery technique in which beads, threads and suchlike can be sewn on to fine materials with a Lunéville hook – a small, thin tambour embroidery needle on a handle. Sewing is done from below through the cloth; while the needle is guided by the left hand, the right hand strings beads or sequins on the thread. The visible side always remains on top but the actual needlework – guiding the stitches with the needle – takes place under the fabric.

03 ÉCHANTILLON N°13 (2025), DETAIL
15 × 21 CM
EMBROIDERED USING LUNÉVILLE HOOK
SILK, GOLD METALLIC THREAD

04 SYMBIOSE (2024), WORK IN PROGRESS
28 × 35 × 12 CM
EMBROIDERED USING LUNÉVILLE HOOK
AND NEEDLE SILK, GOLD METALLIC THREAD,
RAYON, BEADS

05 SYMBIOSE (2024), DETAIL
28 × 35 × 12 CM
EMBROIDERED USING LUNÉVILLE HOOK
AND NEEDLE
SILK, GOLD METALLIC THREAD, RAYON, BEADS

03

04

05

DE Zoé Pignolet ist freischaffende Textilkünstlerin und Stickereidesignerin. Ihre Arbeiten sind Ausdruck einer träumerischen, poetisch überhöhten Natur, die zur kontemplativen Betrachtung einlädt. Pflanzenformen und wechselnde Lichtstimmungen – die Natur ist die unerschöpfliche Inspirationsquelle der 1988 geborenen Pignolet. Durch zarte Stickereien verwandelt sie das Flüchtige in kostbare textile Skulpturen und verbindet traditionelles Handwerk mit einem zeitgenössischen, sensiblen Blick. Sie studierte an der École Supérieure des Arts Appliqués Duperré in Paris, wo sie einen Brevet de Technicien Supérieur (vergleichbar mit einem Diplom) in Textilien, Materialien und Umwelt erwarb, das sie um ein Diplôme des Métiers d'Art in Stickerei sowie ihren Bachelor im Fachbereich Mode erweiterte. Ein Studienjahr an der Escola Massana in Barcelona ergänzte außerdem ihre Ausbildung.

Nach einigen Jahren Berufserfahrung in einem Pariser Haute-Couture-Atelier verfolgt sie seit 2021 ihre eigene künstlerische Praxis als unabhängige Designerin und Künstlerin. Im Zentrum ihrer Arbeit steht die Lunéville-Technik[1] – eine traditionelle französische Methode, die es ermöglicht, mit Präzision und Rhythmus zu sticken. Mit großer handwerklicher Sorgfalt veredelt Pignolet feine Seidenstoffe mit Stickereien aus Perlen, Pailletten und Garnen. Sie bevorzugt natürliche Materialien, die durch Licht, Transparenz und Haptik eine besondere Sinnlichkeit erzeugen.

Ihre Werkzeuge und Materialien bezieht sie wahlweise von spezialisierten Fachgeschäften oder aus kleinen französischen Werkstätten. Pignolets künstlerische Handschrift liegt in der stillen Poesie ihrer Werke. Ihre Stickereien sind zart, organisch, träumerisch – und vermitteln zugleich eine geheimnisvolle Tiefe. An der Schnittstelle von Kunst, Handwerk und Design angesiedelt, tragen die Arbeiten eine besondere Kostbarkeit in sich: Sie veredeln die Natur, ohne sie zu imitieren, und öffnen Räume für Stille, Staunen und feinsinnige Wahrnehmung.

[1] Lunéville: Historische Sticktechnik, bei der mit einer Lunéville-Nadel – einer kleinen Haken-Nadel – Perlen, Garne, etc. auf feinen Stoffen aufgebracht werden. Es wird von unten durch den Stoff gestickt, während die linke Hand die Nadel führt, reiht die rechte Perlen oder Pailletten auf den Faden. Die sichtbare Seite bleibt immer oben, während die eigentliche Handarbeit – das Führen der Nadel – unter dem Stoff stattfindet.

Noushin Redjaian

01 DESIRE (2024)
168 × 42 CM
FLOCKED CARPET OBJECT
STYROFOAM, VARIOUS CARPETS, STAINLESS
STEEL, POTASSIUM ALUMINIUM SULPHATE

Every carpet is a poem that can only be understood by the hand that wove it: a craft with centuries of tradition passed down from generation to generation.

EN Born in 1988, Noushin Redjaian develops in her work various approaches to the medium of textiles. Starting from an interdisciplinary education, studies of transmedia art, graphic art and printmaking as well as fashion design at the Universität für angewandte Kunst Wien, she works on the aesthetic values of physical phenomena and states of being. She unites her various disciplines in an overarching thematic framework and also works freelance on stage and costume projects.

Beginning with what is usually a digital sketch, she always investigates her spatial surroundings as well. This is how she plumbs the analogue realisation of her ideas. It is also how Noushin Redjaian links her education as a carpet and textile restorer with her design studies, thus lending her artworks an artisanal quality. In her Viennese studio there is an area with a chemistry lab, in which she grows crystals and mushrooms or analyses oxidation processes. Her work is based primarily on damaged, often antique carpets that are restored and altered in meticulous precision work. At the same time, her textile artworks create an impression of individuality and sensitivity, although Redjaian develops them in an approach that is almost scholarly. Inspired by nature, poetry and her spiritual praxis, she is always shifting the boundaries between scientific fields, experimentation and aesthetic decision-making.

In all her works she constantly challenges viewers to let their eyes roam, to be observant and to find themselves.

Some of her works reveal an unmediated relationship with nature and the impact it makes. For example, what is the impact made by sunlight and other factors that can be controlled only to a limited extent, and how can the changes thus effected be preserved?

02 YOU CAN'T HIDE, ..ME (2021)
24 × 10 × 9 CM
INSERTED CARPET OBJECT
JALDAR CARPET (PAKISTAN), THISTLE,
POTASSIUM ALUMINIUM SULPHATE

03 YOU'RE GETTING UNDER MY SKIN (2024)
50 × 18 CM
INSERTED CARPET OBJECT
HATSCHLU CARPET (TURKMENISTAN), STEEL,
POTASSIUM ALUMINIUM SULPHATE

04 PROPERTY OF THE SOUL (2023)
60 × 40 CM
INSERTED CARPET OBJECT
KASAK CARPET (AZERBAIJAN), POTASSIUM
ALUMINIUM SULPHATE

02

03

04

DE Die 1988 geborene Noushin Redjaian entwickelt in ihrer Arbeit verschiedene Zugänge zum Medium Textil. Basierend auf ihrer disziplinübergreifenden Ausbildung, dem Studium der Transmedialen Kunst, Grafik und Druckgrafik sowie Modedesign an der Universität für angewandte Kunst Wien, erarbeitet sie körperliche Erscheinungsformen und Verfassungen künstlerisch. Sie verknüpft ihre verschiedenen Bereiche zu einem Gesamtsujet und arbeitet zusätzlich an freien Bühnen- und Kostümprojekten.

Beginnend mit einer meist digitalen Skizze, geht sie immer auch auf die räumliche Umgebung ein. Auf diese Weise lotet sie die analoge Umsetzung ihrer Ideen aus. Ebenso verbindet Noushin Redjaian ihre Ausbildung zur Teppich- und Textilrestauratorin mit ihrem Designstudium und verleiht ihren künstlerischen Arbeiten dadurch handwerkliche Qualität. In ihrem Atelier in Wien befindet sich ein Bereich mit einem Chemielabor, in dem sie verschiedene Kristalle und Pilze züchtet oder Oxidationsprozesse analysiert und diese mit ihrer textilen Arbeit verbindet. Ihr Werk basiert auf vornehmlich beschädigten, teilweise historischen Teppichen, die durch eine akribische Feinarbeit künstlerisch wiederbelebt und verändert werden. Gleichzeitig erzeugen ihre textilen Kunstwerke den Eindruck von Individualität und Sensibilität, gleichwohl Redjaian diese in einer beinahe wissenschaftlichen Herangehensweise entwickelt. Inspiriert von der Natur, Poesie und ihrer spirituellen Praxis bewegt sie sich immer wieder zwischen Feldern der Wissenschaft, dem Experiment und ästhetischen Entscheidungen.

Bei all ihren Arbeiten fordert sie die Betrachter:innen immer wieder auf, den Blick schweifen zu lassen, zu beobachten und zu sich selbst zu finden.

Einige ihrer Arbeiten weisen einen direkten Bezug zur Natur und deren Auswirkungen auf. Was bewirken beispielsweise Sonnenlicht oder andere Faktoren, die nur bedingt steuerbar sind und wie können diese Veränderungen konserviert werden?

01 HERBSTFARBEN VON BACHLÄUFEN UND
FLUSSUFERN (2022)
NATURALLY DYED WITH WILLOW AT HIGH
TEMPERATURE, IRON MORDANT
COTTON CALICO

I always spent a lot of time in nature. It gave me freedom and creative space. I was able to discover things that others didn't see.

EN Born in 1992, Julia Ribic designs work that is distinguished by a close bond with nature and traditional crafts, specifically dyeing with plants. On visits to her native Croatia, she has learnt the centuries-old tradition of dyeing. She has learnt how flax is harvested, fabric woven, decorated with a delicate tracery of embroidery and finally dyed over an open fire. A particularly formative influence has been the knowledge imparted to her by local practitioners of the craft, women who had been handing it down for generations and invited Ribic to participate in this living cultural heritage.

During a carpentry apprenticeship she deepened her sense of form and surface, which she professionalised, as it were, by taking a diploma in product design at Universität Kassel (2022). She established her label, juliwetter_naturgefärbt, in 2021. Her product range encompasses sustainable textiles and textile creations that are made in a seasonal rhythm and dyed with the vegetal substances available at any given time of year. Ecological wearability is central to her designs: everything is used, even the smallest scraps of cloth, which she repurposes by processing them into hand-milled paper. The way natural colours turn out in the creative process has never ceased to amaze her. The date of harvest, temperature, light and fabric texture influence the result and leave ample scope for intuition and chance. Ribic is currently working in three locations: she dyes her textiles in the Black Forest and Croatia, using well water and rainwater while living remote from the mundane rhythms of everyday existence. From a small workroom in the Chiemgau region she produces designs and textile stamps, experiments with dye colours and makes products for her online shop. A studio of her own and a dye garden are pressing priorities for her future as a textile designer.

Be it a project of her own or work done on commission, each piece of hers is a one-off. Ribic's approach unites intuition and planning: she makes full use of available resources, combining old and new while reducing material waste to a minimum. Serendipity is welcome; a mistake becomes an idea. A love for detail lends her work its distinctive character. For her handmade one-offs she deliberately chooses a gradual work process that requires time, devotion and care.

02 PILLOW (2024)
DIFFERENT SIZES
HAND EMBROIDERED WITH THREAD NATURALLY
DYED WITH ACORNS
LINEN, COTTON CROCHET THREAD NATURAL
DYED WITH ACORNS

03 WALNUSS-WEICHE SCHALE, HARTER KERN
(2024)
DIFFERENT SIZES
NATURALLY DYED WITH WALNUT AT HIGH
TEMPERATURE
NATURAL LEFTOVER MATERIALS

04 JUTEGARN TRIFFT EICHELN (2024)
DIFFERENT SIZES
NATURALLY DYED WITH ACORNS AT HIGH
TEMPERATURE
JUTE YARN

02

03

04

DE Die Arbeit der 1992 geborenen Julia Ribic zeichnet sich durch eine tiefe Verbundenheit zur Natur und zu traditionellen Handwerken aus, insbesondere dem Pflanzenfärben. Bei Heimatbesuchen in Kroatien erlebte sie die jahrhundertealte Tradition des Färbens. Sie lernte, wie Leinen geerntet, Stoffe gewebt, mit filigranen Stickereien verziert und schließlich über offenem Feuer gefärbt werden. Besonders prägend war dabei das Wissen lokaler Akteurinnen, die dieses Handwerk schon seit Generationen weitergeben und Ribic einluden, Teil dieses lebendigen Kulturerbes zu werden.

Während ihrer Lehre zur Schreinerin vertiefte sie ihr Gespür für Form und Oberfläche, das sie durch ein Diplom in Produktdesign an der Universität Kassel gewissermaßen professionalisierte (2022). Ihr Label juliwetter_naturgefärbt gründete sie 2021. Es entstehen nachhaltige Textilien und Textilprodukte, die im Rhythmus der Jahreszeiten hergestellt und mit den entsprechend vorhandenen pflanzlichen Stoffen gefärbt werden. Ökologische Tragfähigkeit ist zentral für ihre Designs: Alles wird verwendet, bis hin zu kleinsten Stoffresten, die sie zu handge-schöpftem Papier weiterverarbeitet. Die natürlichen Farben überraschen sie im Gestaltungsprozess dabei stets aufs Neue. Erntezeitpunkt, Temperatur, Licht und Stoffstruktur beeinflussen das Ergebnis und lassen Raum für Intuition und Zufall.

Ribic arbeitet aktuell an drei Orten: Im Schwarzwald und Kroatien färbt sie die Textilien, nutzt Brunnen- und Regenwasser und lebt abseits alltäglicher Rhythmen. Im Chiemgau entstehen im kleinen Arbeitsraum Entwürfe, Stempel, Färbeexperimente und Produkte für den Onlineshop. Ein eigenes Atelier und ein Färbegarten haben große Priorität für ihre Zukunft als Textilgestalterin.

Ob freies Projekt oder Auftrag – jedes Stück ist ein Unikat. Ribics Herangehensweise verbindet Intuition mit Planung: Sie nutzt vorhandene Ressourcen, kombiniert Altes und Neues, reduziert materiellen Ausschuss auf ein Minimum. Zufälle sind willkommen, ein Fehler wird zur Idee. Ihre Liebe zum Detail verleiht ihren Arbeiten Charakter. Für ihre handgefertigten Unikate wählt sie bewusst einen langsamen Weg, der Zeit, Hingabe und Sorgfalt erfordert.

02

01 AMARILLO ES EL BOSQUE (2023)
1100 × 700 CM
NATURALLY DYED WITH WILLOW, BIRCH, OAK,
WALNUT, MULLEIN, NETTLES, FERNS
VARIOUS COTTONS

02 HOJA VERSO (2021)
210 × 150 CM
NATURALLY DYED
COTTON, BEECH PLANK

[179] Belén Rodríguez

EN Born in 1981, Belén Rodríguez has not taken any degrees or diplomas in classic textile design studies, yet her artistic praxis centres on textile materials. She seeks and finds sources of inspiration from observing the natural environment but also draws on art history - from ancient Egyptian animal motifs to Pre-Columbian gold artefacts. Rodríguez first graduated in fine arts from Universidad Complutense de Madrid before going on to study for a master's degree at the Akademie der bildenden Künste Wien, where she also took bachelor's and master's degrees in textual sculpture. She views herself as an exponent of fine art with a pronounced affinity for design and the applied arts, yet what she particularly appreciates about textiles as a medium for artistic expression is the open-endedness they afford. Dyeing and bleaching textiles especially and the requisite techniques have opened up for her a diverse range of patterns and forms that have given her artistic freedom. At first she worked with a lot of chemical bleaches on cotton fabrics, a solution that made it possible for her to work quickly - most notably where large surfaces were concerned. Yet going into materials in more depth, a fundamental change that took place in her through pregnancy and a move to the countryside have led to a conscious break with past practices: now she uses primarily natural pigments from her immediate surroundings, or lemon bleach, and experiments with shibori[1], marbling and ikat techniques[2]. The effect to be achieved by dyeing with a specific colour has lower priority than the underlying idea that organic substances such as leaves, bark and roots become integral elements of the artwork at a molecular level. Rodríguez's works are, as a result, decidedly conceptual and related to the natural environment. She is now living and working in the mountains of Cantabria. A wood she has bought across from her house serves not only as a natural resource she can draw on but also as an (artistic) intervention with the aim of forestalling the very real threat of deforestation.

[1] For an explanation, see p. 120.
[2] Ikat: a traditional resist-dyeing technique that allows patterns to be created even before weaving begins by binding the warp and/or weft yarns and dyeing the remainder in the colour(s) desired. The yarns are not arranged on the loom until after they have been dyed - the distinctive 'washed-out' or blurry look characteristic of the patterns is created by ensuring that the pre-dyed sections are precisely co-ordinated. This demanding technique exacts enormous skill of the practitioner along with a precise feeling for planning, colour and form.

03 HOJA VERSO (2021), DETAIL
210 × 150 CM
COTTON, BEECH PLANK

04 I DANCED MYSELF OUT OF THE WOMB
(2024)
240 × 1000 CM
NATURALLY DYED, SHIBORI
COTTON

05 AVCD + STRBRR + WTRMLN (2015)
227 × 155 CM
BLEACHED
COTTON, BEECH

DE Die 1981 geborene Belén Rodríguez hat kein klassisches Textildesign-Studium absolviert und dennoch stehen textile Materialien im Zentrum ihrer künstlerischen Praxis. Sie findet ihre Inspirationen durch Naturbeobachtungen, aber auch in der Kunstgeschichte - von altägyptischen Tiermotiven bis zur kolumbianischen Goldkunst. Rodríguez schloss an der Universidad Complutense de Madrid ihr erstes Studium in bildender Kunst ab, anschließend führte sie ihr Weg an die Akademie der bildenden Künste Wien, wo sie im Fach Textuelle Bildhauerei zusätzlich Bachelor und Master absolvierte. Sie versteht sich als freie Künstlerin mit einer starken Affinität zu Design und angewandter Kunst, doch schätzt sie gerade die Offenheit des Künstlerischen mit wesentlichem Bezug auf Textilien als Ausdrucksmittel. Besonders durch das Färben und Entfärben von Textilien, und den damit verbundenen Techniken erschlossen sich ihr eine Vielfalt an Mustern und Formen, die ihr gestalterische Freiheit ermöglichten. Zu Beginn arbeitete sie dafür viel mit chemischem Bleichmittel auf Baumwollstoffen, was ihr ein schnelles Arbeiten ermöglichte - besonders bei großen Flächen. Doch die tiefere Beschäftigung mit den Materialien, sowie ein grundlegender Wandel, der sich aufgrund einer Schwangerschaft und durch einen Umzug aufs Land ergab, führten zu einem bewussten Bruch: Heute nutzt sie vorwiegend natürliche Pigmente aus ihrer unmittelbaren Umgebung oder Zitronenbleiche und experimentiert mit Shibori[1], Marmorierungen und Ikat-Techniken[2]. Dabei steht weniger die Farbwirkung als vielmehr der Gedanke im Vordergrund, dass organische Substanzen wie Blätter, Rinde oder Wurzeln integraler molekularer Bestandteil des Kunstwerks werden. Rodríguez' Arbeiten sind dabei dezidiert konzeptuell und naturbezogen. Heute lebt und arbeitet sie in den Bergen Kantabriens. Ein Wald, den sie gegenüber ihrem Haus erwarb, dient nicht nur als Ressource, sondern auch als (künstlerische) Intervention gegen drohende Abholzung.

[1] Erläuterung vgl. S. 120.
[2] Ikat ist eine traditionelle Färbetechnik, bei der die Muster bereits vor dem Weben durch das Abbinden und gezielte Färben der Kett- und/oder Schussfäden entstehen. Erst nach der Färbung werden die Fäden auf dem Webstuhl angeordnet - das charakteristische „verwaschene" Aussehen der Muster entsteht dadurch, dass die vorgefärbten Bereiche beim Weben exakt aufeinander abgestimmt werden müssen. Die Technik erfordert großes handwerkliches Können und ein präzises Gespür für Planung, Farbe und Form.

04

05

03

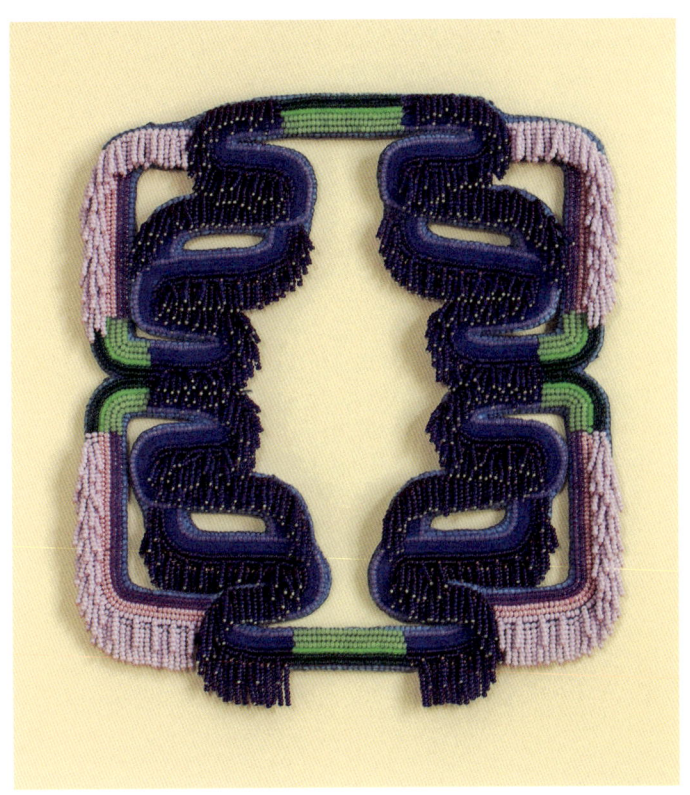

02

01 TAKE CARE (2024), DETAIL
235 × 175 CM
WOVEN
ACRYLIC BEADS, COTTON

02 NIEMANDSLAND (2021)
45 × 45 CM
EMBROIDERED
GLASS BEADS, FELT, COTTON

EN Larissa Schepers, born 1995, took a bachelor's degree in textile design at the Koninklijke Academie van Beeldende Kunsten Den Haag in 2019. In her work she unites traditional and contemporary practices with a special focus on bead work, a design process she has borrowed from historic costumes and the crafts traditions that produced them. This technique, which she links with knitting, weaving and embroidery, enables her to explore the various features specific to textile design and the freedoms it allows. She is particularly fascinated with the contrast between the rigidity of design in knitting with beads and the freedom that embroidery offers her. Her work transcends the boundaries of classic textile art. Schepers uses glass beads, a material traditionally associated with textile art yet one that constantly challenges it, particularly when it comes to functioning on a large scale. By working with beads, she creates soft, ductile textures that evoke manifold visual impressions. Her works are completely handmade. This detailed, time-consuming production process is for Schepers of the utmost importance; the value of a work lies not in the rapidity with which it is completed but rather in intensive involvement with the material itself. Larissa Schepers lives and works in Tilburg, an important textile city in the Netherlands. Her work builds on traditional techniques and develops new approaches to tradition through an experimental, collaborative approach. To execute her works she collaborates with other artists and is particularly interested in communal projects. The way she works often entails beginning with small, explorative pieces with which she tests new materials and techniques before going on to larger works. Her largest work, *Take Care* (2024), which took about a year for the concept to be developed and realised, shows her ability to complete large, complex projects with patient dedication.

03 TRIPPLE KILL (2020)
70 × 100 CM
WOVEN
ACRYLIC BEADS, COTTON

04 HEADSHOT (2020)
105 × 55 CM
WOVEN
ACRYLIC BEADS, COTTON

05 TAKE CARE (2024)
235 × 175 CM
WOVEN
ACRYLIC BEADS, COTTON

03

04

05

DE Larissa Schepers, geboren 1995, erlangte 2019 ihren Abschluss als textile Künstlerin an der Koninklijke Academie van Beeldende Kunsten Den Haag. In ihrer Arbeit verbindet sie traditionelle und zeitgenössische Praktiken mit besonderem Fokus auf verschiedenen Arten der Perlenarbeit – gestalterische Verfahren, die sie historischen Kostümen und deren Handwerkstraditionen entlehnt. Diese Technik, die sie mit Sticken, Stricken und Weben verbindet, ermöglicht es ihr, die verschiedenen Eigenheiten und Freiheiten der Textilgestaltung zu erforschen. Besonders fasziniert sie der Gegensatz zwischen den festgelegten Designs beim Stricken mit Perlen und der Freiheit, die die Stickerei ihr bietet. Ihr künstlerisches Schaffen geht über die Grenzen der klassischen Textilkunst hinaus. Schepers verwendet Glasperlen, ein Material, das traditionell zwar mit Textilkunst in Verbindung gebracht wird, diese jedoch trotzdem immer wieder herausfordert, besonders wenn es darum geht, in der großen Fläche wie Textilien zu funktionieren. Durch das Arbeiten mit Perlen erschafft sie weiche, formbare Texturen, die eine Vielzahl von visuellen Eindrücken hervor-

rufen. Ihre Werke sind komplett handgefertigt. Diese detailreiche und langsame Produktion ist für Schepers von zentraler Bedeutung – der Wert der Arbeit liegt nicht in der Geschwindigkeit, sondern in der intensiven Auseinandersetzung mit dem Material. Larissa Schepers lebt und arbeitet in Tilburg, einer bedeutenden Textilstadt in den Niederlanden. Ihre Arbeit baut auf den traditionellen Techniken auf und entwickelt durch ihr experimentelles, kollaboratives Arbeiten neue Zugänge zur Tradition. Für die Ausführung ihrer Werke kooperiert sie mit anderen Künstler:innen und ist besonders an Gemeinschaftsprojekten interessiert. Ihre Arbeitsweise beginnt oft mit kleinen, explorativen Stücken, mit denen sie neue Materialien und Techniken testet, bevor sie zu größeren Arbeiten übergeht. Ihr größtes Werk, *Take Care* (2024), das etwa ein Jahr in der Konzeptentwicklung und Umsetzung benötigte, zeigt ihre Fähigkeit, große, komplexe Projekte mit Hingabe und Geduld zu realisieren.

Working with textile is a calming ritual and a process that feels meditative – each turn of the yarn around the rope is a quiet, focused act. It is not about speed – it is more about being fully present with the material.

01 EFLORESCENCE (2024)
175 × 85 CM
HAND SEWN, COILED, GYMPED
DISCARDED ROPE, RESCUED, HAND-DYED YARN

[187] Joana Schneider

EN Born in 1990, Joana Schneider has been enthusiastic since childhood about textile techniques that reveal close links to fashion. In her teenage years she produced small works in textiles and was strongly influenced and supported in realising her plans to become an artist by both her mother and her grandmother. Schneider studied fashion and textiles at the Koninklijke Academie van Beeldende Kunsten in The Hague, graduating in 2018 with a bachelor's degree.

Her technique of choice in her work is 'gymping', a circular method of weaving. After finishing her studies, she developed this technique in collaboration with the TextielMuseum Tilburg while she was experimenting with possibilities for wrapping rope in yarn. In this way she creates installations that intervene in space and sculptural environments that interweave themes from natural and fictive worlds. Schneider works mainly with worn-out commercial fishing ropes and storage twines that she procures from a fishing-net maker in Katwijk. The material has to be unravelled and dried before it can be adapted for design. Using this technique enables her to create a wide range of individually coloured ropes, for which she uses natural dyeing methods such as, for instance, those used for dyeing with indigo or rose madder.

Schneider describes working with textiles as a physical and ritualised process that generates a meditative effect through repetitive acts and dealing with materials in a tactile, consistently hands-on way. She experiences wrapping ropes with yarn and hand stitching the wrapped ropes as calming practices and an ongoing attempt to be directly involved with the material she is handling.

Schneider sees herself as an artist rather than a designer. Her focus is on creating worlds and design narratives. To do this she allows herself to be inspired by designs yet does not aim for predefined results. Because her works in large formats, most notably her tapestries, are extremely elaborate and often take months or even years to complete, she works in close collaboration with a small team of assistants.

02 ROYAL BLUE FUTURE FOSSIL (2023)
150 × 160 × 40 CM
HAND SEWN, COILED, GYMPED
DISCARDED ROPE, VARIOUS YARNS

03 MOSS ROCK TOWER (2024)
HAND SEWN, COILED, GYMPED
DISCARDED ROPE, VARIOUS YARNS

04 FUTURE OCEAN #1/2 (2022), DETAIL
DIMENSIONS UNKNOWN
HAND SEWN, COILED, GYMPED
DISCARDED ROPE, VARIOUS YARNS

02

Joana Schneider, geboren 1990, begeistert sich seit ihrer Kindheit für textile Techniken, die einen engen Bezug zu Mode aufweisen. Schon als Jugendliche fertigte sie kleine textile Werke und wurde in ihrer künstlerischen Entwicklung von ihrer Mutter und Großmutter geprägt und unterstützt. Schneider studierte Mode und Textil an der Koninklijke Academie van Beeldende Kunsten in Den Haag und schloss 2018 mit einem Bachelor of Arts ab.

Ihr bevorzugtes Arbeitsmedium ist die Technik des »Gymping«, eine kreisförmige Webmethode. Diese Technik entwickelte sie nach ihrem Studium in Zusammenarbeit mit dem TextielMuseum Tilburg, als sie mit Möglichkeiten experimentierte, Seile in Garn zu wickeln. Auf dieses Weise erschafft sie raumgreifende Installationen und skulpturale Umgebungen, die Themen aus natürlichen und fiktiven Welten miteinander verweben. Schneider arbeitet vorwiegend mit abgenutzten Fischerei-Seilen und Lagergarnen, die sie von einem Netzhersteller in Katwijk bezieht, wobei das Material vor der gestalterischen Adaption entwirrt und getrocknet werden muss. Diese Technik ermöglicht es ihr, eine breite Palette an individuell gefärbten Seilen zu erschaffen, wobei sie unter anderem natürliche Färbemethoden wie Indigo oder Krapp verwendet.

Die Arbeit mit Textilien beschreibt Schneider als einen physischen und ritualisierten Prozess, der durch wiederholende Handlungen und den haptischen Umgang mit Materialien eine meditative Wirkung erzeugt. Das Wickeln des Garns um die Seile und das Handsticken der gewickelten Seile erfährt sie als beruhigende Praktiken und einen stetigen Versuch, im Umgang mit dem Material vollständig präsent zu sein.

Schneider sieht sich nicht als Designerin, sondern als Künstlerin. Ihr Fokus liegt auf dem Erschaffen von Welten und gestalterischen Narrativen, wobei sie sich durch Designs inspirieren lässt, sich aber nicht an vordefinierten Ergebnissen orientiert. Sie arbeitet eng mit einem kleinen Team von Assistent:innen zusammen, da ihre großformatigen Arbeiten, insbesondere die Wandteppiche, sehr aufwendig sind und oft Monate oder Jahre in Anspruch nehmen.

03

04

02

01 LOOK YOUTH (SOIL TO SOIL, 2024)
VARIOUS SIZES
CARDED AND COMBED, NEEDLE FELTED, HAND
EMBROIDERED, MACRAMÉ DETAILS
ALPACA WOOL, LINEN, SILK

02 MATERIAL SAMPLES (2024)
CARDED, MACHINE AND HAND SPUN
ALPACA WOOL

Sabrina Stadlober

Born in 1992, Sabrina Stadlober grew up in Upper Styria, a region of Austria in which closeness to the natural environment is part of everyday life. In her work she unites this profound love of nature with her conceptual design praxis. Driven by an interest in fashion, she started specialist training at an early age at a fashion school in Graz, studied fashion design at ESMOD in Munich and later took a master's degree at Polimoda in Florence in the Textiles from Farm to Fabric to Fashion master's programme, which was designed by Lidewij Edelkoort and Philip Fimmano. There she honed her feeling for textiles, crafts and ecological responsibility. As Stadlober sees it, sustainability is not a zeitgeist-related phenomenon but rather an integral principle of design thinking. Her view of circular design encompasses regenerative agriculture, materials ethics and transplanting pre-industrial techniques and technologies into the present. She views crafts as cultural praxis – as a synthesis of aesthetics, function and community. *Soil to Soil*, the couture collection she launched in 2024 and for which she returned to her native Austria, exemplifies this approach. The collection is based on untreated natural materials, including alpaca wool, linen and silk, showing that she consistently follows the Cradle to Cradle[1] design principle: the starting point is the earth, and that is where the materials are also intended to return after their usefulness has ended. The production process is marked by intensive research into materials and manual skills: they include sheering alpaca fleece and sorting the fibres as well as collaborating with regional spinning mills and with suppliers who produce under ethical conditions. The fabrics are decorated with weaving, needle felting, macramé, hand embroidery and natural dyeing techniques. In this way Stadlober takes on the entire creative process herself, producing tactile surfaces that inspire a conversation between human being, animal and material. *Soil to Soil* thus articulates existential cycles – from birth through growth to decline – in textile form.

[1] Cradle to Cradle (C2C): a concept which strives for a completely circular economy, in which products are designed in such a way that either they are biodegradable after use and return to the natural environment as nutrients, or they remain as technical nutrients remain in the manufacturing cycles and can be reused.

03 LOOK ADULTHOOD (SOIL TO SOIL, 2024)
VARIOUS SIZES
WOVEN ON A SHAFT LOOM AND A LOOM BOARD,
NEEDLE FELTED, HAND EMBROIDERED
ALPACA WOOL, SILK

04 LOOK MATURITY (SOIL TO SOIL, 2024)
VARIOUS SIZES
NATURALLY DYED, NEEDLE FELTED,
HAND EMBROIDERED
ALPACA WOOL, LINEN, SILK

05 LOOK ADOLESCENCE
(SOIL TO SOIL, 2024), DETAIL
450 × 40 CM
WOVEN ON A SHAFT LOOM
ALPACA WOOL

Geboren 1992, wuchs Sabrina Stadlober in der Obersteiermark auf - einer Region, in der die Nähe zur Natur zum Alltag gehört. In ihrer Arbeit verbindet sie diese tiefgreifende Naturverbundenheit mit ihrer konzeptionellen Gestaltungspraxis. Angetrieben durch ihr Interesse an Mode begann sie früh ihre Fachausbildung an einer Modeschule in Graz, studierte Modedesign an der ESMOD München und absolvierte später ihren Master an der Polimoda in Florenz, im Master-Programm Textiles from Farm to Fabric to Fashion, das von Lidewij Edelkoort und Philip Fimmano konzipiert wurde. Dort schärfte sie ihre Wahrnehmung von Textil, Handwerk und ökologischer Verantwortung. Für Stadlober ist Nachhaltigkeit kein zeitgeistgebundenes Phänomen, sondern ein integrales Prinzip gestalterischen Denkens. Ihr Verständnis von zirkulärem Design umfasst regenerative Landwirtschaft, Materialethik und die Überführung präindustrieller Techniken in die Gegenwart. Handwerk versteht sie als kulturelle Praxis - als Synthese von Ästhetik, Funktion und Gemeinschaft. Ihre 2024 entstandene Couture-Kollektion *Soil to Soil*, für die sie in ihre Heimat zurückkehrte, manifestiert diesen Ansatz exemplarisch. Die Kollektion basiert auf unbehandelten Naturmaterialien wie Alpakawolle, Leinen und Seide, womit sie konsequent dem Prinzip »Cradle to Cradle«[1] [dt. wörtl. »von der Wiege zur Wiege«] folgt: Ausgangspunkt ist der Boden - und dorthin sollen die Materialien am Ende der Nutzung auch wieder zurückkehren.
Der Produktionsprozess ist geprägt von intensiver Materialforschung und manueller Expertise: dazu gehörten das Scheren und Sortieren der Alpakafasern ebenso wie Kooperationen mit regionalen Spinnereien und unter ethischen Gesichtspunkten produzierenden Lieferant:innen. Die Veredelung der Stoffe erfolgt durch Weben, Nadelfilzen, Makramee, Handstickerei und natürliche Färbetechniken. Auf diese Weise übernimmt Stadlober den gesamten Entstehungsprozess und lässt taktile Oberflächen entstehen, die einen Dialog zwischen Mensch, Tier und Material anregen. *Soil to Soil* artikuliert so existenzielle Zyklen - von der Geburt über das Wachstum bis hin zur Vergänglichkeit - in textiler Form.

[1] »Cradle to Cradle« (C2C) ist ein Konzept, welches eine vollständige Kreislaufwirtschaft anstrebt, bei der Produkte so gestaltet sind, dass sie nach ihrer Nutzung entweder biologisch abbaubar sind und als Nährstoffe in die Natur zurückgeführt oder als technische Nährstoffe in Herstellungskreisläufen verbleiben und wiederverwendet werden können.

04

03

05

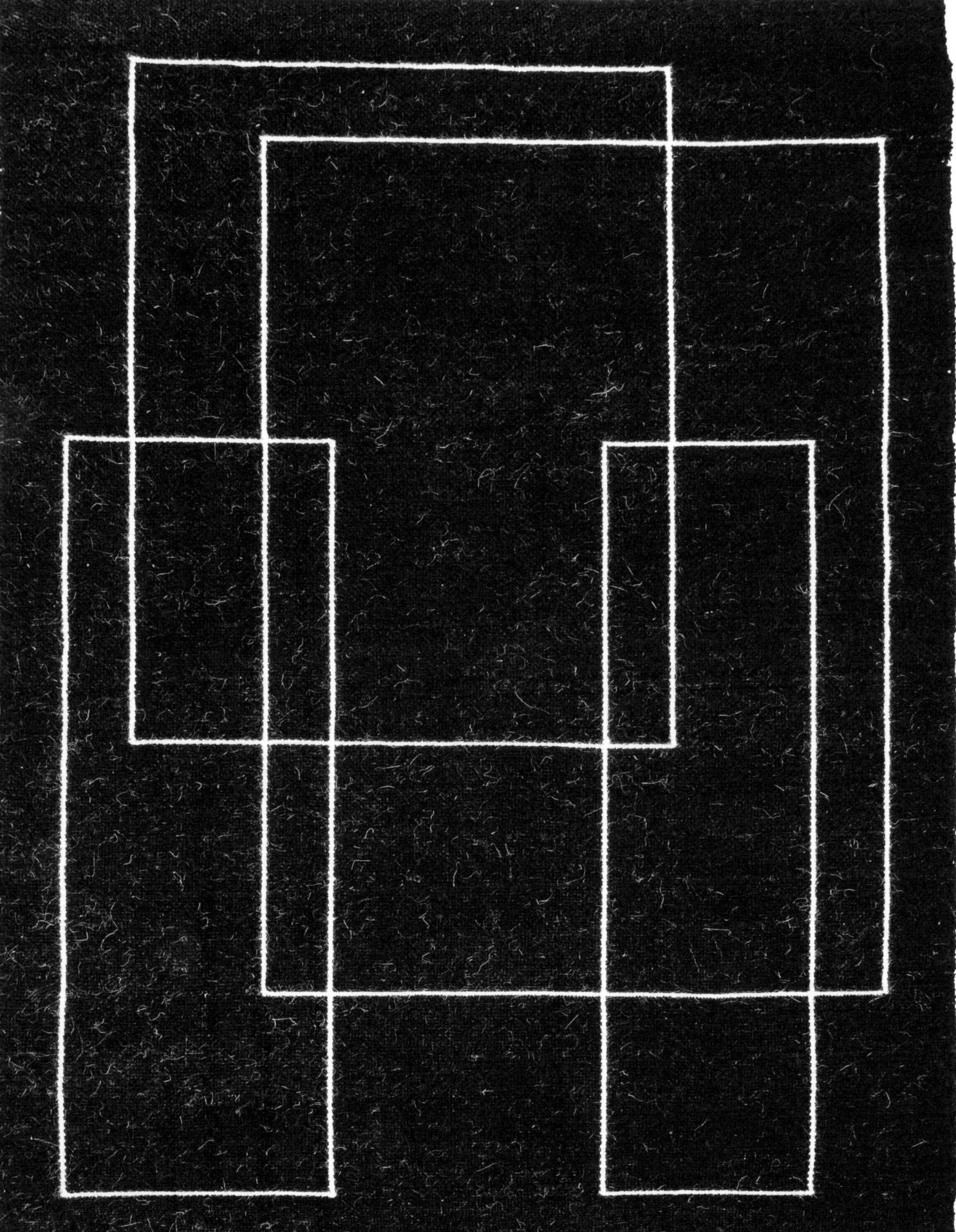

Weaving is the interlacing of threads, the definition of surface, the construction of spatiality. Aesthetics and simplicity find their expression in the woven fabric.

01 SCHICHTEN (2023)
210 × 140 CM
DOUBLE CLOTH WITH PARTIAL LAYER INTER-
CHANGE
GOAT WOOL

[195] Katja Stelz

EN Katja Stelz develops textiles for minimalist living environments in which graphic clarity and sensuous grace are united. The work she has produced in the last few years has focused on carpets in particular. She sees carpets as an architectonic element that defines space and directs movement through the interaction of line and surface. Born in 1960, Katja Stelz started out by serving a hand weaving apprenticeship in 1981 and deepened her interest in crafts by studying textile design at the Fachhochschule Hannover, a step that substantially shaped her development as an artist. At the handloom she creates carpets, woollen blankets, plaids and seat upholstery that are not just functional but also make an impact as art objects. The design of her carpets is based on consistent bicolour combined with an exciting interplay of line, surface and space. She makes these textile objects by applying the technique of double weaving, a traditional method in which a carpet is given two right sides so that it can be turned over – this means it has two faces, as it were. This technique also lends a carpet high durability and a perceptible warm feel. A double-face material also points to the original property of the fabric, that is, space as a surface-creating principle that evokes multidimensionality. The superposition of two layers of fabric by means of this weaving technique and their exchange makes the fabric an architectonic element. For her works she uses only natural materials such as wool, goat hair, mohair or silk, most of which she procures from European suppliers. She lives and works in Mecklenburg, in a small village where she runs her own workshop and weaves all her fabrics, from prototypes through work done on commission to individual carpets on a twelve-shaft table loom.

02 SIC (BELOW), LINE (TOP)(2019), DETAIL
EACH 140 × 210 CM
SIC: OWN TECHNIQUE; LINE: DOUBLE CLOTH
WITH PARTIAL LAYER INTERCHANGE
GOAT WOOL

03 NEUE RÄUME (2024)
210 × 140 CM
DOUBLE CLOTH WITH PARTIAL LAYER
INTERCHANGE
GOAT WOOL

04 M (2010)
150 × 210 CM
COLOUR INTERWEAVING IN PLAIN WEAVE
NEW WOOL

02

03

04

DE   Katja Stelz entwickelt Textilien für ein minimalistisches Wohnambiente, in dem sich grafische Klarheit und sinnliche Anmut verbinden. Insbesondere die Bodenteppiche haben in den letzten Jahren einen Schwerpunkt ihrer Arbeit gebildet. Sie begreift den Teppich als architektonisches Element, das durch den Wechsel von Linie und Fläche Raum definiert und Bewegung lenkt. Geboren 1960, begann Katja Stelz 1981 zuerst eine Lehre zur Handweberin und vertiefte ihr handwerkliches Interesse anschließend in einem Textildesignstudium an der Fachhochschule Hannover, was ihre künstlerische Entwicklung maßgeblich prägte. Am Handwebstuhl entstehen Bodenteppiche, Wolldecken, Plaids und Sitzpolster, die nicht nur funktional sind, sondern auch als künstlerische Objekte wirken. Die Grundlage für die Gestaltung ihrer Teppiche ist eine konsequente Zweifarbigkeit, kombiniert mit dem spannungsreichen Wechselspiel von Linie, Fläche und Raum. Gefertigt werden die textilen Objekte in der Technik des Doppelgewebes, einer traditionellen Methode, die dem Teppich zwei beachtenswerte Seiten verleiht, sodass dieser gewendet werden kann – er hat somit gleichsam zwei Wirkungsflächen. Diese Technik verleiht dem Teppich zudem eine hohe Strapazierfähigkeit und eine spürbare Wärme. Das Doppelgewebe verweist zusätzlich auf die ursprünglichste Eigenschaft des Gewebes als Raum bildendes Element, das mit der Mehrdimensionalität interagiert. Die durch diese Webtechnik entstehende Überlagerung zweier Gewebeschichten und der partielle Austausch macht das Gewebe zu einem architektonischen Element. Für ihre Arbeiten verwendet sie ausschließlich natürliche Materialien wie Wolle, Ziegenhaar, Mohair oder Seide, welche sie zu großen Teilen aus europäischen Produktionen bezieht. Sie lebt und arbeitet in Mecklenburg, in einem kleinen Dorf, wo sie ihre eigene Werkstatt betreibt und auf ihrem 12-Schäfte-Webstuhl alle Gewebe fertigt, von Prototypen über Auftragsarbeiten bis hin zu individuellen Teppichen.

The desire to weave – to create from the material itself – grows from the beginning of each work to its completion. ... I hope that you can feel the heartbeat in my works, the joy of weaving, the delight in creating, the free play of imagination tamed by the technique of weaving.

[199] Gunta Stölzl

EN Gunta Stölzl (1897–1983) was a visionary textile artist who exerted a formative influence on modern textile design, in particular through her unique position as the sole woman instructor to have attained Master status at the Bauhaus - an outstanding example of artistic innovation and female assertiveness in the early twentieth century.

Her works unite crafts, fine art and design in her own inimitable way and reflect the Bauhaus spirit: functional, experimental and radically modern. Stölzl came into contact with art and design early on. After the First World War she began studying at the recently founded Bauhaus in Weimar. There she initially found one of the few possibilities open to women to pursue weaving, yet Stölzl took advantage of the opportunity offered her to radically revolutionise textile design. Turning away from traditional patterns, she developed a new language of forms, characterised by clarity of line, luminous colour and geometric abstraction.

Deploying a marked flair for design and profound technical skill, she made weaving a modern medium for textile design and sought ways to link lofty aesthetic standards and functional production suitable for everyday living. In 1925 she became a Work Master at the new Bauhaus site in Dessau and not long afterwards was officially appointed head of the weaving studio there. Under her management, that division became one of the most innovative, productive and, not least, the most lucrative in terms of sales because, once developed, the product designs appealed to a broad market segment. Nonetheless, for all her successes, she was constantly confronted with prejudice against women. Under political and personal pressure she left the Bauhaus in 1931. In Switzerland she joined other former Bauhaus employees in founding a collective studio of their own, where she continued to design, weave and teach for the rest of her life. Gunta Stölzl revolutionised textile design. Her works are not only significant milestones in art history but also the expression of a visionary outlook: that design can be more than just beautiful, can also be fulfilling and meaningful and, therefore, make a relevant impact on society.

02 MIT GEWENDETEM SCHÜTZEN #1 (1923)
260 × 112 CM
JACQUARD
WARP: COTTON; WEFT: WOOL, VISCOSE

03 DESIGN FOR TEXTILE (1926)
31 × 19 CM ON SHEET 35.8 × 25 CM
DRAWING
WATERCOLOUR, GOUACHE, PENCIL

04 WALL HANGING (1926)
139 × 90 CM
ATLAS, REP AND BASKET (PANAMA) WEAVES
WOOL, RAYON, BOUCLÉ

02

03

04

DE   Gunta Stölzl (1897–1983) war eine visionäre Textilkünstlerin, die das moderne Textildesign maßgeblich prägte, insbesondere durch ihre Position als erste und einzige weibliche Werkmeisterin am Bauhaus - ein herausragendes Beispiel für künstlerische Innovation und weibliche Durchsetzungskraft im frühen 20. Jahrhundert.

Ihre Arbeiten verbinden auf einzigartige Weise Handwerk, Kunst und Design und spiegeln den Geist des Bauhauses wider: funktional, experimentell und radikal modern. Stölzl kam schon früh mit Kunst und Gestaltung in Berührung. Nach dem Ersten Weltkrieg begann sie 1919 ihr Studium am neu gegründeten Bauhaus in Weimar. Dort fand sie in der Weberei zunächst eine der wenigen Möglichkeiten, sich als Frau handwerklich zu verwirklichen - doch Stölzl nutzte diese Chance, um textile Gestaltung grundlegend zu erneuern. Sie wandte sich von traditionellen Mustern ab und entwickelte eine neue Formensprache, geprägt von klaren Linien, leuchtenden Farben und geometrischer Abstraktion.

Mit großem gestalterischen Gespür und technischem Wissen machte sie die Weberei zu einem modernen Medium für Textilgestaltung und suchte Wege, künstlerischen Anspruch und funktionale, alltagstaugliche Produktion miteinander zu verbinden. 1925 wurde sie Werkmeisterin am neuen Bauhaus-Standort in Dessau, wenig später zur offiziellen Leiterin des Webereiateliers ernannt. Unter ihrer Führung wurde dieser Bereich zu einem der innovativsten und produktivsten und, nicht zuletzt, umsatzstärksten der Schule, da die entwickelten Entwürfe und Produkte ein breites Marktspektrum fanden. Trotz ihrer Erfolge war sie immer wieder mit Vorurteilen gegenüber Frauen konfrontiert. 1931 verließ sie das Bauhaus unter politischem und persönlichem Druck. In der Schweiz gründete sie zusammen mit ehemaligen Bauhaus-Mitgliedern ein eigenes Atelier, in dem sie bis zu ihrem Tod weiterhin entwarf, webte und unterrichtete.

Gunta Stölzl hat das Textildesign revolutioniert. Ihre Werke sind nicht nur kunsthistorisch bedeutsam, sondern auch Ausdruck einer Vision: dass Gestaltung nicht nur schön, sondern auch sinnstiftend und gesellschaftlich wirksam sein kann.

I love to build with threads; the fluidity of the line is endlessly inspiring for me.

01 DANGEROUS FOOL (2022)
ONE SIZE
CROCHETED, TUFTED
VARIOUS YARNS

EN threadstories is performatively involved with digital space for the most part anonymously. Very few people know the female-presenting person, born in 1980, behind the name. threadstories creates portraits of an unsettled time, in which identity and information often appear polysemic, constructed and malleable. Viewed against that background, the artistic interest pursued by threadstories targets the mutability of knowledge, appearance and self-image. Handmade art objects – mask-like configurations formed of textile materials – fulfil a dual function: they veil and transform at the same time. These are usually flexible, wearable forms that do not possess a firm shape. They can be constantly remodelled and, therefore, make possible transformation, deception and ambiguity. In a performative act the objects are staged before the camera, with threadstories acting as author, wearer and photographer. With the aid of a cable release, intimate self-portraits emerge to develop an impact that is stunningly sculptural. The masks themselves continue to evolve for years, being reinterpreted and thus becoming the expression of an ongoing artistic process that is constantly changing. The artist draws on traditional textile techniques that she learnt in childhood in her family environment. Studying at the Technological University Dublin from 2000 to 2004 enabled the artist to add a sculptural dimension to the crafts skills she already possessed. Ten years after she finished her studies, these two experiential spaces fused into a unique praxis, where textiles are not just material but also the vehicle for the concept. In the meantime, her works are created in her own studio and are strongly shaped by the idea of the artist conducting a dialogue with the material – not to impose meaning on it but also to develop new narratives from its flexibility, texture and tactility.

02 PERSONA 01 (2021)
ONE SIZE
CROCHETED
ACRYLIC YARN, ROPE

03 PERSONA 14 (2021)
ONE SIZE
CROCHETED, TUFTED, HAND DYED
VARIOUS YARNS

04 PERSONA 05 (2021)
ONE SIZE
CROCHETED, TUFTED, HAND DYED
VARIOUS YARNS

02

03

DE threadstories bespielt den digitalen Raum größtenteils anonym. Nur wenige kennen die weiblich gelesene Person, geboren 1980, hinter dem Namen. threadstories erschafft Porträts einer unsteten Zeit, in der Identität und Information oft mehrdeutig, konstruiert und formbar erscheinen. Das künstlerische Interesse von threadstories gilt vor diesem Hintergrund der Wandelbarkeit von Wissen, Erscheinung und Selbstbild. Die handgefertigten Kunstobjekte - maskenartige Gebilde aus Textil - erfüllen eine doppelte Funktion: Sie verschleiern und verwandeln zugleich. Diese meist flexiblen, tragbaren Formen besitzen keine feste Gestalt. Sie lassen sich immer wieder neu modellieren und ermöglichen so Transformation, Täuschung und Mehrdeutigkeit. In einem performativen Akt werden die Objekte vor der Kamera inszeniert - threadstories agiert dabei gleichzeitig als Schöpferin, Trägerin und Fotografin. Mithilfe eines Fernauslösers entstehen intime Selbstporträts, die eine geradezu skulpturale Wirkung entfalten. Die Masken selbst werden über Jahre hinweg weiterentwickelt, neu interpretiert und so zum Ausdruck eines sich kontinuierlich wandelnden künstlerischen Prozesses. Die Künstlerin greift auf traditionelle textile Techniken zurück, die sie bereits im familiären Umfeld ihrer Kindheit erlernte. Diese handwerklichen Fähigkeiten konnte die Künstlerin in den Jahren 2000 bis 2004 während ihres Studiums an der Technological University of Dublin um die skulpturale Dimension erweitern. Zehn Jahre nach ihrem Abschluss verschmolzen diese beiden Erfahrungsräume zu einer einzigartigen Praxis, in der Textil nicht nur Material, sondern auch Konzeptträger ist. Ihre Arbeiten entstehen inzwischen in einem eigenen Atelier und sind stark geprägt von der Idee, mit dem Material im Dialog zu stehen - nicht um ihm Bedeutung aufzustülpen, sondern um aus dessen Beweglichkeit, Textur und Haptik neue Erzählungen zu entwickeln.

05 PERSONA 04 (2021)
ONE SIZE
CROCHETED, TUFTED
ACRYLIC YARN

04

05

02

01 ANIMATED CORSETRY — DRESS (2025)
VARIOUS SIZES
FALSE LACE (COMPUTER-ASSISTED DOUBLE-
LAYERED PLAIN KNIT WITH RUNNING FLOATS),
FLOATS
POLYAMIDE, POLYAMIDE ELASTIC

02 ANIMATED CORSETRY SERIES (2024)
VARIOUS SIZES
FALSE LACE (COMPUTER-ASSISTED DOUBLE-
LAYERED PLAIN KNIT WITH RUNNING FLOATS)
LINEN, COTTON ELASTIC

Zuzana Vrábeľová

EN Zuzana Vrábeľová, born 2000, grew up in a Slovakian village steeped in folklore. Her approach to textiles was equally shaped by industrial fast fashion and, during her youth, by familial crafts traditions. Crochet laces, coarse hemp fabrics and her grandmother's intricately embroidered linen cloths awakened in her a feeling for material as a vehicle for culture at an early age.

Although she enrolled in the fashion course at the Textilhögskolan in Borås, which she completed with a master's degree in 2025, her praxis is interdisciplinary, moving between textile art, sculpture and the body. Her approach is intuitive, processual and emphatically material-based; decisions are taken on the fly, material samples replace classic sketches. Vrábeľová experiments with unusual fibres such as paper yarn made from Manila hemp[1], unspun wool and water-soluble PVA yarn.[2]

Working with elastic threads has also whetted her interest and she describes such threads as 'invisible forces' that lend textiles tension and liveliness. Her works are generated in a dialogue with the material; she pursues its idiosyncratic properties, its resistance and transformational potential. She views knitting in particular as an organic deceleration process, in which textile organisms slowly grow – without being constrained to a human scale. Vrábeľová sees her time-consuming work process as analogous to physical training. She experiences the slow but steady growth of a textile organism as a ritual through which she gains meditative access to the creative process. Her textile idiom is tactile and intuitive. She is interested in the interstices between human and animal states of being, in organic processes and transgressing natural forms. What began as a material study of a cultural legacy – skin, leather, hide, feathers – has developed into autonomy: the upshot is the emergence of alien skins, odd body parts, textile chimaeras. She envisages her future work as an autonomous experimental intersectional praxis where design, textile and art meet.

[1] Manila hemp: leaf fibre that is obtained from the leaf stalks of the abaca plant, a species of banana that grows mainly in the Philippines. These fibres are extraordinarily tear-resistant, light and durable.
[2] PVA: Polyvinyl acetate, a water-soluble plastic.

03 STUMP ROOT DRAPERY (2024)
VARIOUS SIZES
PLAIN KNIT, FLOATS
MANILA HEMP, COMFIL (THERMOPLASTIC YARN)

04 RUBBER BEAR SUIT (2022)
VARIOUS SIZES
CROCHETED RUBBER BANDS ON A NET BACKING
RUBBER BANDS, COTTON NET

05 DEAD FLOWER BOUQUET (2024)
VARIOUS SIZES
PLAIN KNIT
COMFIL (THERMOPLASTIC YARN), UNTWISTED VISCOSE

DE Zuzana Vrábeľová, geboren 2000, ist in einem folkloristisch geprägten Dorf in der Slowakei aufgewachsen. Ihr textiles Verständnis wurde gleichermaßen durch die industrielle Fast Fashion, während ihrer Jugend, sowie durch handwerkliche Familientraditionen geformt. Gehäkelte Spitzen, grobe Hanfstoffe und kunstvoll bestickte Leinentücher ihrer Großmutter weckten früh ihr Gespür für Material als kultureller Träger.

Obwohl sie im Modestudiengang an der Swedish School of Textiles in Borås eingeschrieben war – den sie 2025 mit dem Master abgeschlossen hat –, bewegt sich ihre Praxis zwischen Textilkunst, Skulptur und Körper. Ihr Ansatz ist intuitiv, prozessorientiert und stark materialbasiert – Entscheidungen entstehen im Tun, Materialproben ersetzen klassische Skizzen. Vrábeľová experimentiert mit ungewöhnlichen Garnen wie Papiergarn aus Manila-Hanf[1], ungesponnener Wolle oder wasserlöslichem PVA-Garn.[2] Auch das Arbeiten mit elastischen Fäden weckt ihr Interesse und sie beschreibt diese als „unsichtbare Kräfte", die den Textilien Spannung und Lebendigkeit verleihen. Ihre Werke entstehen im Dialog mit dem Material – sie folgt dessen Eigenheiten, Widerständen und Transformationspotenzialen. Besonders das Stricken begreift sie als entschleunigten, organischen Prozess, in dem textile Körper langsam wachsen – ohne sich am menschlichen Maß zu orientieren. Vrábeľová begreift ihr zeitaufwendiges Arbeiten analog zu körperlichem Training. Das langsame aber stetige Wachsen eines textilen Körpers erfährt sie als Ritual, wodurch sie einen meditativen Zugang zum Entstehungsprozess gewinnt. Ihre textile Sprache ist haptisch und intuitiv. Sie interessiert sich für Räume zwischen menschlichen und kreatürlichen Verfassungen, für organische Prozesse und für das Überschreiten natürlicher Formen. Was als materielle Auseinandersetzung mit einem kulturellen Erbe begann – Haut, Leder, Fell, Federn – entwickelte eine Eigenständigkeit: es entstehen fremdartige Häute, merkwürdige Körperteile, textile Chimären. Ihre zukünftige Arbeit sieht sie in einer unabhängigen, experimentellen Praxis zwischen Design, Textil und Kunst.

[1] Manila-Hanf: Blattfaser, die aus der Abacá-Pflanze, einer Bananenart, die hauptsächlich auf den Philippinen wächst, gewonnen wird. Die Fasern sind außerordentlich reißfest, leicht und langlebig.
[2] PVA: Polyvinylalkohol, wasserlöslicher Kunststoff.

04

05

Textiles, for me, are a means that serve as a bridge between what our skin knows and technology. In my design practice, I harness the potential of materials as interfaces that respond to touch, temperature and movement.

01 FRISSON (2024)
MADE TO MEASURE
OWN TECHNIQUE
LATEX, TPU, BIOSENSORS, MOTORS

Iga Węglińska

EN   Born in 1986, Iga Węglińska combines fashion, materials science and technology in her work. She focuses on developing smart materials and studying human-computer interaction (HCI). This approach sees textiles function as the interface between the human body and technology; they react to external stimuli, communicate with their surroundings and make possible new forms of interaction that transcend purely aesthetic functions. Węglińska's interdisciplinary background includes training at the Cracow School of Art and Fashion Design, and bachelor (2012) and master (2014) degrees at the Faculty of Industrial Design at the Academy of Fine Arts in Cracow. In 2021 she took a doctorate in art in which she featured her specialisation in new technologies in the fields of fashion and industrial design.

Her artistic praxis centres on developing wearable objects that infringe the boundaries set for classic clothing and function as lively, reactive systems that interact directly with the human body and, therefore, broaden perceptions of it. Węglińska describes her experimental wearables as emotional tools or post-human means of communication that challenge conventional notions of fashion.

To realise the potential of her materials, she combines traditional textile techniques with modern technologies such as prototyping, electronics and 3D scanning. She sees textiles not merely as a visual medium but primarily as a sensory one that reacts to touch, temperature and movement. The tensions between soft materials that are similar to skin - sticky, elastic, flesh-like - and hard synthetic materials such as plastic that represent challenges for the design process are particularly fascinating to her. She is currently living and working in Poznań where she runs her own design studio. In addition, she works as an assistant professor with self-employed status, heads the Fashion Design Department at the Academy of Arts in Stettin. She also teaches Colour, Material, Finish Design and Textile Futures at the SWPS University in Warsaw.

02 RESEARCH ON SAMPLES FOR THE EMOTIONAL CLOTHING (2021)
10 × 10 CM, 6 PIECES
MIXED TECHNIQUE
PE, BIOSENSORS, MICROPROCESSORS, CONDUCTIVE FABRICS, THERMOCHROMIC PIGMENT, POLYMER COATING

03 RESEARCH ON SAMPLES FOR THE EMOTIONAL CLOTHING (2021)
10 × 10 CM
OWN TECHNIQUE
TPU, THERMOCHROMIC PIGMENT, POLYMER COATING

04 EMOTIONAL CLOTHING (2021)
MADE TO MEASURE
MIXED TECHNIQUE: SEWN, CAST, WELDED, EMBROIDERED, SOLDERED, 3D PRINTED
PU, SILICONE, POLYESTER, PLA, BIOSENSORS, MICROPROCESSORS

DE   Iga Węglińska, geboren 1986, vereint in ihrer Arbeit Mode, Materialwissenschaft und Technologie. Ihr Schwerpunkt liegt auf der Entwicklung intelligenter Materialien und der Erforschung der Mensch-Computer-Interaktion (HCI). Dabei fungieren Textilien als Schnittstelle zwischen Körper und Technologie – sie reagieren auf äußere Reize, kommunizieren mit ihrer Umgebung und ermöglichen neue Formen der Interaktion, die über rein ästhetische Funktionen hinausgehen. Węglińskas interdisziplinärer Hintergrund umfasst eine Ausbildung an der Krakauer Schule für Kunst und Modedesign sowie Bachelor (2012) und Master (2014) an der Fakultät für Industriedesign der Akademii Sztuk Pięknych w Krakowie. 2021 promovierte sie im Bereich Kunst mit dem Schwerpunkt Neue Technologien in Mode und Industriedesign.

Das zentrale Anliegen ihrer künstlerischen Praxis ist dabei die Entwicklung tragbarer Objekte, die die Grenzen klassischer Kleidung überschreiten und als lebendige, reaktive Systeme funktionieren. Diese interagieren direkt mit dem menschlichen Körper und erweitern die Wahrnehmung dessen. Węglińska beschreibt ihre experimentellen Wearables als emotionale Werkzeuge oder posthumane Kommunikationsmittel, die ein etabliertes Verständnis von Mode herausfordern.

In der Umsetzung ihrer Materialien kombiniert sie traditionelle textile Techniken mit modernen Technologien wie Prototyping, Elektronik oder 3D-Scans. Sie betrachtet Textilien nicht nur als visuelles, sondern vor allem als sensorisches Medium, das auf Berührung, Temperatur und Bewegung reagiert. Besonders fasziniert sie die Spannung zwischen weichen, hautähnlichen Materialien – klebrig, elastisch, fleischlich - und harten, künstlichen Stoffen wie Plastik, die den Gestaltungsprozess herausfordern. Derzeit lebt und arbeitet sie in Poznań wo sie ihr eigenes Designstudio leitet. Zusätzlich ist sie als selbstständige Assistenzprofessorin tätig und leitet die Abteilung für Modedesign an der Akademia Sztuki w Szczecinie. Zudem unterrichtet sie Color, Material, Finish Design and Textile Futures an der School of Form der SWPS University of Social Sciences and Humanities in Warschau.

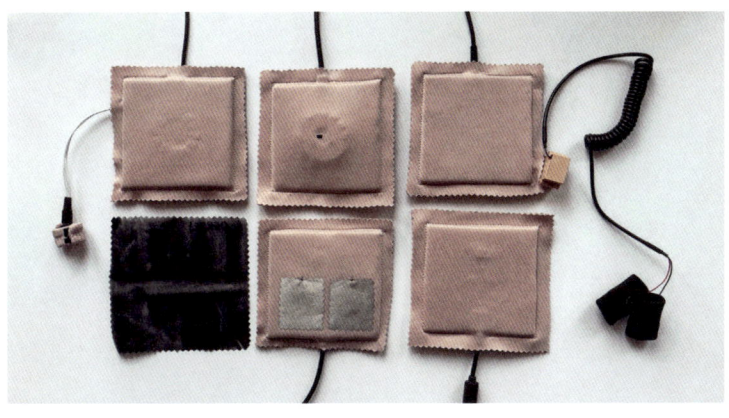

02

04

03

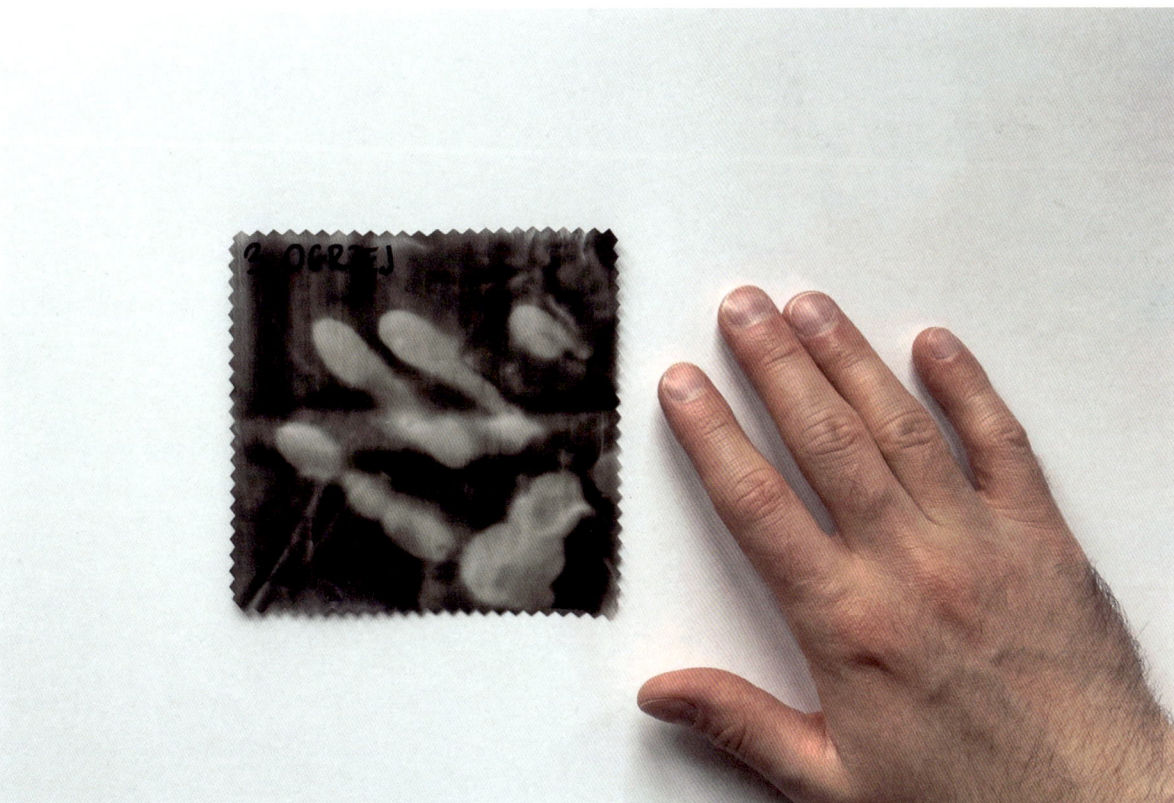

02

01 WIESERGUT (2016), DETAIL
DESIGNHOTEL WIESERGUT,
SAALBACH-HINTERGLEMM
150 × 230 CM (DETAIL)
HAND LAID, NEEDLE FELTED
WOOL

02 MICA 01,02,03 UNIKAT (2018), DETAIL
2 × 160 CM, 1 × 240 CM
HAND LAID IN A CRICLE, NEEDLE FELTED
BY MACHINE
WOOL

EN Lara Wernert, born in 1986, is one of the two minds behind the carpet manufactory 13RUGS by Rohi, alongside Tina Wendler. The company focuses on creating new design products using recycled materials from the textile industry. With a fashion degree from the University of Applied Sciences (HTW) in Berlin and subsequent studies in textile design at the Burg Giebichenstein University of Art and Design in Halle, Lara Wernert began early on to explore sustainable material use and the conscious handling of resources in fashion production. In her thesis, she developed a concept for creating textile products from leftover materials, which led her to connect with the company Rohi, based in Geretsried, Bavaria. Lara made use of wool selvedges – waste materials that are produced in large quantities in the textile industry – and transformed them into textile surfaces. After her initial designs, a collaboration with Rohi quickly developed, one that continues to this day.

Initiated by Katrin Hielle-Dahm, who alongside Tina Wendler is managing director of Rohi, Wernert and Wendler began working closely together and further explored ways to transform the company's production surplus into unique carpets. This process ultimately led to the founding of the 13RUGS manufactory in 2015. To this day, each piece is designed and produced by hand. Once a design is completed, each wool selvedge is loosely placed on a base material and wadding for stabilization, and then basted by hand. These layers are subsequently bonded through a multi-step felting process, with technical support from the Saxon Textile Research Institute in Chemnitz, which has been assisting Lara Wernert since the beginning. Through this collaboration, the production process has been refined over time, resulting in a distinct tactile quality in the textile product. This approach enables consistent local production in Germany – something rare in the carpet industry. The upcycled rugs are characterized by subtle color gradients, exceptional quality, and aesthetics, becoming textile artworks for both the wall and the floor.

03 AQUA AMBER (2015)
150 × 230 CM
HAND LAID, NEEDLE FELTED
WOOL

04 WOLKENGRAU (2020)
220 × 150 CM
HAND LAID, NEEDLE FELTED
WOOL

DE Die 1986 geborene Lara Wernert steht zusammen mit Tina Wendler für die Teppichmanufaktur 13RUGS by Rohi, die mit recycelten Materialien aus der Textilindustrie neue, hochwertige Produkte entwickelt.

Durch ihr Modestudium an der Hochschule für Technik und Wirtschaft in Berlin und das anschließende Studium in Conceptual Textile Design an der Kunsthochschule Burg Giebichenstein in Halle, hat sich Lara Wernert früh mit Möglichkeiten eines nachhaltigen Materialverbrauchs und dem bewussten Umgang mit Ressourcen in der Modeproduktion beschäftigt. In ihrer Abschlussarbeit erarbeitete sie ein Konzept zur Herstellung von textilen Produkten aus Restmaterialien und kam mit dieser Idee mit der Firma Rohi aus Geretsried in Bayern in Kontakt. Wernert machte Gebrauch von Wollwebkanten, die im Bereich der Industrie in großen Mengen anfallen, und verarbeitete diese zu textilen Flächen. Nach ersten Entwürfen entwickelte sich schnell eine Kooperation mit der Firma Rohi, die bis heute anhält.

Initiiert von Katrin Hielle-Dahm, neben Tina Wendler Geschäftsführerin von Rohi, kam es zur Teamarbeit und es wurde weiter an einer Methode geforscht, um Produktionsüberschüsse der Firma zu Teppichunikaten zu verarbeiten. Daraus ging 2015 die Manufaktur 13RUGS hervor. Bis heute werden die Unikate in Handarbeit entworfen und produziert. Nach der Fertigstellung eines Entwurfs wird jede Webkante lose zur Stabilisierung auf einen Rohstoff sowie über ein Hilfsvlies gelegt und von Hand vorgeheftet. Anschließend werden diese Schichten in einem mehrstufigen Filzverfahren verbunden, wofür das Sächsische Textilforschungsinstitut e.V. in Chemnitz Lara Wernert seit Beginn zur Seite steht. Eine durchgehend lokale Produktion in Deutschland wird so möglich, was im Bereich der Teppichproduktion sonst selten der Fall ist. Die Upcyclingteppiche zeichnen sich durch feine Farbverläufe und durch außergewöhnliche Qualität und Ästhetik aus und werden zu textilen Kunstwerken für die Wand genauso wie für den Boden.

03

04

III APPENDIX

59-62 MAGDALENA ABAKANOWICZ
01, 02, 03 ©EAST NEWS, WARSAW, 04 ISABEVLEER, CC BY-SA 4.0 WIKIMEDIA COMMONS, 05 SZCZEBRZESZYNSKI, CC BY-SA 4.0 WIKIMEDIA COMMONS

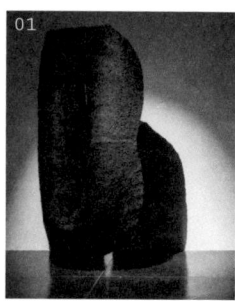 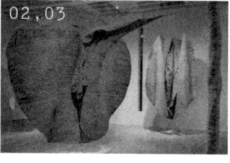  

63-66 CAROLINE ACHAINTRE
01 ANNABEL ELSTON, COURTESY OF THE ARTIST, ART : CONCEPT, PARIS, 02 ANDY KEATE, COURTESY OF THE ARTIST AND VON BARTHA, BASEL/ COPENHAGEN, 03, 05 ROMAIN DARNAUD, COURTESY OF THE ARTIST, ART : CONCEPT, PARIS, 04 INSTALLATION VIEW NEUES MUSEUM NUREMBERG, STEFAN RHONER, COURTESY OF THE ARTIST, 06 JENNA BARBEROT

 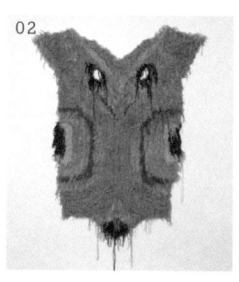 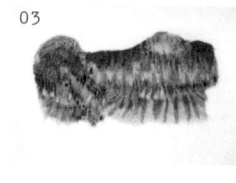   

67-70 ELFI BAUMGARTNER
01 KURT SCHOLZ, 02 PHILIPP SCHÖNBORN, 03 HANS GOSTNER, 04 MARIANNA MOOSBRUGGER

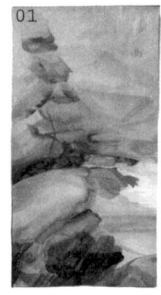   

71-74 OTTI BERGER
01 BPK | KUNSTSAMMLUNGEN CHEMNITZ | MAY VOIGT, 02, 03 © METROPOLITAN MUSEUM OF ART, NEW YORK / CC0 1.0 UNIVERSAL, 04 © ART INSTITUTE CHICAGO / CC0 1.0 UNIVERSAL

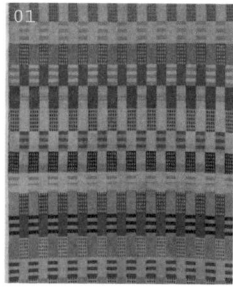 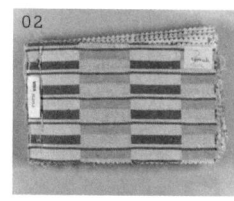 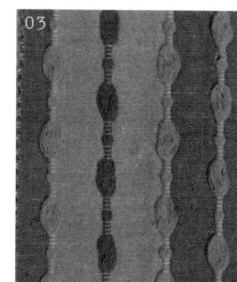  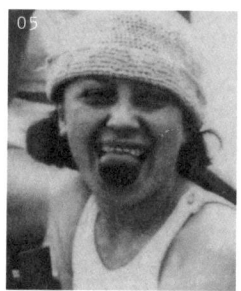

75-78 EMMA DAHLQVIST
01 CLARA BODÉN, 02, 03, 04 EMMA DAHLQVIST

79-82 SOFIE DAWO
01, 02, 03, 04 JOCHUM RODGERS, BERLIN, 05 LABORATORIUM, INSTITUT FÜR AKTUELLE KUNST IM SAARLAND AN DER HOCHSCHULE DER BILDEN-
DEN KÜNSTE SAAR MIT FORSCHUNGSZENTRUM FÜR KÜNSTLERNACHLÄSSE

 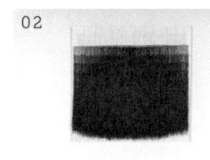 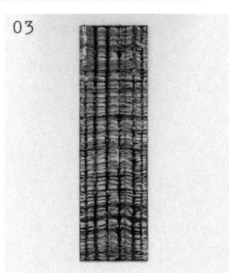 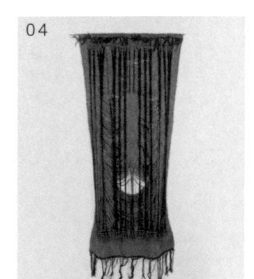 

83-86 LUCIENNE DAY
01, 02, 03 © ROBIN & LUCIENNE DAY FOUNDATION, 04 © ROBIN & LUCIENNE DAY FOUNDATION / JOHN GAY

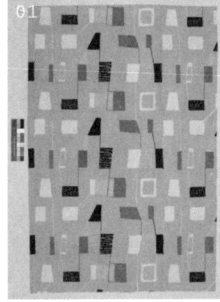 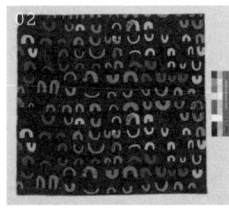 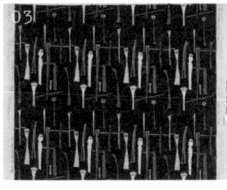 

87-90 PAULINE VAN DONGEN
01 LISELOTTE FLEUR, 02, 03, 05 ANNA WETZEL, 04 LISELOTTE FLEUR, 06 ANOUK MOERMAN

  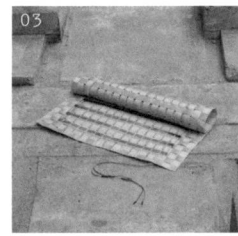   

91-94 ANNETTE DOUGLAS
01 ANNETTE DOUGLAS, 02, 03, 04 MARCEL GRUBENMANN, 05 MIRJAM KLUKA

 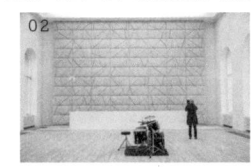  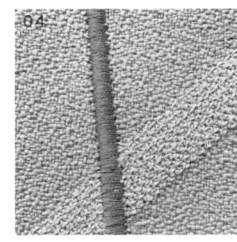 

95-98 MAE ENGELGEER
01, 02, 03, 04 N/J STUDIO, 05 HIDENORI SUZUKI

 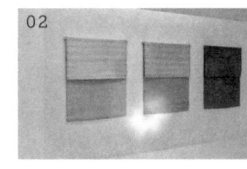   

99-102 CHRISTIANE ENGLSBERGER
01, 03 KURT SALHOFER, 02, 04, 05, 06 CHRISTIANE ENGLSBERGER

 01
 02
 03
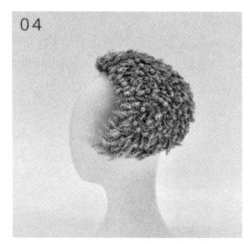 04
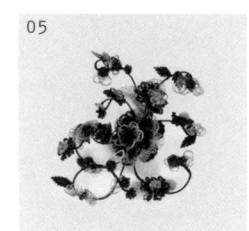 05
 06

103-106 CÉCILE FEILCHENFELDT
01, 04 AURELIE CENNO, PURCHASED BY THE MUSEUM FÜR KUNST UND GEWERBE HAMBURG (MKG), 02, 05 SUSANNE STEMMER,
03 AURELIE CENNO, 06 JULIA VON DER HEIDE

 01
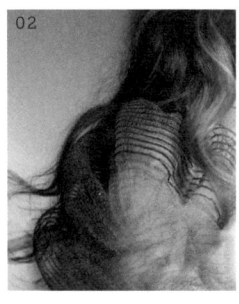 02
 03
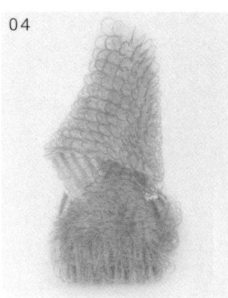 04
 05
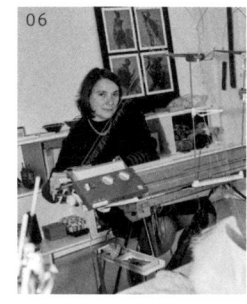 06

107-110 HANNE FRIIS
01, 02, 04, 05 ØYSTEIN THORVALDSEN / VG BILD-KUNST, BONN 2025, 03 ØYSTEIN THORVALDSEN PURCHASED BY MK&G, HAMBURG / VG BILD-
KUNST, BONN 2025, 06 MARIE SJØVOLD / VG BILD-KUNST, BONN 2025

 01
 02
 03
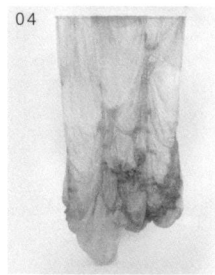 04
 05
 06

111-114 ELSI GIAUQUE
01 ACHIM KUKULIES, TEXTILES: OPEN LETTER, 2013, KUNSTSAMMLUNG DER STADT BIEL, 02, 03 FRANZ XAVER JAGGY & UMBERTO ROMITO,
MUSEUM FÜR GESTALTUNG ZÜRICH, KUNSTGEWERBESAMMLUNG, ZHDK, 04 © ATELIER DE NUMÉRISATION DE LA VILLE DE LAUSANNE. MUDAC,
COLLECTION DE LA VILLE DE LAUSANNE, 05 ELISABETH FUNK, SAMMLUNG ARCHIV ZHDK

 01
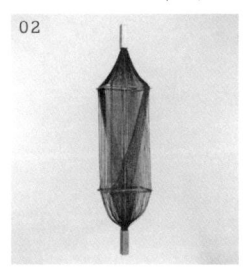 02
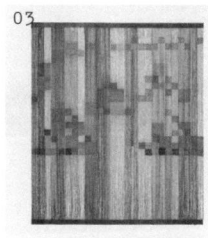 03
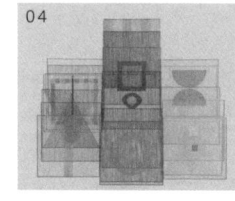 04
 05

115-118 SOFÍA GURIDI
01, 02, 03, 04 VERTTI VIRASJOKI, 05 KRISTINA TSVETKOVA

 01
 02
 03
 04
 05

119-122 JULIA HEUER
01, 02, 03, 04, 05 NEVEN ALLGEIER

123-126 REBEKAH JOHNSTON
01, 04 REBEKAH JOHNSTON, 05 CLARE COE

127-130 HELLA JONGERIUS
01 LAURA FIORIO, 02, 03, 05 ROEL VAN TOUR, 04 MAGDALENA LEPKA, 06 LORAINE BODEWES

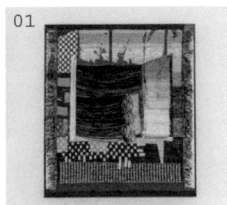  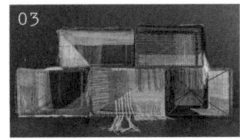   

131-134 STEPHANIE KAHNAU
01 MICHAEL MIESKES/JENNIFER KEUSGEN, 02, 03 STEPHANIE KAHNAU, 04, 05 MICHAEL MIESKES, 06 NILS SCHWARZ

 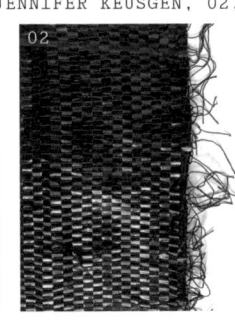 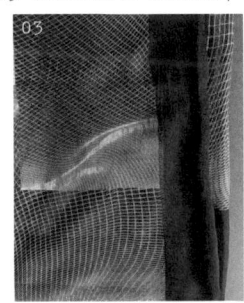 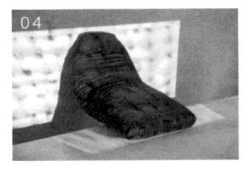  

135-138 SOOJIN KANG
01, 03 BEN HUNTER GALLERY, 02, 04, 05 MARKUS SCHRÖDER

   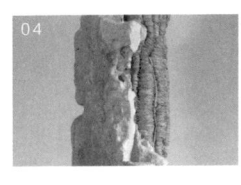 

139-142 MARIANNE KEMP
01 EDDY WENTING, 02, 03 THEO BOS, 04 EDDY WENTING

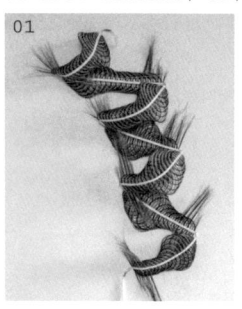

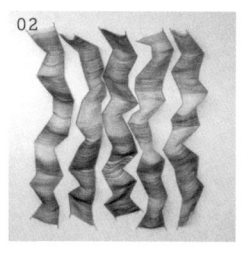

134-146 SONNHILD KESTLER
01, 02 MARION NITSCH, 03 JULIEN VONIER, 04 MARKUS RUF, 05 MICASA SWITZERLAND

147-150 CONSTANZA CAMILA KRAMER GARFIAS
01, 02, 03 CONSTANZA CAMILA KRAMER GARFIAS, 04 LING KHOR

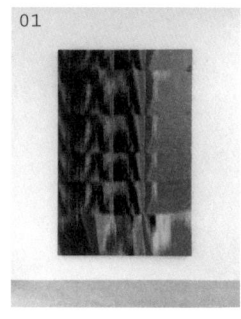

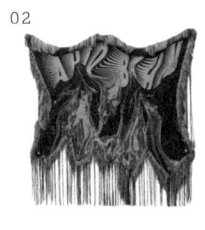

151-154 ALFHILD KÜLPER
01 LUIS CORZO, 02, 03, 04 ARNOUT HULSKAMP, 05 ANNA WEGELIN

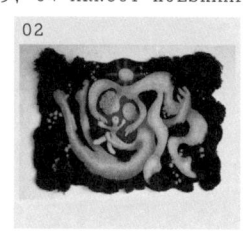

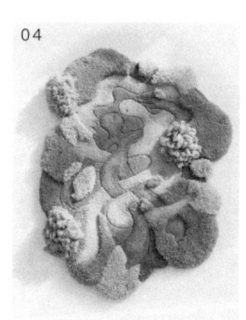

155-158 AURÉLIA LEBLANC
01, 02, 03, 04, 05 ANNE-SOPHIE GUILLET

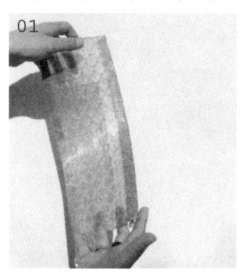

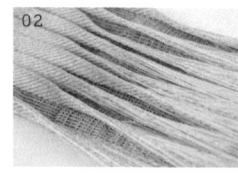

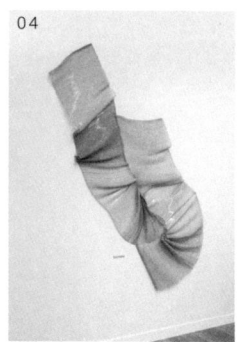

159-162 KAREN MODREI
01 KAREN MODREI, 02, 04, 05, 06 REGINE HEILAND, 03 MATTHIAS HOLZAPFEL

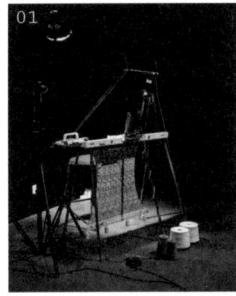   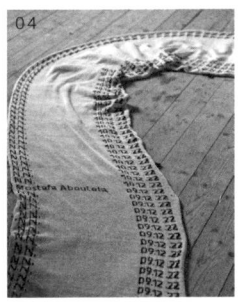  

163-166 EMILIE PALLE HOLM
01, 02, 03, 04, 05 EMILIE PALLE HOLM, 06 MARTIN BRUSEWITZ

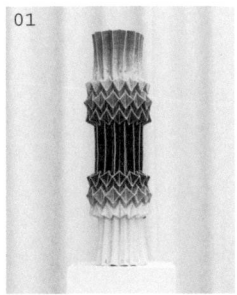     

167-170 ZOÉ PIGNOLET
01 ZOÉ PIGNOLET FOR ATELIER 27 PARIS, 02, 03, 04, 05 ZOÉ PIGNOLET, 06 MARION SAUPIN

 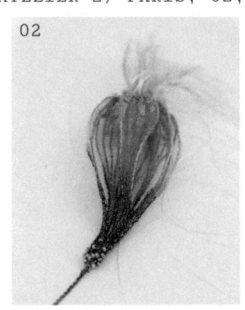  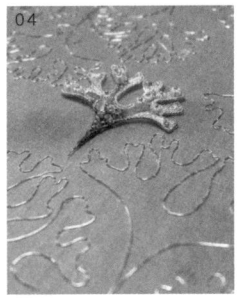 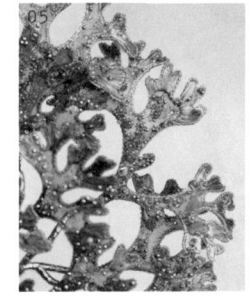 

171-174 NOUSHIN REDJAIAN
01 EVA KELETY, 02, 03, 04 NOUSHIN REDJAIAN, 05 ELSA OKAZAKI

  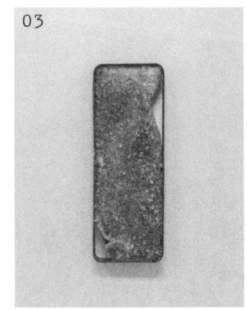  

175-178 JULIA RIBIC
01, 02, 03, 04 JULIA RIBIC, 05 RAFAEL MICHEL

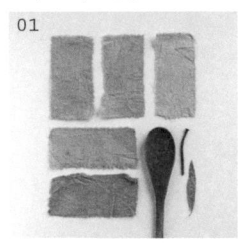    

179-182 BELÉN RODRÍGUEZ
01 ROBERTO RUIZ, 02, 03, 06 SERGIO ALBERT, 04 GINA FOLLY, 05 BELÉN RODRÍGUEZ

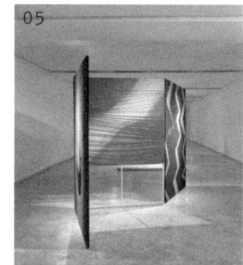

183-186 LARISSA SCHEPERS
01, 03, 04, 05, 06 MERLIJN SPENKELINK, 02 SUNGJAE JOO

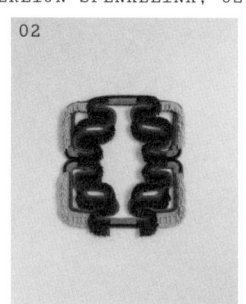

187-190 JOANA SCHNEIDER
01, 02, 03, 04 PEARL SIJMONS, 05 STUDIO PIM TOP

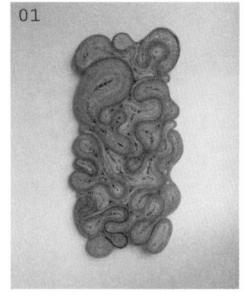

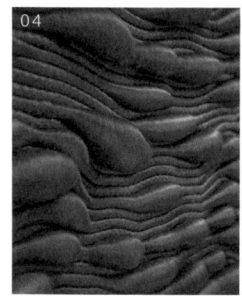

191-194 SABRINA STADLOBER
01, 03, 04 JAKOB KOTZMUTH, FLARE TALENTS, 02, 05 SABRINA STADLOBER, 06 MINA LÖSCHER, FLARE TALENTS

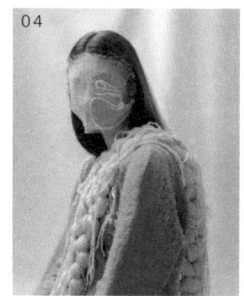
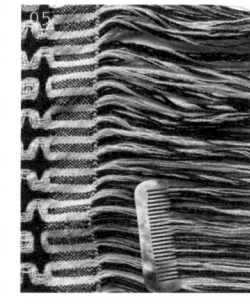

195-198 KATJA STELZ
01, 02, 04 MAX REINHARD, 05 ANDRÉ REUTER

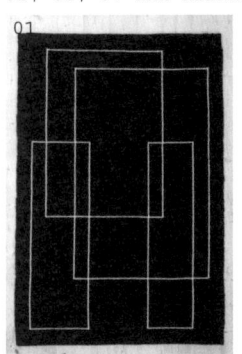

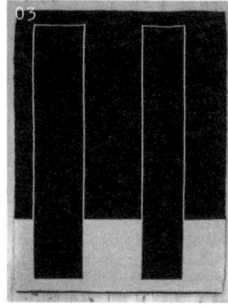

199-202 GUNTA STÖLZL
01 © ST. ANNEN-MUSEUM LÜBECK / © VG BILD-KUNST, BONN 2025, 02, 03, 05 © VG BILD-KUNST, BONN 2025,
04 COURTESY DIE NEUE SAMMLUNG - THE DESIGN MUSEUM, PHOTO: DIE NEUE SAMMLUNG - THE DESIGN MUSEUM (A. LAURENZO),
© VG BILD-KUNST, BONN 2025, 05 © THE GUNTA STÖLZL DIGITAL ARCHIVE / VG BILD-KUNST, BONN 2025

 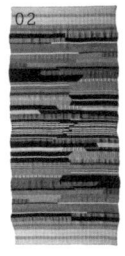 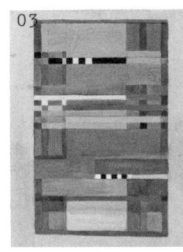  

203-206 THREADSTORIES
01, 02, 03, 04, 05 THREADSTORIES, 06 HAZEL COONAGH

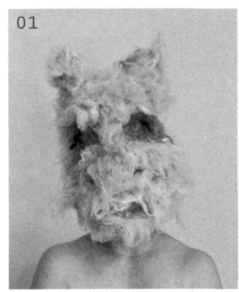 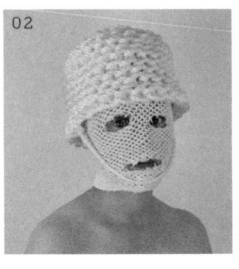 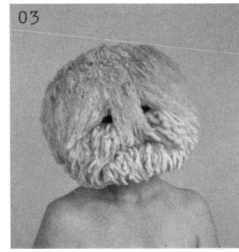 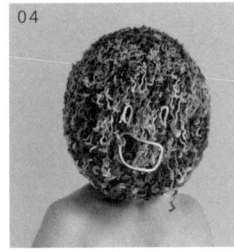 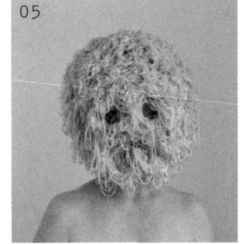 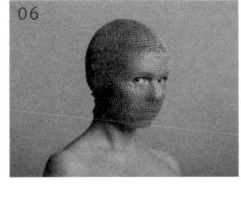

207-210 ZUZANA VRÁBEĽOVÁ
01, 03 ZUZANA VRÁBEĽOVÁ/SHI FAN, 02, 05 ZUZANA VRÁBEĽOVÁ, 04 ANDRA MARTA BABRE, 06 ANDREA REHBEIN

     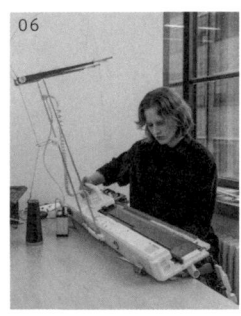

211-214 IGA WĘGLIŃSKA
01, 04, 05 MILA ŁAPKO, 02, 03 IGA WĘGLIŃSKA

   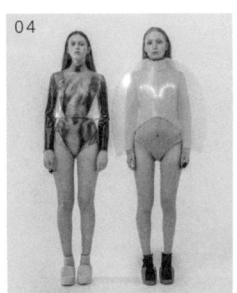 

215-218 LARA WERNERT — 13RUGS
01, 03, 04 13RUGS BY ROHI/ANDREAS HÖRNISCH, 02 13RUGS BY ROHI/STEPHAN FILTGEN, 05 FLORIAN STRANDL

MUSEUMS / GALLERIES / COLLECTIONS	LOCATION		INFO
Bauhaus Dessau	Dessau	[DE]	www.bauhaus-dessau.de
Bayerisches Nationalmuseum	Munich		www.bayerisches-nationalmuseum.de
Deutsches Knopfmuseum	Bärnau		www.deutsches-knopfmuseum.de
Deutsches Textilmuseum Krefeld	Krefeld		www.deutschestextilmuseum.de
Das Esche Museum	Limbach-Oberfrohna		www.esche-museum.de
Draiflessen Collection	Mettingen		www.draiflessen.com
Filzwelt Soltau	Soltau		www.filzwelt-soltau.de
Frauenmuseum Bonn	Bonn		www.frauenmuseum.de
Galerie Handwerk	Munich		www.hwk-muenchen.de
Grassi Museum	Leipzig		www.grassimak.de
Handweberei Kafka	Wuppertal		www.baenderei-kafka.de
Kunstsammlungen Chemnitz	Chemnitz		www.kunstsammlungen-chemnitz.de
Modemuseum im Schloß Ludwigsburg	Ludwigsburg		www.schloss-ludwigsburg.de
Museum für Kunst und Gewerbe	Hamburg		www.mkg-hamburg.de
Münchner Stadtmuseum	Munich		www.muenchner-stadtmuseum.de
Oberfränkische Textilmusem Helmbrechts	Helmbrechts		www.textilmuseum.de
Die Neue Sammlung	Munich		www.die-neue-sammlung.de
Schaustickerei Plauener Spitze	Plauen		www.schaustickerei.de
Staatliches Textil- und Industriemuseum Augsburg	Augsburg		www.timbayern.de
Textilsammlung Max Berk	Heidelberg		www.museum-heidelberg.de
Textilmuseum Mindelheim - Sandtner-Stiftung	Mindelheim		www.mindelheimermuseen.de
Tuch und Technik Textilmuseum	Neumünster		www.tuchundtechnik.de
Tuchmacher Museum	Bramsche		www.tuchmachermuseum.de
Vitra Design Museum	Weil am Rhein		www.design-museum.de
Von Parish Kostümbibliothek	Munich		www.muenchner-stadtmuseum.de
Central Museum of Textiles in Łódź	Łódź	[PL]	www.cmwl.pl
Färbermuseum Gutau	Gutau	[AU]	www.gutau.at
Museum für angewandte Kunst	Vienna		www.mak.at
Museum Alte Textilfabrik	Weitra		www.textilstrasse.at
Schloss Hollenegg for Design	Bad Schwanberg		www.schlosshollenegg.at
Textilmuseum Groß Siegharts	Groß-Siegharts		www.textilmuseum.at
Abegg-Stiftung	Riggisberg	[CH]	www.abegg-stiftung.ch
Landesmuseum Zürich	Zurich		www.landesmuseum.ch
Museum für Gestaltung Zürich	Zurich		www.museum-gestaltung.ch
Textilmuseum Sankt Gallen	St. Gallen		www.textilmuseum.ch
Fondazione Rubelli	Venice	[IT]	www.fondazionerubelli.com
Fortuny Museum	Venice		www.fortuny.visitmuve.it
Lottozero	Prato		www.lottozero.org
Museo del Murletto	Burano		www.museomerletto.visitmuve.it
Museo di Palazzo Mocenigo	Venice		www.mocenigo.visitmuve.it
Museo del Tessuto	Prato		www.museodeltessuto.it
Museo della Seta	Como		www.museosetacomo.com
Palazzo Pitti / Museo della Moda e del Costume	Florence		www.uffizi.it
Benaki Museum	Athens	[GR]	www.benaki.org
The Viktoria Karelias Collection	Kalamata		www.vgkareliascollection.com
Centre de Documentació i Museu Tèxtil	Terrassa	[ES]	www.cdmt.cat
Cristóbal Balenciaga	Getaria		www.cristobalbalenciagamuseoa.com
Museoa	València		www.visitvalencia.com
Museo del Traje	Madrid		www.cultura.gob.es
MUDE - Design Museum	Lisbon	[PT]	www.mude.pt
National Costume Museum	Lisbon		www.museusemonumentos.pt
Association Soierie Vivante	Lyon	[FR]	www.soierie-vivante.asso.fr
Azzedine Alaïa Foundation	Paris		www.fondationazzedinealaia.org
La Galerie Dior	Paris		www.galeriedior.com
Maison des Canuts	Lyon		www.maisondescanuts.fr
Mobilier National - Gobelins	Paris		www.mobiliernational.culture.gouv.fr
Musée Christian Dior	Granville		www.musee-dior-granville.com
Musée des Arts Décoratifs	Paris		www.madparis.fr
Musée de la Mode et du Textile	Paris		www.lesartsdecoratifs.fr

Musée des Tapisseries	Aix-en-Provence		www.aixenprovence.fr
Musée de la Tapisserie d'Aubusson	Aubusson		www.cite-tapisserie.fr
Musée des Tissus et des Arts Décoratifs	Lyon		www.museedestissus.fr
Musée Jean-Lurçat et de la Tapisserie Contemporaine	Angers		www.musees.angers.fr
Musée Soieries Brochier	Lyon		www.brochiersoieries.com
Musée Yves Saint Laurent Paris	Paris		www.museeyslparis.com
BeCraft	Mons	[BE]	www.becraft.org
Les Drapiers	Liège		www.lesdrapiers.be
Modemuseum Hasselt	Hasselt		www.modemuseumhasselt.be
MoMu Fashion Museum Antwerp	Antwerp		www.momu.be
Musée Mode & Dentelle	Brussels		www.museeducostumeetdeladentelle.be
Fashion for Good Museum	Amsterdam		www.fashionforgood.com
TextielMuseum Tilburg/TextilLab	Tilburg		www.textielmuseum.nl
Design Museum	London	[UK]	www.designmuseum.org
Fashion & Textile Museum	London		www.fashiontextilemuseum.org
Josh Lilley Gallery	London		www.joshlilleygallery.com
Newton Textile Museum	Newton		www.newtowntextilemuseum.co.uk
Victoria & Albert Museum	London		www.vam.ac.uk
William Morris Gallery	London		www.wmgallery.org.uk
National Museum of Ireland/Collins Barracks	Dublin	[IE]	www.museum.ie
Design Museum Danmark	Copenhagen	[DK]	www.designmuseum.dk
Nationalmuseet	Copenhagen		www.en.natmus.dk
Tekstil museet Herning	Herning		www.museummidtjylland.dk
Nasjonal Museet	Oslo	[NO]	www.nasjonalmuseet.no
Norsk Folkemuseum	Oslo		www.norskfolkemuseum.no
Nordenfjeldske Kunstindustrimuseum	Trondheim		www.nkim.no
The Röhsska Museum	Göteborg	[SE]	www.rohsska.se
Textilmuseet Borås	Borås		www.textilmuseet.se
Architecture & Design Museum Helsinki	Helsinki	[FI]	www.admuseo.fi
EMMA	Espoo		www.emmamuseum.fi
Forssa Museum	Forssa		www.forssanmuseo.fi
Vapriikki	Tampere		www.vapriikki.fi
Heimilisiðnaðarsafnið – Textile Museum	Blönduós	[IS]	www.textile.is
Heimtali Museum	Heimtali	[EE]	www.muuseumikaart.ee

THE AUGSBURG TEXTILE AND INDUSTRY
MUSEUM AUGSBURG (TIM)

DAS STAATLICHE TEXTIL- UND INDUSTRIE-
MUSEUM AUGSBURG (TIM)

EN Inaugurated in 2010, tim is one of Europe's leading textile museums. In providing a survey of the history of the Bavarian textiles industry, tim illustrates the path taken by the Free State of Bavaria since the eighteenth century in advancing towards the Modern Age – with all its social, economic and political semantic planes. The museum vividly demonstrates how the Bavarian textile industry has actively made use of global interconnections to achieve economic success. However, tim is not just about historical textile technologies; it also showcases the history of design and fashion. At the same time, the museum reflects on the impact made by globalisation on current industrial production and today's overconsumption of clothing. Viewed against this background, the explanation for why the subject of sustainability has assumed major significance at the museum is clear.

tim sees itself as a 'laboratory of the Modern Age' in museum form that offers endless possibilities to all those interested in experiencing the history of (Bavarian) textiles, makes education and knowledge accessible, stimulates reflection and creativity and delights in bringing it all together. A museum whole-heartedly dedicated to a cosmopolitan, democratic society, it is committed to the principles of participation, inclusion and sustainability. Given its social orientation, visitors, who are all welcome – be they present in person or virtual – are the focus of tim's museum activities.

DE Das 2010 eröffnete Staatliche Textil- und Industriemuseum Augsburg, kurz: tim, gehört zu den führenden Textilmuseen Europas. Am Beispiel der Geschichte der bayerischen Textilindustrie demonstriert das tim, wie der bayerische Freistaat seit dem 18. Jahrhundert den Weg in die Moderne beschritten hat – mit all seinen sozialen, wirtschaftlichen und politischen Bedeutungsdimensionen. Das Museum zeigt eindringlich, wie die bayerische Textilindustrie globale Verflechtungen aktiv zu ihrem wirtschaftlichen Erfolg genutzt hat. Das tim verhandelt aber nicht nur historische textile Techniken, sondern gleichermaßen Design- und Modegeschichte. Zugleich reflektiert das Museum die Auswirkungen der Globalisierung auf die gegenwärtige Produktion und den heutigen Konsum von Kleidung. Vor diesem Hintergrund erklärt sich, dass das Thema Nachhaltigkeit eine wichtige Bedeutung im Museum einnimmt.

Das tim versteht sich als ein museales »Laboratorium der Moderne«, das allen interessierten Menschen in der Auseinandersetzung mit der (bayerischen) Textilgeschichte zahlreiche Erfahrungsmöglichkeiten eröffnet: Bildung und Wissen zugänglich macht, Reflexion und Kreativität anregt und alles mit Freude zusammenführt. Als Museum stellt es sich ganz in den Dienst einer ebenso weltoffenen wie demokratischen Gesellschaft und sieht sich dabei den Prinzipien der Partizipation, Inklusion und Nachhaltigkeit verpflichtet. Mit seiner sozialen Ausrichtung stehen die Besucher:innen, die allesamt – gleich ob analog oder virtuell – willkommen sind, im Mittelpunkt der musealen Aufgaben des tim.

	LOCATION		INFO
Burg Giebichenstein Kunsthochschule Halle	Halle	[DE]	www.burg-halle.de
HAW Hamburg	Hamburg		www.haw-hamburg.de
Hochschule Albstadt-Sigmaringen	Sigmaringen		www.hs-albsig.de
Hochschule Hof Campus Münchberg	Hof		www.hof-university.de
Hochschule Niederrhein	Krefeld		www.hs-niederrhein.de
Hochschule Reutlingen - Fakultät Textile und Design	Reutlingen		www.reutlingen-university.de
Staatliche Akademie der bildenden Künste Stuttgart	Stuttgart		www.abk-stuttgart.de
Universität Oldenburg	Oldenburg		www.uol.de
Universität Osnabrück	Osanbrück		www.textil.uni-osnabrueck.de
WHZ Fakultät für Angewandte Kunst Schneeberg	Schneeberg		www.fh-zwickau.de
Kunstuniversität Linz	Linz	[AT]	www.kunstuni-linz.at
Universität Mozarteum Salzburg	Salzburg		www.moz.ac.at
Universität für angewandte Kunst Wien	Vienna		www.dieangewandte.at
Technical University Liberec	Liberec	[CZ]	www.ft.tul.cz
Hochschule für Gestaltung Basel	Basel	[CH]	www.fhnw.ch
Hochschule Luzern	Luzern		www.hslu.ch
Schweizerische Textilfachschule	Winterthur		www.stf.ch
Polimoda	Florence	[IT]	www.polimoda.com
Accademia di Como Aldo Galli	Como		www.accademiagalli.it
École des Arts Décoratifs	Paris	[FR]	www.ensad.fr
École nationale supérieure de création industrielle	Paris		www.ensci.com
L'École Duperré	Paris		www.duperre.org
Académie royale des Beaux-Arts de Bruxelles	Bruxelles	[BE]	www.arba-esa.be
Fashion Institute Amsterdam	Amsterdam	[NL]	www.amfi.nl
Saxon (UAS)	Enschede		www.saxion.edu
Birmingham City University	Birmingham	[UK]	www.bcu.ac.uk
Central Saint Martins	London		www.arts.ac.uk
De Montfort University	Leicester		www.dmu.ac.uk
Norwich University of the Arts	Norwich		www.norwichuni.ac.uk
Royal College of Art	London		www.rca.ac.uk
Bath Spa University	Bath		www.bathspa.ac.uk
Designskolen Kolding	Kolding	[DK]	www.designskolenkolding.dk
Swedish School of Textiles in Borås	Borås	[SE]	www.hb.se
Aalto-universitetet	Helsinki	[FI]	www.aalto.fi
Estonian Academy of Arts (EKA)	Tallinn	[EE]	www.artun.ee
Pallas University of Applied Sciences	Tartu		www.pallasart.ee

STUDIOS / SHOPS / WORKSHOPS	LOCATION		INFO
Blaudruckerei Folprecht	Coswig	[DE]	www.blaudruckerei-folprecht.de
Damastweberei	Munich		www.damasthandweberei.de
Flora und Farbe	Berlin		www.floraundfarbe.de
Fromholzer Textildruck	Ruhmannsfelden		www.fromholzer.de
Giessmann Plissee	Berlin		www.giessmann-plissee.de
HIER–Studio & Store for local Design	Munich		www.hier.studio
HILO textiles	Berlin		www.hilotextiles.com
Handweberei Kafka	Wuppertal		www.baenderei-kafka.de
Material Bank Studio	Stuttgart		www.materialbank.eu
Nanna Textiles	Stuttgart		www.nannatextiles.de
Plissee Schatz	Rechtmehring		www.plissee-schatz.de
Stark und Köppe	Magdeburg		www.stark-koeppe.de
Teppich Bernegger	Munich		www.teppich-bernegger.de
Textillab Berlin	Berlin		www.textilelab.berlin
Beate und Celine von Harten	Vienna	[AT]	www.beatevonharten.at
Juppenwerkstatt Riefensberg	Riefensberg		www.juppenwerkstatt.at
Textiles Zentrum Haslach	Haslach		www.textiles-zentrum-haslach.at
Matrix	Basel		www.matrixbasel.ch
Plisseebrennerei Eva Ott	Basel		www.plisseebrennerei.com
TDS Textildruckerei	Arbon		www.tds-switzerland.ch
Tessandra	Sta. Maria V.M.		www.tessanda.ch
Lottozero Textile Laboratory	Prato	[IT]	www.lottozero.org
Luigi Bevilacqua	Venice		www.luigi-bevilacqua.com
Martina Vidal	Burano		www.martinavidal.com
Giaquinto Tessitura Artigianale	Gagliano del Capo		www.tessituragiaquinto.com
Annie Bouquet	Paris	[FR]	www.anniebouquet.tapisseriedefrance.com
Brochier Soieries Atelier	Lyon		www.brochiersoieries.com
Tapisserie de la Bûcherie	Paris		www.bucherie.com
Wolff & Descourtis	Paris		www.wolffetdescourtis.com
Hand and Lock	London	[UK]	www.handembroidery.com
Macculoch & Wallis	London		www.macculloch-wallis.co.uk
Ray Stitch	London		www.raystitch.co.uk
Wallace & Sewell	London		www.wallacesewell.com
Textile Research Centre	Leiden	[NL]	www.trc-leiden.nl
Icelandic Textile Center	Blönduós	[IS]	www.textilmidstod.is
Kumu Art Museum	Tallinn	[EE]	www.kumu.ekm.ee

AWARDS / FOUNDATIONS / RESIDENCIES	LOCATION	INFO
Baltic Triennial of Miniature Textile in Gdynia	PL	www.muzeumgdynia.pl
British Textile Biennale	UK	www.britishtextilebiennial.co.uk
CSI Colour Award	UK	www.colourindesignaward.org
Danner-Stiftung/Danner-Preis	Germany	www.danner-stiftung.de
Doris Winter-Gedächtnispreises	Germany	-
Europäische Quilt-Triennale	Europe	www.museum-heidelberg.de
European Fashion Award	Germany	www.sdbi.de
European Textile Academy	Italy	www.eurotextileacademy.com
Fondazione Le Costantine	Italy	www.lecostantine.it
Innovate Textile Award	UK	innovatetextileawards.wtin.com
Lotte Hofmann-Gedächtnisstiftung für Textilkunst	Germany	www.lotte-hofmann-stiftung.de
The Lottozero Residence	Italy	www.lottozero.org
Loewe Foundation Craft Prize	Spain	www.craftprize.loewe.com
Task Force Textiles	Germany	www.abk-stuttgart.de
TEXIMUS	Switzerland	www.tafch.ch
Wilhelm-Lorch-Stiftung	Germany	www.wilhelm-lorch-stiftung.de
Wüstenrot Stiftung	Germany	www.wuestenrot-stiftung.de

www.awarewomenartists.com
www.belgiumisdesign.be/designers
www.blog.craft2eu.net
www.blog.fabrics-store.com
www.collectiftextile.com
www.deutsche-manufakturenstrasse.de
www.ditf.de
www.edelkoort.com
www.embroiderymagazine.co.uk
www.etn-net.org/home.html
www.euroweb.uw.edu.pl
www.fashion-council-germany.org
www.fiberartfever.com
www.helsinkidesignweek.com
www.homofaber.com
www.judithbrachem.de
www.masterrat.com
www.mariasigma.com
www.meisterrat.com
www.meredithwoolnough.com.au
www.modesammlung.ch/links
www.nuno.com
www.pallastextiles.com
www.selvedge.org
www.stfi.de
www.tafch.ch
www.texintel.com
www.textile-art-berlin-online.de
www.textileartist.org
www.textile-forum-blog.org
www.textilesociety.org.uk
www.textiletoursofparis.com
www.themakery.de
www.tzurigueta.com
www.wta-online.org
www.wrap.ngo
www.62group.org.uk

Catrin Lorch

EN Born in 1965, Catrin Lorch is a high-profile art historian and art critic, internationally known for her work as a curator, journalist and author. She specialises in contemporary art with a particular interest in interdisciplinary art forms such as video art and textiles.
In 2024 she complete a master's in weaving. An active practitioner of weaving on the handloom, she is the founder of Weberei Kai in Königswinter, organising exhibitions in Germany and the United Kingdom. She also co-ordinates workshops and works on commission, following the thinking of Action Weaving as inspired by Travis Meinolf.

DE Catrin Lorch, geboren 1965, ist eine profilierte Kunsthistorikerin und -kritikerin, international bekannt für ihre Arbeit als Kuratorin, Journalistin und Autorin. Ihr Schwerpunkt liegt auf zeitgenössischer Kunst mit besonderem Interesse für interdisziplinäre Medien wie Videokunst oder Textil.
Sie absolvierte ihre Meister-Ausbildung als Handweberin im Jahr 2024 und als Gründerin der Weberei Kai in Königswinter ist sie in der textilen Praxis aktiv, richtet Ausstellungen in Deutschland und Großbritannien aus. Sie organisiert Workshops und Auftragsarbeiten und folgt dem Gedanken des von Travis Meinolf inspirierten Action Weavings.

Silke Geppert

EN Dr Silke Geppert is an acclaimed historian of art, fashion and costume design who specialises in the history of textiles. Her interdisciplinary work links curatorial praxis, academic research and university teaching and makes her a leading expert on the cultural and social significance of clothing and textiles. Born in 1965, she started out by serving a publishing apprenticeship in Hamburg. In 1991 she became managing director of art publishers Nishen Publishing in London and also curated exhibitions there. She then studied the history of fashion and art in Vienna and wrote her doctoral dissertation on fifteenth-century fashion. Today she is a university lecturer, curates exhibitions internationally devoted to fashion and textiles and publishes regularly on historical and design issues in textile culture. Silke Geppert is also Custodian of the Textiles and Carpets Collection and Curator of Fashion at MAK - Museum für angewandte Kunst in Vienna.

DE Dr. Silke Geppert ist eine renommierte Kunst-, Mode- und Kostümhistorikerin mit einem besonderen Schwerpunkt auf Textilgeschichte. Ihre interdisziplinäre Arbeit verbindet kuratorische Praxis, wissenschaftliche Forschung und universitäre Lehre und macht sie zu einer der führenden Expert:innen für die kulturelle und gesellschaftliche Bedeutung von Kleidung und Textilien. Geboren 1965, absolvierte sie zunächst eine Ausbildung zur Verlagsbuchhändlerin in Hamburg. Ab 1991 leitete sie in London den Kunstbuchverlag Nishen Publishing und kuratierte dort zudem Ausstellungen. Anschließend studierte sie Mode- und Kunstgeschichte in Wien und promovierte 2011 über Mode im 15. Jahrhundert. Heute ist sie als Universitätsdozentin tätig, kuratiert internationale Ausstellungen im Bereich Mode und Textil und publiziert regelmäßig zu historischen und gestalterischen Fragen der Textilkultur. Silke Geppert ist außerdem Kustodin der Sammlung Textilien und Teppiche und Kuratorin für den Bereich Mode am MAK - Museum für angewandte Kunst in Wien

Christina Leitner

EN   Born in 1976, Christina Leitner is a textile artist, curator and influencer. She studied textile design as well as psychology and philosophy in Salzburg and then textil.kunst.design at the Kunstuniversität Linz, where she specialised in paper textiles and also published on the subject. Museum Studies in Graz completed her academic profile. Since 2007 she has worked at Textiles Zentrum Haslach, where she is responsible for the museum, training and production departments and co-ordinates international projects. Alongside this she teaches weaving at the Kunstuniversität Linz and since 2020 has been a board member of the Europäisches Textilenetwork (ETN). Her work combines research and teaching with projects aimed at promoting social participation.

DE   Christina Leitner, geboren 1976, ist Textilkünstlerin, Kuratorin und Vermittlerin. Sie studierte Textiles Gestalten sowie Psychologie und Philosophie in Salzburg, anschließend textil.kunst.design an der Kunstuniversität Linz, wo sie sich intensiv mit Papiertextilien beschäftigte und dazu auch publizierte. Eine museologische Ausbildung in Graz ergänzte ihr Profil. Seit 2007 ist sie am Textilen Zentrum Haslach tätig, wo sie die Bereiche Museum, Ausbildung und Produktion verantwortet und internationale Projekte koordiniert. Parallel dazu lehrt sie Weberei an der Kunstuniversität Linz und ist seit 2020 Vorstandsmitglied des Europäischen Textilnetzwerks (ETN). In ihrer Arbeit verbindet sie Forschung und Lehre mit Projekten zur gesellschaftlichen Teilhabe.

Sabine Flaschberger

EN   Born in 1961, Sabine Flaschberger studied history and art history at the Universität Zürich. She has been a curator of the arts and crafts collection at the Museum für Gestaltung Zürich since 2011. There she conceives exhibitions and publications at the interface of arts and crafts, design and art. In the 2025 exhibition *Textile Manifeste - von Bauhaus bis Soft Sculpture* [Textile Manifestos - From Bauhaus to Soft Sculpture], configured to a large extent on the museum's own collection, she wove textile works with biographical reference points and the principles of the designers to create manifestations of each respective artistic stance. In her contribution she refers to a work by textile artist Lissy Funk and the stimulating relationship between the front and reverse sides of her textile works.

DE   Sabine Flaschberger, geboren 1961, hat an der Universität Zürich Geschichte und Kunstgeschichte studiert. Seit 2011 ist sie Kuratorin der Kunstgewerbesammlung am Museum für Gestaltung Zürich. Dort konzipiert sie Ausstellungen und Publikationen an der Schnittstelle zwischen Kunstgewerbe, Design und Kunst. In *Textile Manifeste - von Bauhaus bis Soft Sculpture* (2025), einer Ausstellung, die weitgehend auf der eigenen Sammlung aufbaute, verwebte sie textile Werke mit biografischen Bezugspunkten und Leitsätzen der Gestaltenden zu Manifesten der jeweiligen künstlerischen Haltung. In ihrem Gastbeitrag nimmt sie Bezug auf eine Arbeit der Textilkünstlerin Lissy Funk und bezieht sich auf das Spannungsfeld von Vorder- und Rückseiten ihrer textilen Arbeiten

EN © 2025 the authors, the artists, and arnoldsche Art Publishers, Stuttgart

Editor and author
Stephanie Kahnau, Munich

Translations
Joan Clough, Penzance

Copy editing
Wendy Brouwer (ENG), Stuttgart
Juliana Müller (DE), Offenbach

Graphic designer
Daily Dialogue, Munich

Offset reproductions
Paladin Design- und Werbemanufaktur, Remseck

Printed by
Schleunungdruck, Marktheidenfeld

Bound by
Schaumann, Darmstadt

Paper
120 g/qm Ovol fine's nature rough zartweiß

arnoldsche project coordination
Greta Garle

Bibliographic information published by the Deutsche Nationalbibliothek
The Deutsche Nationalbibliothek lists this publication in the Deutsche Nationalbibliografie; detailed bibliographic data are available at www.dnb.de.

ISBN 978-3-89790-742-3
Made in Germany, 2025

Quotes
All artists' quotes are taken from correspondence with the author, with the exception of the following:

p. 59, Magdalena Abakanowicz, statement on the occasion of the ceremony of conferring her the Lifetime Achievement Award of the International Sculpture Center, New York, 2005.

p. 71, Gunta Stölzl: *Pionierin der Bauhausweberei*, ed. by Ingrid Radewald and Elke Beilfuß (Wiesbaden: Weimarer Verlagsgesellschaft, 2018), p. 64f.

p. 83, Lucienne Day's quote is taken from: Susan Mansfield, 'Something Completely Different', *The Scotsman*, September 2003; online: www.en.wikipedia.org/wiki/Lucienne_Day.

Further photo credits:
pp. 2, 4, 16, Julia Heuer, photos: Yahui Wang
p. 3, Zuzana Vrábel'ová, photo: the artist
p. 5, Stephanie Kahnau, photo: André Kirsch
pp. 6/7, Cécile Feilchenfeldt, photo: Aurélie Cenno
p. 8, Mae Engelgeer, photo: Hidenori Suzuki
p. 9, Hella Jongerius, photo: Roe van Tour
p. 10, Sofía Guridi, photo: the artist
p. 11, Stephanie Kahnau, photo: Julia Thünemann
pp. 12, 14, Julia Ribic, photos: the artist
p. 13, Marianne Kemp, photo: Eddy Wenting
p. 15, Rebekah Johnston, photo: the artist
p. 17, 21, Zoé Pignolet, photos: the artist
p. 18, Larissa Schepers, photo: Merlijn Spenkelink
p. 19, Katja Stelz, photo: André Reuter
p. 20, Lara Wernert / 13Rugs by Rohi, photo: Rohi Stoffe GmbH
p. 43, photo: Benedikt Ganser
p. 47, photo: © National Gallery of Art, Washington / CC0 1.0 Universal
p. 51, photo: Umberto Romito & Ivan Šuta, Museum für Gestaltung Zürich / Zürcher Hochschule der Künste
p. 55, photo: FF
p. 230, photo: Eckhart Matthäus

Cover illustrations
One of four selected artists' works is featured on the cover of the book:

Julia Heuer: p. 118, 01
Hella Jongerius: p. 127, 02
Noushin Redjaian: p. 172, 02
and: Alfhild Külper, Prism Forest, 2024, 190 × 175 × 4 cm (detail)

This book has been produced with the generous support of:

Danner Stiftung, Munich
Curt Wills-Stiftung, Munich
Rohi, Geretsried
tim – The Augsburg Textile and Industry Museum

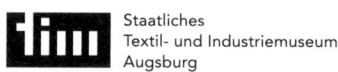

DE   © 2025 die Autorinnen, die Künstlerinnen und arnoldsche Art Publishers,
Stuttgart

Herausgeberin und Autorin
Stephanie Kahnau, München

Übersetzung
Joan Clough, Penzance

Lektorat
Wendy Brouwer (ENG), Stuttgart
Juliana Müller (DE), Offenbach

Grafische Gestaltung
Daily Dialogue, München

Offset Reproduktion
Paladin Design- und Werbemanufaktur,
Remseck

Druck
Schleunungdruck, Marktheidenfeld

Buchbinder
Schaumann, Darmstadt

Papier
120 g/qm Ovol fine's nature rough zartweiß

arnoldsche Projektkoordination
Greta Garle

Bibliografische Information der Deutschen
Nationalbibliothek
Die Deutsche Nationalbibliothek verzeich-
net diese Publikation in der Deutschen
Nationalbibliografie; detaillierte bibliografische Daten sind über www.dnb.de
abrufbar.

ISBN 978-3-89790-742-3
Made in Germany, 2025

Zitate
Alle Künstlerinnen-Zitate entstammen der
Korrespondenz mit der Autorin, mit Aus-
nahme der folgenden:

S. 59, Magdalena Abakanowicz' Statement
anlässlich der Verleihungszeremonie des
Lifetime Achievement Award des International Sculpture Center, New York, 2005.

S. 71, Gunta Stölzl: *Pionierin der Bauhausweberei*, hg. v. Ingrid Radewald und
Elke Beilfuß, Wiesbaden, Weimarer Verlagsgesellschaft in der Verlagshaus Römer-
weg GmbH, 2018, S. 64f.

S. 83, Das Zitat von Lucienne Day
entstammt: Susan Mansfield, „Something
Completely Different", *The Scotsman*,
September 2003; online: www.en.wikipe-
dia.org/wiki/Lucienne_Day.

Weitere Bildnachweise:
S. 2, 4, 16, Julia Heuer,
Fotos: Yahui Wang
S. 3, Zuzana Vrábel'ová,
Foto: die Künstlerin
S. 5, Stephanie Kahnau,
Foto: André Kirsch
S. 6/7, Cécile Feilchenfeldt,
Foto: Aurélie Cenno
S. 8, Mae Engelgeer,
Foto: Hidenori Suzuki
S. 9, Hella Jongerius,
Foto: Roe van Tour
S. 10, Sofía Guridi,
Foto: die Künstlerin
S. 11, Stephanie Kahnau,
Foto: Julia Thünemann
S. 12, 14, Julia Ribic,
Fotos: die Künstlerin
S. 13, Marianne Kemp,
Foto: Eddy Wenting
S. 15, Rebekah Johnston,
Foto: die Künstlerin
S. 17, 21, Zoé Pignolet,
Fotos: die Künstlerin
S. 18, Larissa Schepers,
Foto: Merlijn Spenkelink
S. 19, Katja Stelz,
Foto: André Reuter
S. 20, Lara Wernert / 13Rugs by Rohi,
Foto: Rohi Stoffe GmbH
S. 43, Foto: Benedikt Ganser
S. 47, Foto: © National Gallery of Art,
Washington / CC0 1.0 Universal
S. 51, Foto: Umberto Romito & Ivan Šuta,
Museum für Gestaltung Zürich / Zürcher
Hochschule der Künste
S. 55, Foto: FF
S. 230, Foto: Eckhart Matthäus

Covermotive
Auf jedem Cover dieses Buches ist je ein
Werk von insgesamt vier ausgewählten
Künstlerinnen aufgebracht:

Julia Heuer: S. 118, 01
Hella Jongerius: S. 127, 02
Noushin Redjaian: S. 172, 02
sowie: Alfhild Külper, Prism Forest, 2024,
190 × 175 × 4 cm (Detail)

Dieses Buch entstand mit großzügiger
Unterstützung von:

Danner Stiftung, München
Curt Wills-Stiftung, München
Rohi, Geretsried
tim – Staatliches Textil- und
Industriemuseum, Augsburg

Thank you!

A book is not the work of one individual.
I am therefore even more grateful for all the help, inspiring conversations, valuable advice, professional implementation and financial support, without which this work would not exist.

With Greta and Dirk from arnoldsche Art Publishers, and Malin from Daily Dialogue as graphic designer, I couldn't have wished for a better team to realise this project so close to my heart. Thank you for your enthusiasm, reliability, professionalism and creativity - and for enabling me to develop this book.

My sincere thanks also go to all the artists, designers and creators who so openly and willingly provided me with information and documentation of their work, as well as to Catrin, Sabine, Christina and Silke for their guest contributions. Thank you to Susanne Buch, Jan Andry and Jochum Rodgers gallery, Berlin; Saarländische Galerie, Berlin; Museum Abteiberg, Mönchengladbach; udac, Lausanne; Die Neue Sammlung - The Design Museum, Munich; Fondation Toms Pauli, Lausanne; St. Annen-Museum, Lübeck; and all other institutions involved for their support and such a pleasant and committed collaboration. I would also like to thank Michael Zoller from the Curt Wills Foundation; the Danner Foundation; the Rohi textile company; and Dr. Karl Murr from tim in Augsburg.

Thank you, Juliana, for helping me put my thoughts into clear words. Julia, Isi and the entire HIER- Store team, thank you for your patience over the past few months and for covering for me in the shop.

I would also like to thank Annette, Arnold, Biene, Eva, Elisa, Jennifer, Kata, Katharina Sand and Lara for their many textile tips and advice.

A very special thank you goes to Elfi, Guido, Margit and Andy - without your help, this book would not have been possible. I am infinitely grateful to have people like you around me. Thank you for your trust.

And last but not least: Michi, without whom I would never have dared to tackle such a project, and without whose support in all aspects I would not be where I am today. LY

Stephanie Kahnau

Danke!

Ein Buch entsteht nicht alleine.
Umso dankbarer bin ich für all die helfenden Hände, die inspirierenden Gespräche, die wertvollen Hinweise, die professionelle Umsetzung und die finanzielle Unterstützung, ohne die dieses Werk nicht hätte entstehen können.

Mit Greta und Dirk von den arnoldsche Art Publishers als Verlag sowie Malin von Daily Dialogue für die grafische Umsetzung hätte ich mir kein besseres Team wünschen können, um dieses Herzensprojekt zu realisieren. Danke für euren Enthusiasmus, eure Zuverlässigkeit, eure Professionalität und Kreativität - und dafür, mit mir dieses Buch entstehen zu lassen.

Mein großer Dank gilt auch allen Künstlerinnen, Designerinnen und Gestalterinnen, die mir in so offener und kooperativer Weise Informationen und Dokumentationen ihrer Arbeiten zur Verfügung gestellt haben - sowie Catrin, Sabine, Christina und Silke für ihre Gastbeiträge. Danke an Susanne Buch, Jan Andry, die Jochum Rodgers Galerie, Berlin; die Saarländische Galerie, Berlin; das Museum Abteiberg, Mönchengladbach; das mudac, Lausanne; Die Neue Sammlung - The Design Museum, München, die Fondation Toms Pauli, Lausanne, das St. Annen-Museum, Lübeck und allen weiteren Institutionen, die auf so angenehme und engagierte Weise mit mir kooperiert und mich unterstützt haben. Ebenso danke ich Michael Zoller von der Curt Wills-Stiftung, der Danner Stiftung, der Firma Rohi und Dr. Karl Murr vom tim, Augsburg.

Danke Juliana, für deine Hilfe dabei, meine Gedanken in klare Worte zu fassen. Julia, Isi sowie dem gesamten HIER- Store-Team für eure Geduld in den letzten Monaten und dafür, mir im Shop den Rücken freigehalten zu haben.

Ebenso danke ich Annette, Arnold, Biene, Eva, Elisa, Jennifer, Kata, Katharina Sand und Lara für die vielen textilen Tipps und Ratschläge.

Ein ganz besonderer Dank gilt Elfi, Guido, Margit und Andy - ohne eure Hilfe hätte dieses Buch nicht realisiert werden können. Ich bin unendlich dankbar, Menschen wie euch um mich zu haben. Danke für euer Vertrauen.

Und zuletzt: Michi - ohne den ich mich niemals getraut hätte, so ein Projekt anzugehen, und ohne dessen Unterstützung in jeglichen Bereichen ich nicht da stehen würde, wo ich jetzt bin. LY

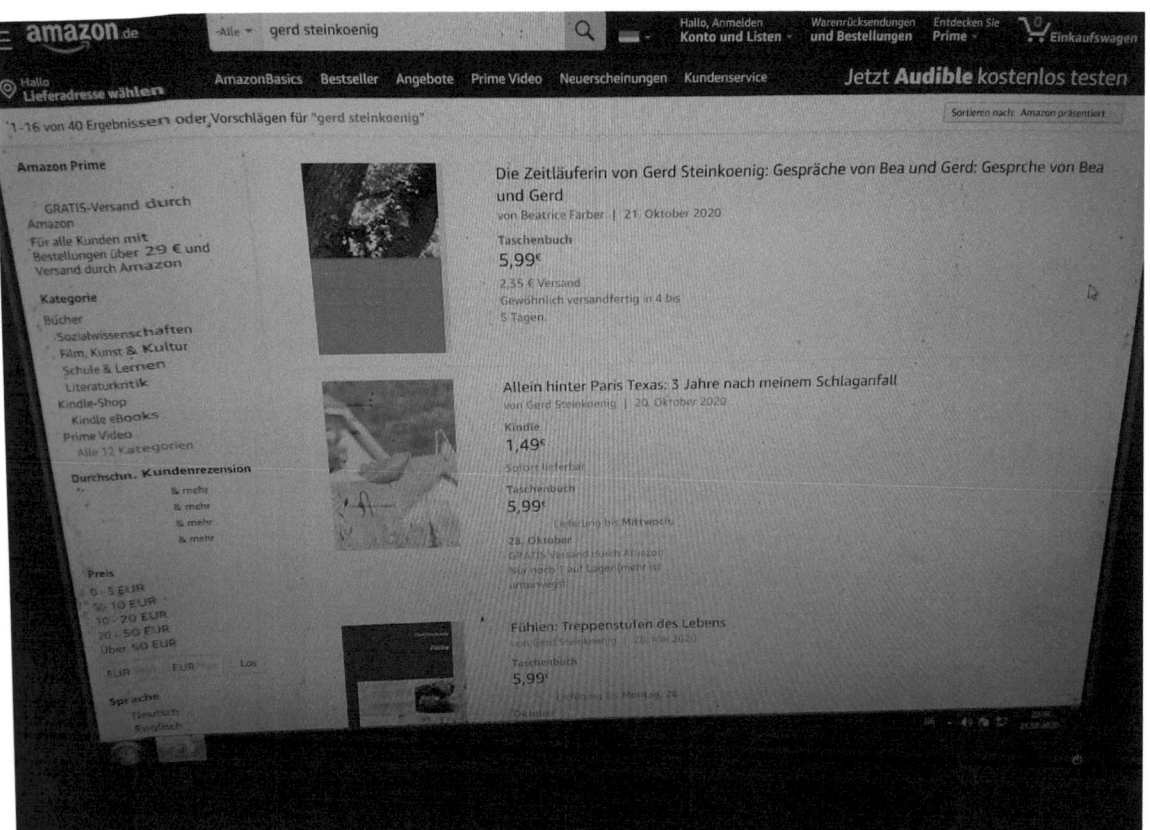

TEIL 2 - ODER 2. AUFLAGE, ODER 2. GESPRÄCH ZWISCHEN BEA UND GERD

Gerd - Wäre toll mit Beatrice wieder zu unterhalten. Aber sie ist irgendwo im Universum. Vielleicht bin ich zu naiv-egoistisch! Oder doch mit meiner Philosophie mit unserem und meinem Leben. Ist ja ein roter Faden bei meinen Büchern, wegen der Musik und Kultur oder der Gesellschaft und Menschheit, Zeitgeist und Zeitmomente. Habe vorhin ein altes One Hit Wonder gehört: Hey Little Girl von Icehouse. Ganz geiler Groove. Aber in 40 Jahren ist der Song total untergegangen... Oder doch wieder das Internet-Archiv-Gehirn? Oder doch Zensur und Meinungsverbote durch die momentanen Nazis, Coronaleugner, Klimaleugner, Trumpisten... Und "meine" Nationalbibliothek wird zerstört...

Bea - Wow! Gerdsche, Positive Vibrations, mach mal locker! Wir hatten so ein tolles Gespräch!

Gerd - Beeaaaaa, jaaaa!!

Gerd umarmt die Zeitläuferin. Es war viel warme Energie und positive Strömungen, es war göttlich!

Bea - Das war eine Ausnahme, wir sind eben vertraut. Du brauchst Gelassenheit, innere Ruhe. Und lache einfach über diese Menschen. Auf der Erde sind wir noch in der Steinzeit. Das menschliche Gehirn ist zu einströmig, keine toleranten Alternativen. Auf meinem Planeten... aber nein, kann ich nicht sagen... Meine 1. Direktive...